OUR
INDIGENOUS
ANCESTORS

OUR
INDIGENOUS
ANCESTORS

A Cultural History of Museums, Science,
and Identity in Argentina, 1877–1943

CAROLYNE R. LARSON

The Pennsylvania State University Press
University Park, Pennsylvania

Library of Congress Cataloging-in-Publication Data

Larson, Carolyne R. (Carolyne Ryan),
1981– , author.
Our indigenous ancestors : a cultural history of
museums, science, and identity in Argentina,
1877–1943 / Carolyne R. Larson.
pages   cm
Summary: "Examines how museum anthropologists'
scientific understandings of indigenous cultures
during the nineteenth and twentieth centuries
impacted creole Argentines' visions of national
heritage and identity"—Provided by publisher.
Includes bibliographical references and index.
ISBN 978-0-271-06696-7 (cloth : alk. paper)
ISBN 978-0-271-06697-4 (pbk : alk. paper)
1. Anthropological museums and collections—
Social aspects—Argentina—History—19th century.
2. Anthropological museums and collections—
Social aspects—Argentina—History—20th century.
3. Anthropology—Social aspects—Argentina—
History—19th century.
4. Anthropology—Social aspects—Argentina—
History—20th century.
5. National characteristics, Argentine—
History—19th century.
6. National characteristics, Argentine—History—
20th century.
7. Indians of South America—Argentina—
Antiquities.
I. Title.

GN36.A75L37 2015
301.07482—dc23
2015003555

The Pennsylvania State University Press is a member
of the Association of American University Presses.

It is the policy of The Pennsylvania State University
Press to use acid-free paper. Publications on
uncoated stock satisfy the minimum requirements of
American National Standard for Information
Sciences—Permanence of Paper for Printed
Library Material, ansi z39.48–1992.

TO ERIC,

without whose constant support and helpful insight this book could not have been written.

Contents

Illustrations

Acknowledgments

Many people contributed to the research and writing of this book. As a student at Lawrence University, I was lucky to have caring and inspiring mentors, especially Paul Cohen, Peter Peregrine, Frank Lewis, Gustavo Fares, and Natasha Gray, who showed me the possibilities of a life in academia and who first cultivated my interests in history and scholarship. At the University of Wisconsin at Madison, I benefitted from the intellectual support and friendship of Ingrid Bolivar Ramirez, Matthew Cosby, Solsi del Moral, Genevieve Dorais, Tamara Feinstein, Julie Gibbings, Jaymie Heilman, Marc Hertzman, Jessica Kirstein, Gabi Kuenzli, Yeri Lopez, Gladys McCormick, Elena McGrath, Andres Matias-Ortiz, Valeria Navarro Rosenblatt, Alberto Ortiz, Yesenia Pumarada-Cruz, Ana Schaposchnik, Vikram Tamboli, and Molly Todd. My advisors, Florencia E. Mallon, Francisco Scarano, and Steve J. Stern, gave freely and generously of their strength, their compassion, their incisive insight, and their humor, all of which helped me grow as a scholar and as a person. The mistakes that remain in this book, despite their best efforts, are entirely my own.

At the University of Wyoming, I have happily found myself among colleagues who inspire me intellectually and who revitalize me with their compassionate collegiality and friendship. My thanks to Michael C. Brose, Leif Cawley, Isadora A. Helfgott, Douglas Johnson, Marianne Kamp, Renée Laegreid, Barbara E. Logan, Jeffrey D. Means, David A. Messenger, JoAnna Poblete, Phil Roberts, Ronald Schultz, and Cheryl Wells. I also owe thanks to a wide circle of colleagues who have offered support, ideas, and sympathetic ears, depending on the situation. Among this large group, I would like to especially thank Bill Beezley, Christina Bueno, Steve Bunker, Julia Rodriguez, and David Sheinin for stimulating conference panels, good conversations, exciting professional opportunities, and inspiring scholarship.

My archival research in Argentina was made possible by immensely capable archivists and welcoming scholars, including Vivian Spoliansky, Yolanda Velo, and Mónica Ferraro at the Museo Etnográfico "Juan B. Ambrosetti";

Irina Podgorny and Máximo Farro at the Museo de Ciencias Naturales de La Plata; Maria Marta Rotondaro at the Biblioteca del Congreso Nacional; and Alejandra Korstanje at the Instituto de Arqueología y Museo in San Miguel de Tucumán, as well as all the people with whom they work. My work would also not have been possible without the universally helpful staff at the Academía Nacional de la Historia, the Archivo General de la Nación, the Biblioteca Nacional, the Universidad Nacional de Tucumán, and the Centro Cultural Rougés. My research in Argentina began well and continued smoothly thanks to the consistent support of Lidia Nacuzzi and Ingrid de Jong, both of the Universidad de Buenos Aires. I would also like to thank Mónica Quijada and Jesus Bustamante, who took the time to meet with me and offer invaluable advice early in my fieldwork.

Finally, I have many personal debts to acknowledge—people who have offered their unflagging support over the years and have been precious sources of laughter, support, and friendship. Very special thanks are due to Julie Gibbings and Paul Jenkins, who have been my constant companions in this journey and have been forced to read and hear far too much about this book. I am deeply grateful to my family, who have patiently listened to my unsolicited stories about Argentina and museums longer than anyone. Above all, I want to thank Eric, who has played an irreplaceable role in the writing of this book and in my life. Thank you, all.

Introduction

On September 5, 1929, the popular Buenos Aires newspaper *Crítica* ran the bold-lettered headline "Man Has Inhabited the Santiagueño Chaco for More than 5,000 Years." Claiming exclusive rights to the story, *Crítica* covered its front page with photographs and drawings of artifacts uncovered during a recent archaeological expedition in the northern province of Santiago del Estero. The newspaper punctuated the page with dramatic subtitles such as "Don't Fail to Read It" and "A French Scientist Has Made a Sensational Discovery," referring to the expedition's lead archaeologist, Emilio Wagner. The next day, *Crítica* ran a follow-up story with the provocative title "An Unknown Race Predominated in the Argentine North?," enticing its readers to "Read Tomorrow" for the answer to the question "Where Did the Man Who Inhabited the Santiagueño Chaco in Remotest Times Come From?"[1]

In many ways, the existence of a five-thousand-year-old human culture hardly seems newsworthy. Why did *Crítica* devote its front page to an archaeological find and not, for instance, to the all-time high reached by the U.S. stock market only two days before, a subject of considerable interest to the many Argentines involved with U.S. companies? The publication of this story—one among many reports on anthropological discoveries that were regularly printed by popular newspapers and magazines in Argentina's early twentieth century—shows that anthropology commanded the kind of widespread interest that sold newspapers, making it newsworthy indeed.

Such newspaper stories revealed a groundswell of popular interest in anthropology as a science and especially in indigenous cultures of Argentina's past and present. They also highlighted the complex and sometimes contradictory role of science in modernizing Argentina. Professional scientists—a self-defined community of experts and educated scholars—and nonscientific actors—a much broader and more flexible category encompassing those without academic scientific credentials—shared a strong interest in scientific studies of indigenous cultures. However, popular and scientific actors expressed this shared interest very differently. While the popular press often presented indigenous cultures in sensationalized terms, pairing romance and science in ways designed to attract an ever wider readership, professional scientific publications were written for an increasingly exclusive audience by the early twentieth century and were characterized by technical analyses of stratigraphy, morphology, typology, and statistics. This emphasis underscored the importance of anthropology's scientific nature to its practitioners. Anthropologists clearly identified their work as a hard science, minimizing its qualitative and interpretive elements and stressing its factual and quantitative basis. The titles of professional scientific publications capture, perhaps most succinctly, the nature of the differences between popular and scientific writings about indigenous cultures. Rather than promising answers to tantalizing questions about "remotest times" or "unknown races," titles of professional scientific publications more commonly ran along such sober lines as "The Chaco-Santiagueña Civilization and Its Correlations with Those of the Old and New World"—a landmark study published by Emilio Wagner and his brother Duncan on the same discoveries reported by *Crítica*.[2]

While professional scientists and newspaper editors may have disagreed on how best to write about Argentina's ancient indigenous civilizations, they nonetheless agreed on three important points. First, both clearly saw Argentina's indigenous cultures as subjects worthy of their attention and expended considerable energy writing about them. Further, scientists and nonscientists alike couched indigenous cultures as a part of Argentina's cultural heritage and an inheritance of an authentic creole nation, and they made romantic connections between indigenous cultures and contemporary creole-dominated Argentine national culture. Third, popular and scientific writers both acknowledged the importance of scientific authority for making claims about indigenous cultures. When popular newspaper and magazine writers such as those for *Crítica* strove to appropriate scientific knowledge and authority for themselves, they also acknowledged and reinforced its power in contemporary Argentine society. Science wielded substantial social influence in late nineteenth- and early twentieth-century Argentina. Under the aegis of a progressive Liberal state, Argentine elites championed an agenda of national modernity and employed scientific tools to "improve" the nation, expanding national infrastructure to facilitate transportation and communication and practicing eugenic science to "cure" social ills. Science also permeated everyday decisions and social norms. During this period, Argentina—especially its cities and large towns—supported a growing and diversifying class of physicians; a rising tide of electricity, indoor plumbing, and other innovative modern conveniences in private homes; and a vibrant civic scientific culture of museum visiting, scientific reading, and private collecting.[3] In this modernizing moment of deliberate preoccupation with progress, science also became a vehicle for understanding indigenous cultures in strategic connection with the Argentine nation-state, even as mainstream national narratives suggested that a new creole Argentina was emerging, composed of Argentine-born and European-descended citizens and destined to triumph over the "barbarous" influences of Afro-Argentine and indigenous peoples.

The scientific authority to interpret indigenous cultures during the late nineteenth and early twentieth centuries was housed primarily in museums. Museums appeared across Argentina during this period, embodying contemporary national orientations toward science and institution building and also creating spaces for new interpretations of national history, nature, and aesthetics.[4] In natural science and anthropology museums, anthropologists linked indigenous cultures with nature, displaying them as natural adaptations and mounting indigenous bodies like zoological specimens. Museums offered ideal spaces for the cultivation of anthropological authority and knowledge, as many subfields—especially archaeology, physical anthropology, and ethnography—did object-based work, easily suited to museum exhibition and publication. In displaying their growing collections in vaulting exhibition halls and lavishly illustrated museum journals, museums in Argentina carved out niches as authorities on scientific understandings about indigenous people.

In addition to their scientific research, museums defined themselves as institutions that educated "the public." This amorphous category encompassed a cross-class array of politicians, educators, lawyers, collectors, artifact dealers, businessmen, journalists, workers, newspaper audiences, school groups, women's groups, foreign travelers, and others. Members of this complex "public" interacted very differently with museums, responding to their own political, economic, and social agendas. As scientific institutions that facilitated public access to indigenous artifacts and human remains, and even very occasionally to living indigenous people on display, museums spoke to a spectrum of popular interests in science and worked to shape national understandings about indigenous cultures through their displays. Popular actors, however, did not always accept museum scientists' interpretations or decisions. Argentine museums during this period received a growing stream of requests, demands, and objections from members of the public, and their displays and publications were criticized in the popular press and retooled by nonscientists in support of other agendas. In this back and forth, museums lost some of their ivory luster and became social spaces that fueled interest in scientific understandings of indigenous cultures but were not always able to control public debates over how these cultures connected with Argentina's modernizing nation-state.

Within a self-consciously creole national imagination—"creole" being a very flexible term that in Argentina included those who self-identified as being of European descent and born in Argentina—museum-driven scientific understandings of indigenous cultures played important symbolic roles in crafting notions of national distinctiveness and history.[5] Through museums and science, Argentines could imagine and embrace an indigenous national heritage, while simultaneously maintaining ethnically European, creole identities. *Crítica*'s front-page story on the Wagners' discovery, for instance, spoke to contemporary debates about Inca cultural expansion into Argentina's pre-Columbian north, a scientific question that for scientists and nonscientists alike became entangled with national identity and pride. Creole Argentine readers were encouraged to see the photographed artifacts and human remains in *Crítica* as evidence of their country's ancient pedigree and to think of the Inca as foreign invaders and aggressors against an older and more elevated "Argentine" indigenous culture, framing themselves—rather than the indigenous people living in the north—as inheritors of this remote and romantic past. Through museum-based anthropological science, creole Argentines expressed a connection with indigenous cultures and bodies, simultaneously possessing and cataloguing them as artifacts belonging *to* the nation but not necessarily *within* the national community. Such contradictory visions of indigenous connections to the nation-state were possible largely because many creole Argentines maintained a distinction, to borrow Rebecca Earle's very useful phrase, between indigenous cultures (which were abstract and embraceable) and indigenous people (who lived in the present and were often seen as troublesome and backward).[6]

The notion of strategically embracing indigenous cultures as part of national identity and politics is not new in modern Latin American history. Earle's comparative work has illustrated the multiple symbolic roles that indigenous cultures played for creole elites crafting heritage and identity throughout Spanish America in the tumultuous century after independence. Other scholars have drawn out the implications of scientific, cultural, and official state adoptions of indigenous cultures for nationalist and *indigenista* projects in countries such as Mexico and Peru, where indigenous cultures have often been strategically linked with state-making projects.[7] In Mexico, for example, national history has been connected with the indigenous past— in one way or another—since independence, and anthropological collecting has been an official, state-sponsored part of Mexican patrimony making at least since the creation of the National Museum in 1825.[8] As Christina Bueno has shown, Mexican anthropologists during the later nineteenth-century Porfiriato collected pre-Columbian artifacts as markers of Mexican heritage and brought them to state-operated museums for interpretation and transformation into objects of national patrimony or "objects believed to embody the nation's culture and identity."[9] Nineteenth-century scientists collecting archaeological artifacts in national museums connected ancient cultures such as the Mexica with the nation-state and lent the modern Mexican nation a desired sense of unity and permanence. Later, in postrevolutionary Mexico, *indigenista* movements incorporated contemporary indigenous bodies and cultural practices into possessive expressions of nationally and regionally distinctive identities that often simultaneously celebrated and sought to control the meanings of indigeneity within national society.[10] Such connections between national identity and indigeneity, patrimony and science, have made anthropology a fruitful avenue for recent historical research.

In light of the often-cited importance of a "white" Argentine identity that emerged during the later nineteenth and early twentieth centuries, creole Argentines' strategic engagement with indigenous cultures during these decades prompts important questions about race, science, nation, and identity in Argentina. This connection also puts Argentina's nation-state formation process in dialogue with broader movements in Latin America, rather than framing it as an exceptional case. Nicolas Shumway has argued that nineteenth-century Argentine state makers and intellectuals crafted a foundational "mythology of exclusion" that imagined Argentina as a negatively defined space, identified as much by what was not Argentine as by what was.[11] Argentine state makers constructed national identity through inside-outside relationships that identified Argentina as European, white, and progressive, while their opposites—non-European, nonwhite, and backward—became accordingly un-Argentine. Mid-nineteenth-century liberal statesman Juan Bautista Alberdi illustrated this inside-outside thinking in 1852 when he wrote, "Who among us would not prefer a thousand times over to see his daughter marry an English shoeman rather than an Araucanian prince? In America everything that is not European is barbaric; there is no division other than this one: Indian which is synonymous with savage, and European which means those of us born in America, who speak Spanish and believe in Jesus Christ."[12] Alberdi exhorted Argentines to seek political unification by appealing to a shared identity as European-descended creoles and as Christians. As the nineteenth century progressed, Alberdi's division between creole Argentines and others—including indigenous peoples—acquired new urgency. Likewise, Domingo Faustino Sarmiento's midcentury exhortation that Argentines escape from the clutches of barbarism and enter into the light of Western civilization became a generational clarion call, and indigenous peoples were pushed decidedly into the former, politically undesirable category. Insightful studies focusing on the marginalization of a variety of deviant behaviors and groups, including Afro-Argentines, federalist caudillos, prostitutes, and the mentally ill, have borne out the importance of these and other inside-outside identities to nineteenth-century Argentine politics and culture.[13]

In this vein, scholars have compellingly explored the extent to which indigenous peoples were excluded from Argentina's modernizing economy, educational system, and political agendas during the nineteenth and twentieth centuries.[14] Because Argentine national identity is most often associated with these narratives, Argentina is not generally recognized as a nation shaped by an interest in indigenous cultures, much less one that would seek to connect indigenous cultures to its national identity and heritage. And yet, as Mónica Quijada has shown, indigenous cultures were critically involved in constructions of Argentine patrimony and narratives of nationhood during this period.[15] This book argues that while many creole Argentines participated in the everyday construction of a "white" or creole Argentina, they also helped create strategic and possessive connections with Argentina's indigenous heritage in the scientific and public spaces of museums, as well as newspapers and magazines, schoolrooms and congressional sessions, public monuments and antiquities markets.

Cultural History: Nation, Science, and Objects

It should be noted from the outset that this is not an institutional museum history, nor is it a scientific history of the discipline of anthropology. Other scholars have written a great deal about the institutional development of Latin American museums, the evolution of scientific methodologies, and the scientific biographies of anthropologists discussed here.[16] The aim of this study, by contrast, is to use the insights of cultural history to explore the everyday social life and meaning making of museums and anthropological science. Museum scientists' approaches to anthropology as scientific practice will play an important part in this history but will do so in dialogue with how their scientific work impacted and was shaped in return by other people's feelings about science, museums, and indigenous cultures. Key here will be the relationships between professional science and popular science, especially dialogues between professional attempts to control scientific knowledge and popular expressions through correspondence, the popular press, public events, private collecting, and other avenues.

Cultural history's heterogeneous methodologies and theoretical base offer an aptly flexible framework for exploring something as multivocal (and even cacophonous) as the meanings of scientific ideas about indigenous cultures to an entire country. Cultural history draws together scholars interested in diverse topics, from consumerism to religion, national identity to childhood.[17] While cultural history embraces many topics and various approaches to them, one central tenet holds them together: cultural history seeks to address the idea that human life is about meaning.[18] Cultural historians contend not only that symbolic and everyday social practices are "as" important to understanding history as more traditional political and economic questions, but that these cultural practices form a foundational context within which other historical questions take on more complete meaning.[19] From within the wide field of cultural history, this study draws particular inspiration from scholarship on nation, science, and the intersections between elite and popular culture. Benedict Anderson's foundational study of nations as "imagined communities" has inspired a generation of new scholarship that sees nations and states as socially constructed understandings rather than stable realities.[20] Anderson's notion that all human communities—from small towns to nations and beyond—are held together not by preexisting or static likenesses but rather by communally crafted narratives of shared history and character shows identity to be a flexible and contested thing that is shaped not by an objective "truth" but by ever-changing human perceptions and priorities.

Anthony Smith has developed this idea in connection with national identity, arguing that national identities combine both "civic" and "ethnic" elements, building multifaceted identities that appeal to a wide base of human sensibilities, both political and legal (civic) and cultural and genealogical (ethnic). Smith locates Argentina among nations whose identity after independence formed "without immediate antecedent ethnie"; instead, Argentine state makers deliberately coded their nation in civic terms, embracing Atlantic revolutionary ideals such as liberalism, citizenship, and popular sovereignty as part of Argentine national identity, even if those ideals were not fully realized in practice.[21] Nineteenth-century Argentine national identity, from this perspective, was based on political character and conviction rather than inherited traditions, memory, or ancestry.

This book argues, however, that Argentina's national identity also relied on a carefully constructed ethnie, whose first chapter lay in the pre-Columbian world. Along with creole elites across Latin America, Argentina's Liberal state makers and intellectuals carefully selected useful elements of indigenous cultures to reinforce and authenticate the nation's unique ethnic identity.[22] Argentina's indigenous peoples, viewed through the lens of museum anthropology, responded to calls for national identity and heritage. In this pursuit, creole Argentines coded themselves as the rightful heirs to the deep indigenous past and sometimes also claimed connections with indigenous peoples in the present, thus creating a largely symbolic ethnic foundation for a liberal, civic nation willfully throwing off the tarnished vestiges of Spanish colonialism. The social utility of this strategic embrace also begins to explain why, at the end of the time period examined here, creole Argentines moved away from indigenous imaginings of their national heritage as alternative models—particularly colonial Spanish heritage and *criollismo*—gained political and social ascendance.

Much of the most visible national imagining in modern nation-states has been driven by political and socioeconomic elites, who have constructed national images that reflect their own aspirations and self-perceptions. Mary Louise Pratt has argued that elites in modern nation-states have often engaged in "autoethnography," actively creating their own cultural identities through mechanisms of national representation such as national anthems and world's fairs, folklore festivals and public monuments.[23] Scholars have often seen museums as crucial institutions of elite autoethnography and have analyzed them in Foucaultian terms, emphasizing elite efforts to control visibility and to use it as a form of power through the languages of knowledge, science, and art. Through museums, scholars have demonstrated, elites learned to control what was seen, how it was seen, and who might see it.[24] These insights have proven invaluable for understanding how museum scientists and their savvier elite patrons used museum spaces and exhibit technologies to send specific messages to specific audiences. Such approaches also help us understand how museum scientists constructed their own authority as "experts" during the nineteenth century, as museum objects became invested with unique types of knowledge and power. In the more specific realm of museum anthropology, scholars have underscored that indigenous bodies on display were not willing collaborators in their own exhibition, nor did they often return the visitors' gaze. Rather, they were acted upon, exposed to public examination without their consent in the name of furthering Western scientific knowledge.[25]

There are, however, some limits to this kind of analysis. At their best, Foucaultian-inspired studies have interrogated the flow of power, vision, and knowledge through the institutional framework of the museum. On the other hand, focusing on the circulation of power as the primary goal of museums runs the risk of transforming these institutions into what is by now a familiar stereotype of museum scholarship: museums become cogs within abstract elite machines of social control, and the human beings within them morph into one-dimensional accomplices of social domination.[26] Such a focus can also suggest that elite control over national imaginings in museums and elsewhere was absolute, a notion that recent cultural historical scholarship has largely deflated. Answering calls in the 1990s from scholars such as Gilbert M. Joseph and Daniel Nugent, cultural historians have recognized the importance of popular cultures as primary factors in defining national identity and culture. Scholars have identified popular culture as the broad sphere of everyday actions of nonelite or subaltern people, as well as the meanings that are attached to those actions.[27] Moreover, most cultural historians emphasize that there is no cut-and-dried boundary between elite and popular cultures, but rather that these arenas are created in dialogue with one another, in ways that reveal power inequalities in a given society and also create space for negotiations, appropriations, and transformations.[28] The everyday dialogues between elite and popular sectors have revealed culture making that is neither top-down nor bottom-up, but rather a negotiation between.

Museum science is a valuable window onto exchanges between elite and popular culture during this period in part because of how museum scientists saw the objects they studied. Museums of the late nineteenth and early twentieth centuries exhibited objects as direct conduits to knowledge, which could be understood not just by trained scientists but by anyone who observed them carefully. This perception of objects as carriers of knowledge, which Steven Conn has called an "object-based epistemology," opened the door to popular interpretations and appropriations of museum science.[29] In essence, by understanding museum objects as universally comprehensible, without the need for professional mediation, and by defining itself in relation to those self-explanatory objects, museum science cast itself as open to all, even as museum scientists continually contradicted this idea by insisting on their own scientific authority. Thus, while science and museums are generally understood as a part of elite histories, cultural history allows for fruitful analysis of negotiations between elite and popular understandings of science, as well as examination of fractures within these large categories.

Museum objects were sometimes physical—as in artifacts and human remains, or photographs that served as proxy objects—while others were more abstract—as in the scientific language, data, and theories that identified indigenous cultures as ancient and autochthonous. These physical and abstract objects enjoyed distinct social lives in Argentina; they operated as contested commodities that circulated between scientific and popular hands, gaining and losing different sorts of value. As Arjun Appadurai has noted, an object or idea can be considered a commodity when "its exchangeability (past, present, or future) for some other thing is its socially relevant feature."[30] There is no concrete distinction, then, between commodities and other things, because all things acquire and lose exchangeable value through the mercurial mechanisms of human desire.

Analytically approaching indigenous artifacts and even human remains as commodities calls attention to their constructed and contested values and meanings and to the processes of recoding that transformed them into exchangeable commodities. Moreover, scientists and popular actors attributed conflicting sets of scientific, cultural, and economic value to indigenous artifacts that translated these objects into powerful commodities and patrimonial symbols and also disassociated them from indigenous lives and cultures.[31] These different sorts of value were often couched as mutually exclusive, and yet, in practice, scientists and nonscientists alike often invoked them together, revealing complex and often contradictory understandings of what these objects, and the ideas they were seen to embody, actually meant. Although human skulls were collected, sold, and displayed as objects in the period under study here, important questions remain about the moral implications of describing them as such. In transforming human remains into museum objects, scientists and collectors often subtracted something of their humanity and distanced the scientific practices of collecting, researching, and displaying from cultural considerations of sanctity or privacy of the body in death. This book employs the language of objects and commodity value to underscore the historical processes under analysis, but it also works wherever possible to call attention to the humanity of these remains.

Through the tangible objects of museum science, indigenous cultures became malleable and meaningful indicators of authentic *argentinidad*. Shelley Garrigan has argued that acts of collection often involve processes of "emptying," in which objects are disassociated from earlier meanings in order to recode them as part of new collections and their narratives. The power of museum objects to embody abstract ideas such as national identity, heritage, and patrimony lay in the multiple meanings that could be imprinted onto them, making them elastic symbols in ongoing conflicts over what, precisely, the nation was.[32] Objects associated with indigenous cultures in Argentina—ceramic jars and human remains, weapons and musical instruments—came under scrutiny by museum anthropologists, newspaper writers, politicians, schoolteachers, field guides, and a diverse array of other actors, who emptied them of connections with individual indigenous people and recoded them as bearers of creole heritage and identity. This ability to recode objects' meanings was coupled with a prismatic array of possible interpretations, making indigenous cultures powerful points of contention. Scientists in different parts of Argentina interpreted the same indigenous artifacts in conflicting and impassioned ways, popular texts made different claims about the ancient human past than academic sources did, and scientists became popular celebrities and national icons even as their theories were debunked by professional scientists.

This study explores everyday meaning making about indigenous cultures through the individual objects collected by museums, along with the stories of scientists and others who engaged with them. In exploring the variable meanings of indigenous cultures, science, and objects, this book contends that "big ideas" like national identity are shaped by small, quotidian actions like reading a newspaper or visiting a museum, and that these ideas must be examined from multiple perspectives—geographical, socioeconomic, political, generational—in order to understand their full importance. My research took me into museum libraries and archives, where I found records of daily museum operations, including reams of correspondence and telegraphs, shipping receipts documenting collections exchanges, employment records and complaints, working drafts of speeches and publications, field journals and sketches, requests and petitions from people outside the museum, and museum supply catalogues and order forms. These archives also contain photograph collections that offer visual evidence of museum display techniques and spaces, public events in museums, anthropological fieldwork, and collections analysis. I also worked in state, university, city, and private archives and libraries, where I found a wealth of published anthropological studies from the nineteenth and twentieth centuries, university publications and operations records, newspapers, art and literature, and current Argentine scholarship on museums and anthropology. Finally, I spent time in the museums themselves, exploring them and connecting my own experiences to historical documents and events that occurred decades ago in these spaces. I saw how each museum presents its own history—in both text and museum display—and studied the changes that these museums have undergone during their histories.

Museums in Argentina, 1877–1943

Susan Sheets-Pyenson and other scholars have often framed their work on museums by defining a "museum age," a period during the nineteenth and twentieth centuries in which museums gained and exercised authority as dominant scientific institutions in areas of both professional research and public education, giving them potent influence over civic, regional, and national cultures.[33] The time frame under analysis here is more specific, addressing the development of an idea within museums, rather than the rise and fall of museums themselves. The period between 1877 and 1943 captures a window of unprecedented state support for museums in Argentina and complex alignments between liberal political and scientific interests, in addition to the professionalization of museums and anthropology in Argentina and the popularization of science on local, regional, and national scales, which transformed anthropology into a "national" science—one deeply involved in national identity and heritage. This period was marked by a contentious and conditional affiliation between museum anthropology and the Liberal Argentine Republic, whose political philosophy ideologically aligned with museums as part of wider mantras of progress and civilization. This was, however, a very changeable relationship. At times museum anthropologists supported liberal state agendas, and at other times they broke with state interests to adhere to their own plans for museum professionalization. Museums during this period emphasized the rational, orderly organization of their collections, the seriousness of scientific research conducted in their libraries and collections repositories, and the importance of public education and improvement as part of their mission.[34]

This was also a period of transition in Argentina, characterized by indigenous conquest, European immigration, political radicalism and agitation, the emergence of mass politics and oligarchic struggles to retain control, civilian uprisings and military coups, regional tensions, and economic swings. As scholars such as Marial Iglesias Utset have noted, periods of political and economic transition can intensify the meanings of ordinary social practices; everyday decisions take on new meaning, old assumptions are called into question, and the search for identity or purpose assumes a conscious social importance.[35] During the sixty-odd years under study here, Argentina experienced a series of important political, social, and economic transitions, whose impact on creole Argentine identities was shaped by and reflected in changing ideas of national indigenous heritage in museums and popular science.

This book focuses on three museums: the Museo de Ciencias Naturales de La Plata, the Museo Etnográfico "Juan B. Ambrosetti" in Buenos Aires, and the Instituto de Etnología at the Universidad Nacional de Tucumán in northwestern Argentina. I have chosen these museums because they offer a range of institutional size and focus, and they are situated within different geographical and social contexts. Because of their differences, they constitute a compellingly representative sample of the priorities and challenges faced by different kinds of museums in Argentina, including state-funded and university-run museums, large and small museums, anthropology and natural science museums, museums that were open to the public and those dedicated largely to academic research, and museums whose collecting focused on a specific region and those with broader national or international ambitions. They are not, of course, the only museums I might have chosen for this study; interesting anthropological museums and museum departments also existed during this period in Santiago del Estero and elsewhere, among them the Museo Nacional de Ciencias Naturales in Buenos Aires. Additionally, I have chosen these three museums because of their palpable influence on museum anthropology in Argentina: the Museo de La Plata became a national icon and an internationally recognized scientific center during the late nineteenth and early twentieth centuries; the Museo Etnográfico served as a highly visible institution of Argentine archaeology and of *porteño* cosmopolitanism in the early twentieth century; and the Instituto de Etnología identified itself as a center for northwestern regional studies during the early twentieth century, often standing in contrast to coastal institutions in Buenos Aires and La Plata. This book does not aim to be a comprehensive or exhaustive history of museums in Argentina, but rather to offer a detailed analysis of a group of carefully chosen museums and to use those museums as a platform for broader comparative analysis. I examine each museum in turn, while also comparing and highlighting the connections between them, exploring the internal dynamics of anthropology museums as well as their impact on broader understandings of indigenous peoples, popular actors' impact on museums, and, where possible, indigenous peoples' reactions to anthropological scrutiny.

This study begins in 1877 with the opening of the short-lived Museo Antropológico y Arqueológico in Buenos Aires, founded and directed by naturalist Francisco P. Moreno and dedicated to the anthropological study of Argentina's indigenous peoples. The new museum reflected the tensions of its day, including the Liberal preoccupation with museums and science as part of cultivating civilization and the creole Argentine anxieties about the "unconquered" indigenous peoples of the southern pampas, who by the 1870s were responding to southward creole expansion with increasing violence. Less than a year after the Museo Antropológico y Arqueológico opened its doors, the Argentine Republic mounted the Conquest of the Desert, a military campaign aimed at the "subjugation or eviction of the barbarous Indians of the Pampa" and the clearing of these fertile grasslands for creole Argentine occupation.[36] At the time of the Conquest, Argentina's southern regions were populated by a number of largely nomadic and seminomadic indigenous groups, who had resisted conquest by Spanish and Argentine forces since first contact in the sixteenth century. A complex and flexible frontier society existed between Argentine settlements to the north and indigenous territories to the south, forging trade networks, social exchange, and fragile peace agreements punctuated by outbursts of violence. Estimates suggest that more than 40,000 indigenous people occupied the territory south of the Argentine settlement frontier in 1870, as compared to an estimated 170,000 people living in Buenos

Aires at that time. Official figures claim that 1,271 warriors were taken prisoner and 1,313 were killed during the Conquest; in addition, 10,513 women and children were "placed under state supervision," which often meant relocation to Buenos Aires as service laborers, forced adoptions of indigenous children by creole families, or captivity in state prisons. These figures are not exact, nor do they encapsulate the range of destinations and fates faced by displaced indigenous peoples after the Conquest. Some escaped southward or westward into Patagonia and Chile, at best temporary refuges against the expanding Argentine and Chilean states. Others were relocated to state-created *colonias*, where it was hoped they would become Western-style agriculturalists and shed their indigenous identities.[37]

In addition to a legacy of violence and erasure, the Conquest spurred interest in scientific knowledge about indigenous peoples. The same interethnic tensions that built support for military conquest in the 1870s also prompted the growth of scientific studies of *indios amigos* ("friendly" or treaty-bound indigenous peoples) and *indios no sometidos* ("unconquered" indigenous peoples).[38] Francisco Moreno himself sent information about indigenous cultures and politics back to Buenos Aires and later advocated for the relocation of indigenous groups he knew personally after their expulsion during the Conquest. Argentine anthropologists from the 1870s to the turn of the century focused most of their attention on the contemporary indigenous cultures of the southern pampas and the northern Chaco, who had recently been subdued by the Argentine military. In these conquered landscapes, anthropologists and others amassed vast collections of the remains of recently deceased indigenous people. Argentina's largest and most impressively displayed physical anthropological collections were housed in the Museo de La Plata, opened in 1884 by Moreno, who took his original collections from the Museo Antropológico y Arqueológico with him (see chapter 1).

After the turn of the twentieth century, Argentine anthropologists shifted their focus from the bodies of the recently conquered to the ancient indigenous civilizations of the Argentine northwest. These cultures had left behind stonework structures, worked bronze and stone artifacts, and strikingly beautiful ceramic vessels, meeting contemporary sensibilities about "advanced" ancient civilizations. This sliding scale, which differentiated glorified civilizations like the Maya and the Inca from "lesser" groups like the seminomadic peoples of the pampas and the Amazon, identified the pre-Columbian indigenous cultures of Argentina's northwest as indicators of a splendid and ancient national past (see chapters 2 and 3). Between the beginning of the 1900s and the early 1940s, northwestern archaeology attracted significant state funding, regional support, and popular interest. This popularity was finally overshadowed in the 1930s and 1940s by a rise in conservative politics and nationalism that championed colonial Spanish and rural criollo folklore as the "true" seat of national heritage, rather than indigenous cultures.

Also during the early decades of the twentieth century, Argentines joined impassioned international debates over human evolution in scientific publications and the popular press. These debates were brought home by Argentine scientist Florentino Ameghino, who contended that humankind had originally evolved in Argentina. Ameghino's highly provocative and much-debated theories drew out divisions between popular scientific enthusiasm, which overwhelmingly embraced him as a national hero and scientific visionary, and professional scientists, many of whom worked to distance themselves from his increasingly outlandish claims. Between the 1910s and the 1930s, Ameghino's scientific celebrity highlighted the fissures within the social life of science in Argentina, as well as the highly emotional payload carried by a purportedly "objective" field of knowledge (see chapter 4).

This study closes with the military coup of 1943, following a decade of resurgent conservative politics in the 1930s that shifted national focus and scientific resources away from indigenous-focused anthropology and toward alternative national identity markers.[39] While the period under analysis here begins with the opening of a museum, it concludes with a coup d'état; I have chosen this ending point not because anthropologists ceased to study indigenous cultures in 1943, but rather because the coup signaled a turning away from nationalist politics and culture making that imagined Argentina as a creole nation with an indigenous heritage. Instead, strategic political adoptions of criollo folk culture and the colonial Spanish past were embraced as truer indicators of authentic Argentine heritage.[40]

$$\boxed{1}$$

Magic in the Desert: Indigenous Bodies on Display in the Museo de La Plata, 1877–1906

Introduction

In October of 1877, the Buenos Aires provincial government created a museum under the direction of twenty-five-year-old naturalist and explorer Francisco P. Moreno.[1] This museum, the Museo Antropológico y Arqueológico, was composed of Moreno's personal anthropological collections and was initially housed in Moreno's private downtown residence at 128 Avenida Florida. After a few months of preparation, Moreno opened a public exhibit hall on the fourth floor of the Teatro Colón (then located on the Plaza de Mayo), to enthusiastic public acclaim.[2] Domingo Faustino Sarmiento, in 1877 already a former president of the Republic and now the general director of schools for the province of Buenos Aires and a senator for San Juan, wrote a glowing review of the new museum in which he enthused, "What a story these skulls tell!"[3] This story, as creole Argentine scientists, statesmen, and others were arguing with increasing efficacy by the late 1870s, was that of Argentina's deep and ancient past. Upon seeing the prehistoric artifacts on display in Moreno's museum, Sarmiento voiced a reversal of his own binary of civilization and barbarism, writing with great patriotic verve, "What barbarians those Europeans were! They lived in caves, scaring off the hyenas, while *we* were already making guanaco stew! The remains are there in the Museum, in earthenware, ashes, charcoal, and the chewed bones."[4] This unexpected "we" reveals a strategic and possessive identification not with European culture, or even with a gauchesque or criollo folk tradition, but with the indigenous populations who inhabited the pampas and Patagonia during humankind's prehistory. Argentina was imagined here as a "vast necropolis" of mankind, a human cradle (and even more so, a grave) of deep antiquity from which the Argentine nation-state could draw a prehistoric genealogy through its indigenous forebears and thereby derive a sense of its own worth and pedigree. Moreno also saw the significance of his museum in terms of patriotic service. "The fruit of my labors," he wrote in 1879, "has been the collection that I have formed and which I have had the honor of donating to the *patria* in order to found the Museo Antropológico y Arqueológico de Buenos Aires, of which I am the director and to whose development I destine all the years of my life."[5]

While Moreno organized his collections for display, however, the Argentine state was also preparing for war against the indigenous peoples of the south. In the closing months of 1878, the Argentine military invaded the southern pampas and Patagonia, aiming to drive indigenous peoples from the fertile pampean pasturelands and open the way for creole ranchers and cereal growers.[6] This campaign, known as the Conquest of the Desert, was described by contemporaries as a glorious victory and "one of the most prolific expeditions mounted by the Argentine army since the heroic times of Independence."[7] The Conquest marked a breaking point in the rising tensions between indigenous communities to the south and largely creole Argentines to the north, who were eager to expand ranching and agricultural interests into indigenous-controlled pampas lands and to exert effective control over the entire claimed national territory. After 1880, when the Conquest's military commander, General Julio A. Roca, was elected to the presidency, contemporaries also celebrated the Conquest of the Desert as marking Argentina's passage between eras. Before the Conquest, Argentine national histories were characterized by social disunity, economic stagnation, and political instability. Afterward, by contrast, Argentina entered into what was often described as a "golden age" of social progress, economic growth, and national unity. The Conquest facilitated this abrupt national turnaround, according to contemporaries, by eradicating the indigenous peoples of the southern pampas and Patagonia, thereby helping "resolve" Argentina's long-standing "Indian problem" alongside parallel campaigns in the Argentine north and the Chaco.[8]

Although the Conquest took credit for solving the "Indian problem," Argentine interest in indigenous cultures did not abate after the campaign officially ended in 1880. If anything, frontier indigenous cultures and bodies inspired *more* popular and scientific interest, as evidenced by the transformation of Moreno's small anthropology museum in the Teatro Colón into the much larger, lavishly designed and decorated, nationally celebrated Museo de Ciencias Naturales de La Plata in 1884. As Mónica Quijada has argued, indigenous conquest and nation-state formation became mutually enforcing in late nineteenth-century Argentina. Argentine scientists and statesmen effectively transformed the indigenous people of the southern pampas and Patagonia into proper objects for conquest and, simultaneously, into adoptable figures of national history, as they disappeared from the national present.[9] Building on this insight, this chapter explores the conflicted and ambivalent display of indigenous bodies in Moreno's second museum, the Museo de La Plata, during the years surrounding the Conquest of the Desert, 1877 to 1906. This chapter uses Foucaultian ideas about power, visibility, and biopower to analyze scientific practices surrounding the display of indigenous bodies in the Museo de La Plata; it also, however, argues that there are limits to these analytical tools, and it highlights not just the smooth operation of Foucaultian-style exercises of power and knowledge but also moments when anthropologists in the museum contradicted these models in significant ways. The Conquest shaped creole Argentine interest in indigenous cultures between the 1870s and the turn of the century, focusing scientific and social attention on the physical bodies of contemporary indigenous people who were understood generally as receding into the past. In Moreno's short-lived Museo Antropológico y Arqueológico, and later in the Museo de La Plata, physical anthropologists rhetorically relegated indigenous cultures to the national past using international languages of progress and science, a strong example of biopower at work.[10] And yet their everyday words and actions often contradicted these clean lines, presenting indigenous human bodies as abstract racial specimens but also as individual people and even popular celebrities. The presence of celebrity specimens and living indigenous people on display in the Museo de La Plata pulled indigenous cultures into the national present, complicating museum anthropology's alignment with Argentine state–driven narratives of whiteness and indigenous eradication.

Anthropology and the Conquest of the Desert

Argentine military officer, writer, and scientist Estanislao Zeballos offered a revealing glimpse into contemporary creole perspectives on the indigenous cultures affected by the Conquest, writing in his popular frontier memoir *La Conquista de Quince Mil Leguas*, "These Indians live by theft and make War against the Christian with cruelty and implacable hatred, as if it would satisfy a horrible vengeance sworn by their ancestors against the injustice with which they were treated. Their invasions of our lands leave traces stained in blood and marked by fire and plunder; and in their own *toldos* the disgraced prisoners or *cautivos* are made to suffer horrible and indescribable tortures." Despite his swift allusion to the "injustice" suffered by indigenous peoples, Zeballos's evident focus was on indigenous savagery and the cruelties inflicted upon "Christian" communities along the frontier. These desecrations, Zeballos wrote, were being avenged by the Conquest campaign: "The military power of the barbarians is totally destroyed because the Remington [rifle] has taught them that a battalion of the Republic can cross the entire pampa, leaving the field seeded with the corpses of those who dared to oppose them."[11]

Few today would argue that the Conquest eliminated indigenous peoples in Argentina. Indigenous communities still exist throughout the country, and many have joined hemisphere-wide campaigns to assert their cultural and legal rights as First Peoples. Historians *have* argued, however, that indigenous peoples disappeared from the national imaginary in the decades following the Conquest, a disappearance that had important political, social, and economic consequences. For example, in the wake of the Conquest, relocated indigenous peoples were recorded by national census takers according to their occupation—as laborers, servants, or *colonistas*—rather than as Tehuelches, Ranqueles, or Pampas. Traditional indigenous lifeways were dismantled, broken by military conquest or slowly eroded through contact with, and often coercion by, creole Argentine communities and economic systems. In most existing histories of Argentina, indigenous cultures fade from national historical narratives beginning in the late nineteenth century and reemerge in the last quarter of the twentieth century, often in connection with indigenous revitalization movements.[12] Indigenous peoples' connections with national histories, then, also pivot around the Conquest of the Desert: before the Conquest, they are portrayed as relevant to national histories, given that they effectively controlled part of the national territory, while afterward their importance to national histories is often closely circumscribed. Indigenous peoples after the Conquest are most often considered apart from the national mainstream, and questions of how indigenous cultures impacted the nation, or were impacted by it, fall from view.[13] Moreno's anthropology museum, created in this nineteenth-century context and on the eve of the Conquest, raises complicating questions about the place of indigenous peoples in a creole Argentina. This project was surely inspired in part by desires to control, contain, and even colonize indigenous peoples, but it also reveals something more complex about relationships between indigenous peoples and creole society. The same Conquest that facilitated the supposed "disappearance" of indigenous cultures in Argentina also spurred their scientific study as part of the national and natural landscape, possessively and strategically reincorporating them into creole national identities.[14]

During the 1860s and 1870s, the Argentine Republic faced almost constant challenge, from within and without, heightening national interest in frontiers. Federalist rebellions in the country's interior provinces continually rose up against the centralized government in Buenos Aires, and state military resources were needed to quell these revolts at least until 1880.[15] In addition, the Triple Alliance War, which pitted Paraguay against Brazil, Argentina, and Uruguay, proved to be the bloodiest international war in the history of Latin America, costing between 150,000 and 200,000 lives between 1865 and 1870.[16] Although Argentina emerged victorious, the draining of military and other resources required by the war had called forces away from other problem areas and created new internal problems. Finally, the question of boundary lines, both among Argentine provinces and between Argentina and neighboring countries, promoted the necessity of mapping out national landscapes and cultivated rising interest in exploration and knowledge about the boundaries of the national territory.

National interest in frontiers and frontier expansion found cultural expression in travel writings and scientific exploration. Frontier travel narratives flooded Argentina during the 1870s, offering a potpourri of geography, ethnographic data, and anecdotal tales of travel. The authority of the traveler was often augmented by the scientific information he conveyed.[17] Recourse to science, in a very real sense, separated the narrator from the "savage" indigenous peoples and untamed landscapes that he encountered and made the wilderness comprehensible to "civilized" readers. Anthropology, as a scientific lens through which to view indigenous peoples, became increasingly connected with frontiers and national expansion, generally accompanied by prophesies of indigenous extinction in the face of creole advance. As the nineteenth century progressed, national expansion and anthropology became mutually enforcing, creating a positive feedback loop that attracted more state funding and public interest to anthropological study.

Anthropology proved directly useful to the expansionist Argentine state and military. First, the Argentine state was actively engaged throughout the nineteenth century, as had been the Spanish colonial government before it, in networks of peace treaties and negotiation with indigenous cultures along settlement frontiers. Ethnographic knowledge about indigenous communities in unconquered terrains helped the Argentine state deal, if not with greater sensitivity, certainly more knowledgeably with indigenous leaders and political systems. Moreover, anthropologists could provide tactical information to the military about who controlled what territories, when warriors were likely to attack or to be separated from their home communities, and how large the fighting forces of various caciques were at any given time. Anthropologists could serve as the eyes and ears of the Argentine state as they traveled less conspicuously (in comparison with a heavily armed company of cavalry, for example) through uncontrolled territories, reporting on the movement of indigenous and other peoples. For example, the minister of foreign relations wrote to Moreno in June 1877, requesting to know whether, in his most recent voyage through Patagonia, Moreno had seen any Chilean settlements "north of the Strait [of Magellan] or south of the Santa Cruz River."[18]

Anthropology's utility to an expansionist Argentine state came into increasingly sharp focus during the 1870s. Exploration was coded as patriotic, and scientific curiosity was paired with military expansion as part of a modern national destiny. The state effected its expansionist agenda by sending out expeditions to explore, catalogue, and subdue the untamed territories at the margins of the nation-state. In light of Argentina's costly victory over Paraguay in the Triple Alliance War and continuing national disunity between Buenos Aires and interior provinces, campaigns against unconquered indigenous peoples addressed a sorely felt need to exert national prowess and dominance. In these campaigns, scientific information gathering became as instrumental to national power as military strength. The self-vindicating flavor of the campaigns was captured by Estanislao Zeballos, for example, who wrote of the conquest of the pampas in 1879, "Happily the day to make felt the iron hand of the power of the nation has come, and everything will be settled when the frontier has as its natural line the Río Negro."[19]

The close ties between expansionism and anthropological science in the nineteenth and early twentieth centuries, in Argentina and beyond, have been well studied in the context of "skull science." Scholars have convincingly connected skull science's preoccupation with measuring non-Western physical bodies and quantifying racial traits with Western nation-building narratives, and especially with efforts to tie present nation-states to longer histories of the territories they occupy. Scientists and state makers during this period reinterpreted ancient human remains as well as contemporary non-Western cultures as evidence of a long-standing human presence in the landscape, coding the nation-state as rightfully inheriting that tradition. Skull science has also played an undeniable role in reifying the racial hierarchies and violent oppression of imperialism around the globe. Especially insofar as the remains of indigenous or other non-Western peoples have been taken by force, without the permission or participation of the individuals or cultures involved, skull science has often underscored the perceived inferiority of the "studied" to the "studier." Finally, skull science emphatically placed indigenous cultures in a universal human past, defining them as contrary to the forward motion of progress and civilization. Scholars have compellingly argued that scientists coded themselves in these studies as denizens of the present and their subjects as part of the past, creating hierarchies of race and time.[20]

Museum anthropologists employed methodologies and theories reflecting deeply racist assumptions, without question, and this kind of racism played a formative role in how museum anthropologists in Argentina and elsewhere understood indigenous peoples. However, these perceptions were neither cleanly defined nor uncontested. Moreno and the anthropologists working in the Museo de La Plata dealt with indigenous cultures and bodies in contradictory and revealing ways. Indigenous bodies on display in the Museo de La Plata were sometimes treated as generic specimens that reaffirmed tenets of skull science such as racial hierarchy and development. At other times, anthropologists emphasized the individuality of indigenous bodies on display, presenting them not as anonymous specimens but as dynamic and unique human beings and even as public figures or celebrities. There were also occasions when these categories overlapped, and contradictions arose between indigenous bodies' scientific anonymity as specimens and their individuality as human beings in the past and present. In the late nineteenth century, when the creole-indigenous violence of the Conquest of the Desert and similar campaigns in the north was still very recent and even ongoing, these tensions between specimen and person had social salience that played into questions of Argentine identity and politics. It is perhaps unsurprising that narratives of national whiteness were not so well ordered during this contentious moment in Argentina's history—nor were indigenous peoples detachable from the emerging national community.

La Plata: City and Museum

Moreno's lifelong dedication to the Museo Antropológico y Arqueológico was thwarted after less than two years when the city of Buenos Aires was federalized in 1880. With the relocation of Buenos Aires's provincial government to the newly established city of La Plata, Moreno's museum was also moved and transformed into the Museo de Ciencias Naturales de La Plata. La Plata was envisioned as a model city, the embodiment of the progressive ideals toward which Argentina was rapidly advancing. The new capital city also filled a yawning gap in Buenos Aires's geographical identity. Aside from the port city that had been its anchor for decades, if not centuries, Buenos Aires province in 1880 was a very rural place. Proximity to the inner nexus of Argentine railroad lines and a broad Atlantic coastline had not, outside of Buenos Aires itself, resulted in an urban-centered population, but rather in a mostly rural-dwelling and widely spread populace. Until quite recently, the southern frontier had extended well within what was now defined as the province's boundaries; the Conquest of the Desert was, in fact, still ongoing during the early 1880s. Many of the towns and settlements that lay south of Buenos Aires had a haphazard frontier quality to them that did not live up to progressive standards. These frontier towns were actively springing up throughout the pampas at this time, appearing along railroad lines and in connection with economic nodes of activity. In 1881, only eight municipalities in the province possessed between 4,000 and 10,000 inhabitants.[21]

La Plata, unlike other frontier urban centers being established during the 1880s, did not emerge organically according to changing needs of the moment. It was explicitly planned, practically stone by stone, and as such captured how provincial and national elites saw their society as it was, as well as their hopes for its future. The cityscape of La Plata was designed by Argentine architect and engineer Pedro Benoit, who arranged the urban center on a perfect grid system; it was dotted with urban plazas and crosshatched by diagonal avenues designed to facilitate more direct and rational travel across the city. Benoit, together with a committee in charge of public buildings, crafted an urban space that impressed both Argentine and foreign visitors. North American naturalist Henry A. Ward visited La Plata in 1889 in order to see Moreno's museum and commented that "La Plata is a city unique of its kind; in certain respects, its equal probably does not exist in the entire world."[22]

La Plata accomplished more than keeping pace with recognized world powers, Ward contended. The city, and the country that created it, actually outstripped the urban achievements of other civilized nations. In contrast with the new cities then being built in the North American West, for example,

> this city, which was raised by magic in the desert, is not a collection of wooden houses, with boards for walls . . . as are nearly all our settlements of rapid creation to the west of the Mississippi. On the contrary, it consists of wide, long, and majestic streets, at whose margins are found, without interruption, lines of elegant businesses and private homes; in large part these consist of carved stone and stucco, with beautiful facades and artistic cornices. Many of these streets are shaded by rows of trees at the edge of their spacious sidewalks along sumptuous avenues and boulevards.[23]

In an internationally comprehensible architectural language of progress, La Plata declared loudly and clearly that Argentina had come of age and stood poised to claim its place among the advanced nations of Europe and North America.

Behind the face of La Plata's self-spun narrative of progress and bustling urbanity, however, was a peculiar hollowness; La Plata, as an entirely new city, had no economic base. Thus, just as Buenos Aires province lost its political center when the port city federalized in 1880, so too it would lose the economic hub that had been the foundation of provincial prosperity. All the urban-oriented economic activity of the province had focused resolutely on Buenos Aires, the first and last stop in Argentina's radiating web of railroad lines and the only truly viable large-scale Atlantic seaport in the country. How was La Plata to support itself? Part of the city's budgetary allotment from the federal government included the rechanneling of the nearby Riachuelo River, which was intended to foster river-borne shipping and trade in conjunction with the railroad lines connecting the new provincial capital with the old. These attempts, however, lagged far behind provincial expenses and the pace of construction in the city. As a result, La Plata was, at least at first, largely a *symbolic* city, rather than an economically solvent or independent one. As Susan Sheets-Pyenson has noted, during its first years "La Plata still looked deserted, with many houses remaining unoccupied and grass growing up in the streets."[24] Without a ready-made economic base, La Plata struggled to fill its own shoes.

Despite these economic false steps, however, La Plata symbolized to many Argentines in the 1880s a clean break with the past and the beginning of a new chapter for national civilization. As Domingo Faustino Sarmiento remarked in a July 1884 speech given in La Plata, the legacies of Spanish colonialism had isolated Argentines from their true national character; cramped in the superstitious, backward-looking confines of Spanish colonial ideas, cultural values, and cities, the "true" Argentina had had insufficient room to breathe. The "tyranny that weighed down on her for four centuries," Sarmiento argued, "separated us from the paths upon which the human spirit marches in search of scientific truth." La Plata, which he described as having appeared "in what was until yesterday the Pampa, clean as on the map," effectively constituted the first opportunity for the "Argentine Spirit" to evince itself fully and without the fetters of colonial entanglement. "It is an ideal city," Sarmiento declared, "constructed not for the present, but for a generation yet to come, and a great envisioned city."[25]

Among the many public buildings constructed in La Plata during the 1880s, the Museo de La Plata occupied a conspicuous position within a civic and national pantheon of celebrated, symbolic sites. Moreno's museum was the first in South America to be built specifically as a museum, rather than finding itself housed in repurposed space above a bank, in a private home, or in the basement of a government building. With Moreno's insistent guidance, Swedish architect Henrik Aberg and German architect Karl Heynemann designed the Museo de La Plata to be an eclectic, neoclassical and baroque temple that glorified city, state, and science together in marble steps and soaring windows, stone sculptures and fluted iron columns.[26] The overflowing richness and ostentation in the aesthetic elements of the museum's design in some ways contradicted contemporary museum design. Museum scientists such as William Henry Flower of the British Museum, whose ideas about museum design influenced a generation of museum builders on both sides of the Atlantic, were at this moment advocating simplicity as the surest way to focus visitors' and researchers' attention on individual objects and the knowledge that might be gleaned by their examination. This "principle of sparseness" called for the simple and uncluttered presentation of high-quality specimens within an atmosphere of nondistracting austerity. However, the Museo de La Plata did not gently envelop its visitors within the clean canvas of open space and plain walls that Flower called for; rather, it astonished them with riotous display and color before inviting them to peruse the collections. If Flower proposed the controlled sampling of individual objects between meticulous palate cleansings, Moreno offered visitors to La Plata an uninterrupted sensory smorgasbord. On the other hand, as a civic monument commemorating the heights reached by Argentine civilization, the museum perhaps served its purpose most effectively by displaying a combination of science and art, logic and beauty. The presence of sculpture, paintings, and architectural flourishes in the design of the Museo de La Plata shored up the cultural stature of the museum and elevated it within Argentina's symbolic national landscape.

The Museo de La Plata's carefully conceived architectural and artistic design portrayed Argentina as a progressive and modern nation, and yet it also inextricably bound Argentina's national heritage with indigenous cultures of the past and present. As Jens Andermann has noted, the museum's central rotunda displayed murals of Argentine flora and fauna alongside paintings of ancient, or perhaps simply timeless, indigenous scenes, such as *La vuelta del malón* (The return of the raid, painted by J. Bouchet), *La caza del guanaco* (The guanaco hunt, by J. Speroni), and *Descuartizando un gliptodonte* (Quartering a glyptodont, by L. de Servi).[27] In addition, the museum's baroque tendency toward effusive interior decoration was seen in indigenous American motifs throughout the building, running along the base moldings, skirting the ceilings, and climbing the walls of the grand central staircase. Moreno incorporated these images—drawn from Andean, Mesoamerican, and specifically Argentine archaeological records—into the decoration of his museum in an attempt to "give [it] an archaic American character that does not disagree with its Grecian lines."[28] In this, it seems, he was successful. Ward enthused that "above all, this is an *Argentine Museum*; and it is this distinctive characteristic that gives this collection special interest for the foreigner who visits the country, just as it also constitutes its principal importance for this nation."[29] Indigenous iconography played an integral role in making the Museo de La Plata uniquely "Argentine," and in the process indigenous cultures were claimed and possessed by the nation, just as they were incorporated into its natural being.

While the museum's artwork presented indigenous cultures as timeless elements of Argentina's natural world, its displays and publications offered a

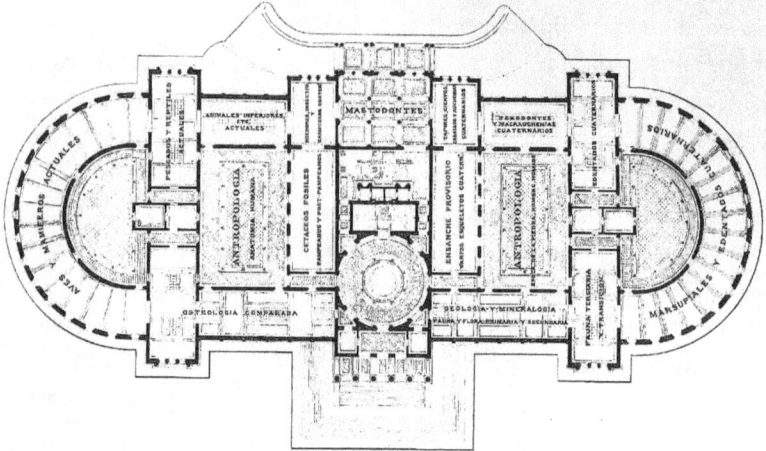

MUSEO DE LA PLATA — (Primer piso)

Fig. 1 Floor plan of the Museo de La Plata, ground floor. Francisco P. Moreno, "El Museo de La Plata. Rápida ojeada sobre su fundación y desarollo," *Revista del Museo de La Plata* 1 (1890–91): plate 2.

more contradictory understanding of indigenous peoples' connections with creole scientists and visitors. Moreno designed the Museo de La Plata as an ellipse, a plan inspired by European museum scientists such as Albert Gaudry of the Paris Museum. Gaudry, a paleontologist, advocated the presentation of specimens in long, continuous galleries designed to accommodate contiguous series of objects. These linear displays would carry the visitor along an evolutionary progression, through chronological time and biological changes. Moreno adapted this idea for his own museum. Whereas Gaudry advocated a linear progression of halls, which would presumably require the visitor who reached the end or apex of the exhibit to turn around and travel backward in time/space in order to exit the museum, Moreno constructed his museum in the shape of an "elongated hoop," measuring approximately 135 meters in length and 70 meters in width (see figs. 1 and 2). Moreno argued that the elliptical floor plan represented "the biological ring, which begins in mystery and terminates with man."[30] Thus, the visitor who began by turning from the rotunda into the mineralogy hall (which also contained early flora and fauna) would make his way around the ring of exhibits and eventually emerge on the opposite side of the central rotunda, after passing through the final gallery of

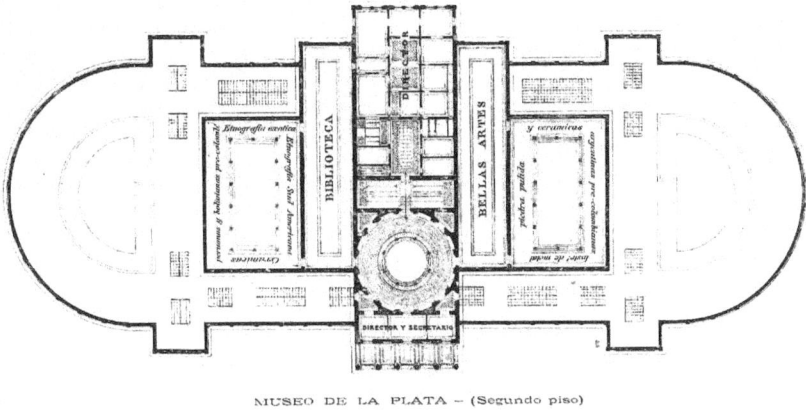

MUSEO DE LA PLATA – (Segundo piso)

Fig. 2   Floor plan of the Museo de La Plata, second floor. Francisco P. Moreno, "El Museo de La Plata. Rápida ojeada sobre su fundación y desarollo," *Revista del Museo de La Plata* 1 (1890–91): plate 2.

contemporary comparative osteology; he was now prepared to contemplate the pinnacle of the natural world, represented in La Plata by the anthropology halls at the center of the museum.[31]

Indigenous Bodies on Display: Racial Specimens and Personal Acquaintances

Upon entering the two central galleries, visitors discovered the single-story architecture of the outer halls replaced by soaring two-story galleries of marble, glass, and iron. Sunlight filtered to the ground floor through second-story skylights and down into lower-level laboratories through translucent glass-block floors (see fig. 3). Visitors' shoes clicked faintly against the marble and glass, each sound amplified by the sensitive acoustics in the gallery's reverberating echo chamber. The Museo de La Plata, particularly its central anthropology halls, typified the internationally popular, striking neoclassical and baroque style of late nineteenth-century museum architecture, which has prompted scholars to so aptly describe these structures as "cathedrals of science."[32]

One of the Museo de La Plata's two central halls contained its collections of comparative human anatomy, with its ethnographic and archaeological collections displayed on the upper balcony (see figs. 4 and 5). This hall surrounded viewers with a glittering gridwork of custom-designed glass, iron, and wooden display cases, in and around which were mounted hundreds of geometrically arranged human skulls, skeletons, face casts, and typological portraits, all facing inward toward the visitor's gaze. The exhibit's proliferation of human remains and representations entailed several different types of display, each designed by a succession of anthropologists working in the Museo de La Plata between 1884 and 1910 to convey specific meanings to the viewer.

First, a dizzying array of human skulls, displayed in glass wall shelves and freestanding cases, was designed to facilitate physical comparison between individuals of different ages, sexes, ethnicities or races, and eras, and with various cranial deformations (see fig. 4). The viewer was invited to participate actively in tracing the similarities and differences between these different human "types" through direct examination of their craniums, the most scientifically meaning-laden part of human anatomy. Late nineteenth-century physical anthropology emphasized quantitative measurement of the human body as the means of identifying diagnostic human traits. The head occupied a central place within these analyses; anthropologists measured skull size and shape, cranial capacity, and facial features, connecting their findings with race, intelligence, and personality. Anthropologists compared humankind across continents and through time, creating scales of development and regression. Unsurprisingly, perhaps, the modern European male stood at the pinnacle of these calculations, as a standard against which all other bodies were measured and generally found wanting.

Even more visually striking than the serial displays of skulls lining the walls of the physical anthropology hall was a freestanding glass case running down the center of the room. This two-story case displayed a double series of fully articulated human skeletons, one on top of the other, exposed to view on four sides by panes of glass. These skeletons belonged to native peoples from different parts of Argentina, and the case was crowned with a row of busts depicting notable anthropologists. The case strongly invoked the full-length, rigid, frontal typology photographs so common among anthropologists and criminologists around the world during the later nineteenth century, as marginalized bodies were lined up—here with the aid of mounting wire and metal supports rather than compensation or coercion—for scientific examination. Full skeletal analysis often complemented nineteenth-century skull science, as physical anthropologists, criminologists, and eugenicists

Fig. 3 Glass-block floor tiles in the Museo de La Plata. These thick tiles were designed to allow light to pass into basement-level workshops through the main-level exhibit spaces. Photograph by author.

Museo de La Plata

Sección antropológica; vista parcial

Fig. 4   Physical Anthropology Hall at the Museo de La Plata, 1910. Archivo General de la Nación, Departamento de Documentos Fotográficos, Buenos Aires.

studied correlations between mental faculties and extracranial physical parameters in order to determine links between intelligence and physicality, or to discover markers of physical adaptation that tied particular populations to their natural environments (see fig. 5).

Other elements of the exhibition supplemented these displays: smaller, free-standing cases were built to display specimens in flat-top glass compartments, while other objects were concealed and stored in drawers beneath. Smaller still were glass cases constructed to house single objects, such as the mummified remains visible in fig. 4, and eye-level carousels of photographs that allowed the visitor to peruse human types and specimens not housed in the museum itself but connected to it by the global ties of professional anthropology. Meanwhile, the walls above and between display cases and above door frames were hung with series of face casts and drawn portraits, further representations of human types that invited side-by-side comparison. The visitor to the physical anthropology hall of the Museo de La Plata, in short, moved through a carefully arranged catalogue of human bodies and representations of human bodies that was designed to facilitate the scientific analysis of the physical form along comparative and racial lines.

Fig. 5   Physical Anthropology Hall at the Museo de La Plata. Francisco P. Moreno, "El Museo de La Plata. Rápida ojeada sobre su fundación y desarollo," *Revista del Museo de La Plata* 1 (1890–91): plate 7.

In the decades immediately following the Conquest of the Desert, anthropology in the Museo de La Plata focused notably on the physical bodies of indigenous peoples of the southern pampas and Patagonia. Indigenous bodies were incorporated and possessed within the Argentine natural world, showcased in the museum's largest and most central galleries. Museum display abetted indigenous conquest in that it provided a scientific basis for the narratives of racial superiority and conquest then in use by the Argentine state and military; however, it also prevented discursive indigenous erasure by presenting indigenous peoples as a natural part of the Argentine nation in the past and present. The possessive and strategic claims over indigenous bodies on display in the Museo de La Plata cut in multiple directions, serving to control indigenous presence within the national space through the sanitizing and codifying language of scientific analysis and yet also defining Argentina in tangled connection with its indigenous cultures. The visitor to the Museo de La Plata, when considering the presence of indigenous peoples within Argentina's national borders, certainly did not see them as equal citizens. However, as they passed through ornate and spectacular exhibit halls decorated with indigenous-themed artwork and decor, filled with anthropological collections, and even physically occupied from the 1880s to the turn of the century by indigenous captives living in the museum, visitors did not experience an indigenous-free Argentina either, nor one in which indigenous peoples were easily segregated from the national landscape. Rather, they saw their nation connected with indigenous bodies and cultures, and they saw creole culture as the rightful leader of a national domain, of which these indigenous cultures formed one part.[33]

When the Museo de La Plata was established in 1884, Moreno's personal collections, including some fifteen thousand anthropological pieces and smaller paleontological holdings, were transferred from the short-lived Museo Antropológico y Arqueológico to form the core of the Museo de La Plata. Moreno himself served as the museum's first curator of anthropology, as well as its general director. Throughout his directorship of the Museo de La Plata (1884–1906), anthropology remained Moreno's primary scientific passion, and his personal collections and interests bolstered anthropological study at the museum. During the 1880s and 1890s, physical anthropology, in particular, was gaining international scientific cachet. Interest in human evolution, spurred by a series of dramatic discoveries of fossilized human remains in Asia, Africa, and Europe, catapulted physical anthropology to the front pages of newspapers around the world and began transforming human remains and ancient archaeological finds into objects of hotly contested national importance. Argentines responded to this combination of scientific and political relevance with intensifying interest in physical anthropology and indigenous bodies, an interest that gave anthropological exhibits and research in the Museo de La Plata and elsewhere a broader consequence that was often denied to other natural sciences.[34]

Moreno contended that Argentina was a uniquely fertile field for anthropological exploration and scientific inquiry, arguing in the internationally read *Revista del Museo de La Plata* that "there is not a single point [within Argentina], no matter how inhospitable a desert it may seem today, that does not hold traces of the passing of man. In the heart of the forests, in the deserts without water, in the highest, craggy, and icy mountains, [ancient man] has established his home since times that can be calculated in the thousands of years."[35] As he had done in his first museum in Buenos Aires, Moreno linked the ancient indigenous past with the modern national present through scientific study. He and his colleagues at the Museo de La Plata sought to demonstrate that Argentina was emerging as a center of international scientific study, thanks to its rich natural landscape, and that their museum was an institution worthy of Argentina's potential. Anthropology—and the study of Argentina's indigenous cultures specifically—formed a keystone of these claims.

Anthropologists at the Museo de La Plata displayed and wrote in contradictory and telling ways about the indigenous bodies in the museum's impressively scaled anthropology halls. At times indigenous bodies were identified as generic racial specimens without individual agency, and at other times anthropologists treated them as dynamic individuals to whom they felt bound by complex human ties. Most of the human remains in the Museo de La Plata's collections were displayed as representative of racial types, without any individual markers other than race, sex, and sometimes age. The display of these anonymous or generic specimens coded them as examples of racial group norms, lacking in individuality or unique traits, in keeping with contemporary scientific norms. In effect, through the display of their physical remains, these human beings became bodies, their bodies became objects, and these objects became symbols of scientifically defined types. These bodies no longer "belonged" to individual people; they were recreated as scientific objects invested with significance through their ability to convey information about human subgroups to the trained scientific eye. In other words, they became vehicles of information for scientists, who were the only ones capable of extracting that information. In a very real sense, these bodies ceased to belong to their life owners, instead passing into the rightful possession of science and its practitioners. In displaying and studying indigenous human remains, Argentine museum scientists located themselves and the mostly creole and European visitors to their museums along a universal human scale of progress and civilization, in which creole Argentines became the scientific stewards of these indigenous bodies, capable of understanding them in ways that their original owners had purportedly been unable to. The visual impressiveness of these remains' display en masse, moreover, consolidated the Museo de La Plata's cultural position as a repository of national heritage and scientific knowledge.

In 1887, only three years after the Museo de La Plata was established, the physical anthropology collections already contained "some 60 skeletons and more than 700 human craniums of distinct races but especially South American, already mounted and conveniently organized."[36] By 1910, the collections had grown to include 5,588 objects, primarily skulls, skeletons, and assorted loose bones, as well as smaller collections of face masks, mummified remains, plaster skull casts, scalps, preserved brains, and other specimens. Within the physical anthropology collections, a compelling majority came from the pampas and Patagonia. These regions were represented by 902 skulls, 61 skeletons, and 3,068 loose bones (*huesos sueltos*), as compared to the 327 skulls, 41 skeletons, and 391 loose bones that the museum housed from every other region of the country.[37] These pampean and Patagonian specimens were organized into a series of indigenous racial groups and types and facilitated the museum's research and publications hypothesizing the racial relationships and hierarchies between different groups. Many of the indigenous remains were casualties of the Conquest and conflicts surrounding it, having been taken from battlefields or exhumed from burial grounds by creole Argentine travelers, scientists, and military men.

The representational power of the genericized remains went beyond their scientific value. Within a larger Argentine cultural context, these human bones were transformed into dense nodules of knowledge, sentiment, and history. Foucault's notion of biopower—of a state exerting control over the lives and bodies of its population in ways both literal and symbolic—can be extended here to scientists, whom scholars have often seen as being in league with the state during the late nineteenth century. In this light, scientists such as Moreno and his cohorts at the Museo de La Plata controlled how indigenous bodies were seen and what they meant to national history and progress. Museum scholars have also explored the question of how objects displayed in museums acquire value. Does a museum object—whether it be a famous painting or a biological specimen or a cultural artifact—hold value because of its inherent qualities, such as material or structure? Or does a museum object acquire value because of external cultural principles that deem it beautiful, interesting, or enlightening?[38] In the Museo de La Plata, external circumstances determined the worth of the museum's physical anthropology collections. Creole Argentines emptied indigenous bodies of their associations with violence, conquest, and individual human lives and reimagined them as symbols of a deep national past that became entangled in the years surrounding the Conquest with contested and often uncomfortable elements of the national present. The indigenous remains on display in the museum invoked a sense of temporal movement—not a simple linear advance from past to present, but the jumbled presence of both. To museum anthropologists, contemporary indigenous remains represented a less advanced step along a Western evolutionary ladder, making them denizens of the universal human past while they also represented still-living, contemporary indigenous societies of the present. Each specimen in the museum's hall also represented a personal human past, as each bone belonged to a deceased human being. On the other hand, many of these specimens invoked the present, as some contemporary indigenous skulls and skeletons on display had been taken from fresh graves by collectors who had known the individuals and their families in life. These individuals, then, belonged both to a personal past (their own) and to a personal present, in the memories of those who still remembered them.

The entanglement of past and present in contemporary indigenous remains came into especially sharp focus during the years surrounding the Conquest of the Desert. As Susana Rotker has argued in connection with captive creole women among indigenous peoples along the Argentine southern frontier, there was a concern in late nineteenth-century creole Argentine culture that while it was possible to bring people and landscapes into the progressive present through assimilation and conquest, it was also distinctly possible for the civilized to be dragged back into the barbaric past through the corrupting influences of backward places and people, if these degenerative elements were allowed to remain intact or even if one spent too much time in the company of "savage" peoples. This anxiety sharpened calls and justifications for conquest of the southern frontier, and it drew an imperative line beneath the evolutionary and progressive narrative of anthropological studies. The "pasting" of indigenous bodies, then, even those from contemporary indigenous societies, served to buffer the Argentine present from a still-menacing and potentially damaging indigenous past. Although indigenous specimens collected from the recently deceased might represent an ongoing continuum of indigenous life and culture, they nonetheless also represented archaic forms of human life.[39]

The Museo de La Plata answered the national call for forward progress along Western models, and yet it also captured within its glass displays the underlying anxieties of these positivist ideas. If indigenous bodies collected from the recently deceased signified control over an archaic race, as well as creole Argentines' ability to claim dominance over all those living in the Argentine territory, they also suggested the continuing living presence of these groups along the unconquered frontiers of the nation. Anthropologists in the Museo de La Plata did not consign these indigenous bodies and the cultures they represented entirely to the past or detach them from national history and heritage. On the contrary, many late nineteenth-century anthropologists in Argentina contended that national heritage was tied to indigenous peoples. Early in his career, Moreno argued that his anthropological collections portrayed "the history of the first inhabitants of our soil" and that in his museum "their descendants will be able to study their progress."[40] Given that museumgoers in nineteenth-century Buenos Aires and La Plata were overwhelmingly identified as creole or European, the connection drawn here between Argentina's "first inhabitants" (that is, indigenous peoples) and these museumgoers as "their descendants" suggested an understanding of the deep indigenous past as part of the story of the Argentine nation, rather than a separate story of "other" people. Moreover, Moreno argued that indigenous people formed not just any part of Argentina's national history, but its oldest and original chapter.

Although late nineteenth-century physical anthropology emphasized morphology and racial types, the anthropologists of the Museo de La Plata seemed to follow these rules with one hand and to break them with the other. Amid its collections of generic scientific specimens, the Museo de La Plata also displayed a series of distinctly individual indigenous bodies, whose meanings complicated the message conveyed by anonymous racial types. Anthropologists recorded specimens' race and age and, where available, descriptions of the individual in life. These living details were generally intended to draw connections between the physical body and an individual's psychological tendencies. For example, the cranium of a half-Araucanian, half-African woman named María, who had died from unknown causes in a Patagonian ravine called Trolopen in 1888, was given to the museum by botanist Carlos Spegazzini, who "knew her personally at the end," on October 27, 1905. The skeleton of a nameless Mataco man was donated to the museum in 1906 by a medical doctor in San Pedro de Jujuy named William Peterson, who had "known the Indian personally and had treated him." And, in 1888, Santiago Pozzi donated the remains of an indigenous man named "Michel," identified as a member of the "Tribe of Calachú," whom his expedition had killed, for reasons unmentioned in the catalogue records, during the museum's expedition near Corpen Aiken, in the Patagonian territory of Santa Cruz. Pozzi evidently decided to collect the man's remains as a specimen for the museum and therefore recorded some observations of his appearance. "According to Sr. Pozzi's notes," the catalogue disclosed, "when they killed him this Indian had his face painted with ochre, and above a black triangle."[41] In these and other cases, personal acquaintance and experience—phrases repeated often in the catalogue and in contemporary published anthropological studies dealing with the living and recently deceased—became important elements of museum object provenance and were dislodged in some sense from other understandings of "personal" relationships. Personalities became data, and even close friendships with eligible subjects were to be turned toward scientific ends, when the occasion presented itself.

In some cases, the life details recorded in the catalogue went beyond psychological observations and entered the realm of detailed biography. This was especially true when remains belonged to an individual of public prominence, whose actions in life were known to museum scientists and visitors. There were, in fact, "celebrities" among the physical anthropology collections—famous caciques, warriors, and members of their families, enemies of the Argentine state and its allies—whose remains became, in essence, trophies on display for the public. The catalogue included specific references to famous indigenous caciques such as Panquitruz Guor, Chipitruz, and Calfucurá, whose skulls and skeletons had come to rest in the museum, and it linked them with written accounts of their activities in life—travel writing and scientific accounts by Europeans like British naval officer George Chaworth Musters and creole Argentines like Francisco Moreno, Estanislao Zeballos, and Lucio Mansilla. These specimens' value, in part, clearly did not derive from their anonymity or representative typology, but rather from their individuality and the unique experience of seeing their famous remains on display. These specimens represented dense nexuses of scientific, nationalist, and historical meaning that transformed the anthropological halls of the Museo de La Plata into a complex stage of nation making and a forum for often contradictory impulses toward education and entertainment.

One such celebrity specimen was the skull of Ranquel cacique Cipriano Catriel. Moreno collected the skull during one of his earliest expeditions, while traveling through Buenos Aires province in 1875. He wrote to his father on April 5, "I already have the skull of the celebrated Cipriano [Catriel], and the complete skeleton of his wife, Margarita." Although Moreno intended to send a number of indigenous skulls and other specimens he had collected back to Buenos Aires, he stipulated in his letter that "the head [of Catriel] remains here with me; it has been a while since I examined it, but although I have cleaned it a little, it retains always a very foul smell. It will accompany me to Tandil because I do not wish to be separated from this jewel, for which I am much envied."[42] He wrote similarly to his brother Josué, "You will already know that I have a good quantity of craniums and that the tiger Catriel is in my power, more secure than in the great office safe."[43]

The value of Cipriano Catriel's skull was not located solely in its physical qualities. As an osteological specimen, the skull was neither unusual in its physical dimensions nor remarkably well preserved for a representative specimen (quite to the contrary, according to Moreno's olfactory protestations). Yet it was nonetheless a "jewel" that Moreno bragged about to his family and prided himself on possessing. The appeal of Catriel's skull was, in fact, partly scientific, although its true value was created through a triangular relationship between science, history, and nation. The skull was a scientific specimen that pertained to contemporary physical anthropology and, because the individual mind of Catriel was to a certain extent known to history and could therefore be connected with his physical remains, psychology. However, the skull was also a historical marker. The Catriel dynasty of Ranquel caciques had maintained a complex and conflicted relationship with the Argentine state and military, and with individuals living close to the southern frontier, for three generations by the time Moreno obtained the skull. Finally, in passing into Moreno's custody, Catriel's skull also became a nationalist trophy, the possession of which demonstrated expanding Argentine dominance over the frontier zone. Although the Catriel dynasty had a history of cooperating with the Argentine state as *indios amigos* in frontier conflicts—indeed, Cipriano had died the previous year while fighting with the Argentine military—possessing the skull nonetheless extended Argentine mastery over the as-yet unsettled frontier, through Moreno as an individual agent.[44]

In addition to its scientific and national-historical importance, moreover, Moreno emphasized the value of Cipriano Catriel's skull as a commodity, not in a strictly capitalist sense, as an object produced or processed for monetary sale, but as an object with appreciable exchange value, akin to a treasure meriting careful protection. In Moreno's reflections, the skull was emptied of its original meaning in connection with Catriel's life and recoded in order to express scientific, historical, and commodity values.[45] Tellingly, while Moreno's accounts of his expedition were published by newspapers and scientific societies in Buenos Aires, indigenous responses to such common practices of "collection"—which very likely seemed more like grave robbing than science—were not.

Yet these clear narratives of nation and science, history and indigenous extinction, were at times complicated by anthropologists' conflicting impulses to aid indigenous people whom they knew personally and to slow the destruction of the cultures they studied. Indigenous individuals and communities sometimes accepted this interference on their behalf and at other times came into conflict with their would-be scientific benefactors. For example, Moreno worked to convince the national government to restore the "good Indians" he knew from his southern explorations to lands of their own in Patagonia, with some success. The Tehuelche cacique Foyel and his followers were eventually relocated to the valley of Súnica in Chubut, thanks in part to Moreno's vocal support, and a number of other indigenous groups were also relocated to *colonias* in the south, where legislators hoped they would adopt Western lifeways and become agricultural producers.[46] In the 1880s, the Museo de La Plata staged another attempt at reconciliation between creole Argentina and the frontier indigenous peoples it was in the process of conquering, this time by "rescuing" a group of indigenous prisoners of war from the Conquest of the Desert and bringing them to live in the museum as "live ethnographic exhibits." In the contradictions between anthropologists' intentions and actions, and between their visions of themselves and their indigenous subjects' responses to them, it is possible to reconstruct some of the complexity of anthropology in this historical moment—in the civic environment of La Plata, in frontier-fractured Argentina, and for indigenous communities in the upheaval of conquest.

Living Indigenous Bodies: Ethnographic Captives in the Museo de La Plata

The first chapter of this story was recorded retrospectively in 1905 by Herman Ten Kate, a Dutch anthropologist who worked in the Museo de La Plata between 1893 and 1897. According to Ten Kate, in July 1884, an Argentine garrison at Fortín Villegas, in the newly conquered Patagonian territory of Chubut, watched the approach of some 180 indigenous men, women, and children, with their horse herds and material possessions in tow. This group, the living remnants of the two tribes of caciques Incayal and Foyel, had come "in order to swear their fidelity and peaceful intentions toward the national government." In response to a request for instructions sent to the capital by the fort's commander, the national government ordered that the indigenous "rebels," as they were described by the commander, were to be stripped of their material goods and put aboard a steamer bound for Buenos Aires, as prisoners of war. Once the steamer arrived in Buenos Aires, many prisoners were separated from their children, who were distributed among waiting Argentine families. "Deprived of their children and their friends," the remaining indigenous prisoners were taken to the island prison of Martín García, where they remained for nearly a year and a half.[47]

On October 2, 1886, Moreno wrote two letters—one to Marcelino Vargas, a medical doctor with connections to the military, and one to Antonio Muratorio, an official at Martín García prison—setting in motion the transfer of a number of indigenous prisoners to La Plata. According to his letters, Moreno had already obtained permission from Minister of War Carlos Pellegrini for "the delivery of the Caciques Incayal and Foyel with their siblings, wives, and children—that is to say Incayal, a brother, his wife, and three or four children, Foyel, his brother, his wife and children, and the translator who accompanies them—in total fifteen persons large and small," all of whom were to live in the museum.[48] It was Moreno's hope that these prisoners, once transferred to the museum, would find some relief there from the harsh conditions of their imprisonment. They were to be provided with "good rooms, horses, etc.,"[49] and allowed freedom of movement within the museum grounds and the broader cityscape of La Plata. Furthermore, Moreno hoped that the captives would be useful to the museum's scientific research. It was expected that the women, as Ten Kate explained, "would enrich the ethnographic collections by their weaving work, and at the same time their manners [of both men and women] could be studied." In addition to these functions, Moreno intended for the captives to be submitted to examinations by the museum's physical anthropologists, which, in connection with prolonged observation of their behavior and mental capacities, would provide invaluable data for anthropological study. The prison released the captives, and they made their way to La Plata, where they took up residence in the quarters Moreno had provided for them on the grounds of the Museo de La Plata.[50]

Despite Moreno's high hopes, however, the behavior of the captives living at the museum often clashed with anthropologists' expectations. For example, they actively resisted anthropologists' efforts to measure their bodies scientifically. Ten Kate wrote that "neither kindness, nor the attentions with which he [Moreno] surrounded them, nor even the attraction of a remuneration, could overcome their apathy." Ten Kate described the difficulty he had in measuring and photographing the captives in 1896, some ten years after their arrival in La Plata. He wished to take a number of physical measurements and to photograph each individual from the front and in profile, according to anthropological methodologies of the time. This style of photography, as

mentioned earlier, had strong connections to emerging criminological practices of photographing and measuring detainees, especially the system developed by French scientist and police officer Alphonse Bertillon. The similarities
between criminological and anthropological practices were apparent and
alarming to many of the indigenous captives, who "believed that my [Ten
Kate's] investigations had some relationship with the police and, not wanting
to be treated like common criminals, refused to submit themselves to the
measurements." Rufino Vera, Incayal's interpreter, finally allowed himself to
be photographed, setting an "example" that his daughter and a second man
followed voluntarily. "The others persisted in their rejection," Ten Kate
recorded, although he added without further explanation that, in the end,
"all allowed themselves to be photographed." Although the captives were
encouraged to think of La Plata as a haven and an escape from imprisonment and were ostensibly granted freedom of movement within the museum
grounds and the city of La Plata, this silence suggests that they also experienced a degree of coercion that prevented even their collectively voiced
resistance from overriding the desires of their scientific rescuers. At least in
this moment, the captives' agency and individuality were overruled by a scientific vision of them as racially representative specimens, to be measured and
possessed.[51]

The double-edged nature of their scientific sanctuary did not, however,
stop these indigenous captives from asserting their own agency in other ways.
Not long after the captives' arrival in La Plata, for example, Moreno was
forced to abandon his hopes for their ethnographic utility. The captives
refused to give demonstrations of weaving or other cultural arts for public
visitors and evinced symptoms of collective trauma that made them unfit for
ethnographic "display" and even, according to their anthropological observers, unsuitable as sources of ethnographic information in general. The men,
Ten Kate complained, were frustratingly uncommunicative and spent the
majority of their time sitting together, either smoking and talking quietly
among themselves or drinking excessive quantities of alcohol that led to bouts
of unpredictability and violence. The women, meanwhile, were readily talk-
ative but unreliable. According to Ten Kate, the same question asked of the
same woman two days in a row might produce very detailed, but very different, answers.

Although museum anthropologists could not convince the indigenous
captives to offer weaving demonstrations for the public, the women evidently
did weave ponchos, sashes, and other textile goods while in the museum.

However, rather than adding these items to the museum's ethnographic collections (and despite the fact, Ten Kate noted somewhat testily, that the wool and dyes for these weavings were provided by the museum), the women sold them "clandestinely, at a cheap price," in the city. The money made from these exchanges, Ten Kate believed, was spent entirely on alcohol for the men, in which they indulged to dangerous excess. Men and women alike smoked tobacco, to which they added ground calafate, and indulged in refined sugar sweets "of any kind." All of this behavior seemed to Ten Kate reflective of deep depression, which the captives expressed individually and as a group. The Tehuelche cacique Incayal was particularly prone to verbal outbursts, which Ten Kate approximated in broken French: "Me chief, son of this land, white robbers . . . to kill my brothers, to steal my horses and the lands that have seen my birth, now unhappy prisoner . . . I [am] wretched!" Incayal's facial expressions in these moments reflected "the greatest sadness." As a group, the indigenous captives expressed their grief through communal action, notably the singing of lengthy songs that Ten Kate described as "extremely lugubrious."[52]

Although some indigenous captives eventually left La Plata to return southward, others never left the museum. A number of captives died in the Museo de La Plata, including Incayal, his unnamed wife, Margarita (Foyel's daughter), an Alacaluf woman named Eulltyalma or Tafá, and a Yámana man named Maishkensis. In 1905, Ten Kate published a physical anthropological study in the *Revista del Museo de La Plata* that addressed these four captives, whose deaths within the confines of the museum after years of in-depth, daily anthropological observation had transformed them into optimal physical anthropological specimens. Ten Kate's analysis of the Fuegian captive Maishkensis, whom he had known personally and called Maish for short, offered a more personal and individualized window onto the life of one of the captives. Maish existed, through Ten Kate's eyes, as a rigorously analyzed scientific specimen and also as a human being complete with his own suite of flaws and endearing eccentricities. The juxtaposition between these two facets of Ten Kate's understanding reveals an irrepressible tension between progressive impulses to distance and contain and the simultaneous impulses to understand and connect, although these too contained elements of inequality and possession (see fig. 6).

Maish came to the Museo de La Plata as part of Foyel and Incayal's retinue, though his precise role in the group has not been recorded. His physical abilities and proclivities were closely studied through everyday observation and more directed forms of testing. Ten Kate described Maish's hearing and

long-distance vision as "striking" and commented on his affinity for horse-
back riding, bird hunting, tobacco smoking, and sugar as racially pro-
grammed proclivities. Ten Kate also described Maish's mental abilities at
great length. His attention span, his capacity for abstract thought, and his
natural curiosity were all evaluated according to measures both quantitative
and qualitative. His memory, for example, was tested by showing him a series
of images and then asking him to recount what he had seen. Ten Kate mar-
veled that while Maish failed these and similar tests miserably, he was at the
same time capable of recalling "the smallest details" of a wilderness trail
without hesitation, a sort of memorization that Ten Kate presumed was more
closely adapted to his natural life. Ten Kate described Maish's attention span
as short and his capacity to complete complex and long-term projects as
accordingly low. He never learned to read or write, for example. On the other
hand, Maish's verbal linguistic abilities were apparently quite developed: "He
spoke Spanish easily, [spoke] a little English, and pronounced French well."
Even Maish's taste in women was recorded for scientific posterity. According
to Ten Kate, "He did not like brunettes and he liked black-haired [women]
even less. He had a very marked preference for blondes, who were generally
the objects of his enterprises."[53]

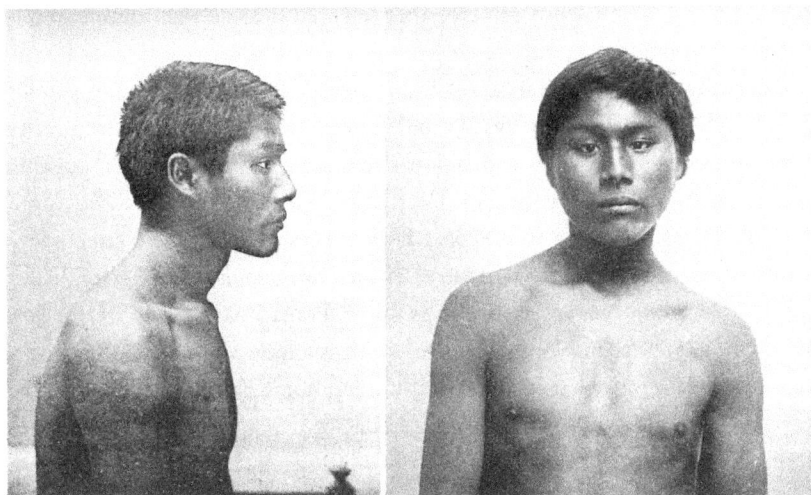

Maishkensis (Yahgan)

Fig. 6   Maishkensis, or Maish, in front and profile. Ten Kate, "Matériaux pour servir à
l'anthropologie des Indiens de la République Argentine," *Revista del Museo de La Plata*
12 (1905): plate 1.

Ten Kate's observations on Maish's physical and psychological attributes were, however, vastly outnumbered by more qualitative and even intimate discussions of his character, which revealed a more personal day-to-day relationship between the captive and the scientist. Ten Kate contended that Maish had undergone vast changes during his captivity; unsociable and "even savage" when he arrived at the Museo de La Plata, Maish had gradually grown accustomed to life in the museum and in the city, eventually becoming "a useful auxiliary for the Museum" and a model for contemporary Argentine projects of native reformation. Maish was, by Ten Kate's account, good-natured and "timid; obedient and faithful." He had received some formal education at a Christian mission in Ushuaia and was familiar with Christian morality and beliefs, which Ten Kate identified as having become Maish's own. By way of example, Ten Kate cited Maish's tendency in a dispute to respond with reason, rather than emotion, and to forgive his opponent rather than hold a grudge. Some of Ten Kate's observations also contained an undertone of anecdotal affection and even humor. He recalled, for example, Maish's "marked taste" for Western fashion. He was apparently often to be seen "strolling the streets of La Plata," perfumed and pomaded, wearing "a black redingote [a great coat] which Mr. Moreno had given him." Ten Kate described Maish more generally as a kind and warm-hearted person who enjoyed playing with Moreno's children in the museum, a mark of trust from the museum director that fell well outside the bounds of scientific observation.[54]

Moreno was by no means alone in his project to install living indigenous people in his museum. Displays of non-Western, "exotic" peoples were already a recognized device within exposition circuits, from internationally touring American Wild West shows to international expositions across western Europe during the 1870s and 1880s. Many of these displays were largely sensational and nonscientific in nature, but anthropologists were nonetheless often involved in their creation. For example, Franz Boas, widely viewed as a foundational figure in North American anthropology, was personally instrumental in creating what was dubbed an "ethnological zoo," alongside the better-remembered ethnographic material culture collections that were to form the basis for the Field Museum of Chicago, for the 1893 Columbian Exposition. This exhibit displayed native peoples from throughout the Americas, West Africa, and Asia. Anthropologically oriented live native displays were also nothing new to South America. Moreno's project was predated by four years by the Anthropological Exhibition of 1882 in Rio de Janeiro, where a group of Xerente and Botocudo Indians were displayed and figured prominently in press coverage of the event.

Within this international context, the human remains of indigenous celebrities and living individuals on display at the Museo de La Plata suggest that indigenous bodies were not only interesting to creole Argentines from a scientific perspective; they also attracted attention as spectacles, entertainment, and curiosities. Creole Argentines came to the museum to see these captive indigenous bodies, visually possessing them by transforming them into objects of spectacle and neutralizing their individual agency through their scientific analysis as specimens. The contradictions in this process were felt by anthropologists in La Plata. Ten Kate, although often baffled and even irritated by the behavior of the museum's indigenous captives, also sympathized with their plight, as they were held in captivity far from their homelands and isolated within a strange and often hostile culture. Having left the museum while several captives were still in residence, Ten Kate wrote regretfully from afar that although he knew the fate of the four deceased individuals, "what became of the other Indians, men and women, interned within the Museum, I do not know."[55] Ten Kate joined Moreno in believing, as the latter wrote in 1897, that "the nation has the duty to give landed property to those indigenous peoples" exiled by the Conquest and deserving of resettlement.[56] The contradiction between Ten Kate's expressions of compassion and his efforts to measure and study the indigenous captives at the Museo de La Plata during the 1890s, despite their clear resistance, reveals the multiple layers of intention and action at work in anthropology in the museum. Along with many of his contemporaries, Ten Kate was aware that the situation of indigenous peoples in Argentina was problematic and that responsibility for addressing it rested in the hands of creole Argentine state makers and intellectuals, and yet he did not seem to recognize his own role in this situation, nor any connection between his desires to measure and photograph indigenous captives and their resistance or feelings of disempowerment.

Scholars examining the Museo de La Plata's indigenous captives have disagreed fundamentally on the nature of their confinement in La Plata and their relationship to the anthropologists studying them. Some have contended that Moreno's motives for relocating Incayal, Foyel, and their retinues were primarily humanitarian, "inspired by the sad situation in which he encountered those men and women, whom he had known a short time earlier enjoying their liberty and the lands of their birth." From this perspective, it has been argued that the scientific justifications that Moreno offered the authorities for his interest in the indigenous prisoners were, in fact, a blind for his true personal motivations. Knowing that his influence as a museum scientist was more likely to produce fast results than his personal friendship with the prisoners, Moreno "appealed to science to legitimate" his deeper humanitarian motivations.[57] Others have interpreted the captivity of these indigenous people in a different light, referring to Incayal's death in the museum as an "ultimate act of resistance" against his involuntary confinement by Moreno and the unjust situation of his people.[58]

Taken individually, each of these perspectives offers valuable insight into the conflicting realities of anthropologists' actions and intentions, but combining them yields an even richer appreciation for the situation.[59] If Moreno was not an altruistic hero, rescuing Incayal and Foyel from prison for purely humanitarian reasons, and it seems unlikely that he was—we might well ask, to this effect, why he allowed the remains of deceased captives to be publicly displayed, studied, and published after their death, despite his intimate knowledge of these individuals personally and their cultural beliefs regarding the sanctity and privacy of human remains—neither did he or other anthropologists witness Incayal's death (or that of other captives) without any compassion or human feeling. As their words in professional publications, museum catalogues, private correspondence, and memoirs attest, museum anthropologists such as Moreno and Ten Kate thought of the indigenous bodies and individuals they studied as generic specimens on one hand and as people on the other, often with contradictory and conflictive results. In negotiating this contradiction, museum anthropologists in La Plata did not erase indigenous peoples from Argentina's natural landscape but rather incorporated them into it, locating these peoples and cultures within Argentina's natural panorama and within the scope of the Museo de La Plata's purview as an inextricable element of the national past and present.

Conclusion

For Moreno, and through him in the Museo de La Plata, the links between science and the Argentine nation-state were deeply drawn. "Without its own science," he wrote frankly, "there is not a strong Nation."[60] True science must be patriotically motivated, and true modern nationalism must also cherish and facilitate scientific progress. The Museo de La Plata, as a symbol of Argentina's scientific progress, occupied a prominent space within a progres-

sive national pantheon during the "golden age" of the late nineteenth century, embodying the progressive ideals of a civilizing state that pictured itself
and its people as moving toward the high-cultured accomplishments of
western Europe. Moreno and other anthropologists in the museum deliberately stationed themselves as stewards of Argentina's national mission, which
was embodied scientifically in the museum's exhibit halls and research
publications.[61] Moreno also infused the Museo de La Plata with a vision of
the Argentine natural landscape in which indigenous peoples were inextricable from Argentina's national heritage. Through the scientific display of
indigenous bodies as both generic specimens and dynamic individuals,
anthropologists played both sides of an often contradictory line that possessively and strategically coded these bodies as part of Argentina's past and
present.

In 1905, the national government proposed the creation in La Plata of a new
national university, which would expand the Museo de La Plata's mission of
public education and cosmopolitan progress but also absorb the museum
within the organization of the university. The museum would report directly
to the university and restructure itself according to the dictates of university
curricula. The independent public museum Moreno had designed twenty
years earlier was now in danger of losing its independence, as well as its direct
connection to the broader public. Moreno protested what he saw as the hijack-
ing of his personal museum but was ultimately overruled. In 1906, he resigned
his post as director of the Museo de La Plata, which he had created from his
own collections and largely through his own personal efforts, and to which he
had envisioned dedicating "all the years of my life." Moreno went on to a second career as a congressional representative for the province of Buenos Aires,
founded Argentina's first national parks, and became a devoted advocate for
public education.[62]

The Museo de La Plata, the first purpose-built natural science museum in
South America, also became one of the first museums in Argentina to bow to
the rising power of universities as rival institutions of scientific education and
research. Throughout the world, museums were fighting an increasingly uphill
battle against the encroachment of universities on their educational and
research territories. In 1906, the Museo de La Plata capitulated to the newly
created Universidad Nacional de La Plata, marking a new period in Argentine
museum science. During the early twentieth century, the demands of both
public- and university-oriented education would drive museum scientists in
increasingly insistent and unexpected ways.

In no small sense, this new arrangement, so unacceptable to Moreno, was largely of his own making. So successful had he and other museum scientists been in spearheading rising interest in science and museums within broader spheres of Argentine society that museums were now crowded with outside actors, all pronouncing opinions about—and even claiming a right to influence—how museums functioned. In 1904, a new anthropology museum opened in Buenos Aires, under the auspices of the Universidad de Buenos Aires and under the directorship of Argentine naturalist-turned-anthropologist Juan B. Ambrosetti. Ambrosetti's museum would demonstrate an expanding national and public interest in museums, anthropology, and the study of indigenous Argentina that carried well into the twentieth century.

national politicians, wealthy businessmen, and others constituted a group of outside "elites," drawn from Argentina's upper and middle classes, who often claimed ties of equality with museum anthropologists along lines of social status, education, or relative wealth (although museum anthropologists did not always acknowledge these claims). This group can be distinguished from a second group of outside "popular" actors: workers, newspaper audiences, school groups, and others who could not or did not claim such ties of equality with museum scientists. The members of both groups, however, tended to identify themselves as Argentine citizens and creoles. These basic commonalities proved vital to the incorporation of indigenous heritage into Argentine national identity through the mechanism of museum anthropology. These terms of belonging also appeared prominently in outside actors' efforts to gain access to the Museo Etnográfico's resources on grounds of nationalism, citizenship, and scientific interest.

Museum scholars have long puzzled over how to access and interpret outside actors in museums. Most commonly, cultural scholars and historians have focused on analyzing the efforts made by museum scientists and administrators to engage with their public visitors in changing ways during the nineteenth and early twentieth centuries, in keeping with internationally shifting priorities toward public education and scientific popularization. These studies have effectively detailed museum administrators' and scientists' visions of the changing relationship between museums and broader publics, but fewer studies have given comparably critical attention to the words, actions, and thoughts of public audiences. Recently, historians have attempted to address this omission, but they have had difficulty identifying "the public" as an analytical unit capable of expressing collective opinions or desires because, as Kenneth Hudson wrote in his foundational work on museum visitor history, "the public, as a homogeneous unit, does not exist; and it is a waste of time to look for it or to attempt to cater for its needs. For museums, as for libraries, concerts and airlines, there are many publics, each made up of individuals with roughly similar interests, abilities, backgrounds and temperaments."[3] Public visitors are notoriously difficult to study because little source material exists that reveals their own thoughts or actions. Historians generally find that the thoughts and actions of museum scientists and administrators are much better represented in museum archives than those of visitors. Even the source materials most often used to glean public response to museums—newspaper reviews, incident reports, visitor surveys, and personal accounts written by travelers and authors—provide only anecdotal, and largely exceptional rather than representative, information.

The archives of the Museo Etnográfico offer an opportunity to address these silences. The museum did not maintain more detailed visitor statistics than other museums of the time, but it did archive correspondence sent to the museum by outside actors, who wrote to donate objects, attempt to sell their collections to the museum, or ask for copies of museum publications, special visiting privileges, or assistance with scientific questions. The existence—to say nothing of the volume—of this surviving correspondence, in addition to the museum's diffusionary publications and newspaper writings about itself, indicates that the Museo Etnográfico was an institution of considerable public interest and that creole Argentines in Buenos Aires and beyond saw it as a resource within their grasp, not an inaccessible ivory tower.

In the Museo Etnográfico, academic and popular impulses played against one another in the construction of a larger consensus. On one hand, the museum's stated mission focused on academic anthropology, an endeavor that catapulted Argentine anthropology, and especially pre-Columbian archaeology, into international scientific prominence during the early twentieth century. On the other hand, despite the museum's explicitly academic character, outside actors thronged the museum, inspired by more spectacular models of museum anthropology (such as Moreno's Museo de La Plata); captivated by a rising tide of colorful, anthropologically themed newspaper and magazine spreads; and drawn with progressive, modernist zeal to the museum's academic pedigree and scientific authority. Perhaps ironically, the museum's success in cultivating a reputation for scientific professionalism, which was intended to help distance its practices from the amateurish pursuits of popular hobbyism, became one of its strongest attractions for outside actors in Buenos Aires and beyond. In the sometimes harmonious, sometimes conflictive relationships between Museo Etnográfico insiders and outsiders, Argentines constructed an ever-stronger sense of creole Argentine identity in which indigenous cultures played a vibrant and multifaceted role.

Manuel Antequeda's letter to the museum in 1918 exemplified the complexity of these inside-outside negotiations. Antequeda, a schoolteacher in Tio Pujio, Córdoba, offered an object from his personal collection of antiquities in donation to the museum. Debenedetti had expressed his interest in this artifact—which Antequeda described simply as a "tablet"—through a mutual acquaintance. "I know that you have an interest in the tablet," Antequeda wrote in clear, careful cursive. "As my purpose was only to form a small collection that would serve me in the school as illustrative material, I do not mind giving it to you."[4] Antequeda acknowledged the Museo Etnográfico as a center of professional, academic anthropology; however, as his appeal also demonstrates, recognizing these divisions did not necessarily discourage efforts to dialogue between professional and popular spheres. Antequeda framed his donation in two distinct ways, one of which identified Debenedetti as a museum-based scientific authority to whom he dutifully acquiesced and the other of which linked the two men as members of the same collegial network.

First, Antequeda underscored his pleasure at donating the tablet, because "to you it will be more useful than to me and science will come out ahead." He thus cast Debenedetti as an emissary of "science" and the proper custodian for the tablet. On the other hand, Antequeda also plainly felt that through this donation he entered into a relationship of collegiality and even reciprocity with Debenedetti. He reminded Debenedetti that the two men had previously met socially, "in something of a hurry" through a mutual friend, and that he also knew Debenedetti by sight "from having attended the Universidad de La Plata for several years" while Debenedetti had also been in residence there. Building on these social and academic connections, Antequeda suggested that Debenedetti might consider transforming his donation into an exchange. "If you unearth some pottery pieces of those [types] that by being common are of scarce interest," he hinted, "I beg that you might contribute them to the *museo escolar* that I am proposing to form in the school that I direct here."[5] In this way, Antequeda deftly located himself within a wide-ranging museum network that encompassed Debenedetti's state-funded, university-run Museo Etnográfico as well as Antequeda's much more modest "museo escolar." Antequeda's suggestion that Debenedetti send him ceramics of the most commonly found types reflected his awareness of his lower station within the hierarchy of this imagined museum network. But even in his deference to Debenedetti's superior authority, Antequeda underscored that, as a member of this museum network, he saw himself as authorized to make this kind of request. To Antequeda, the Museo Etnográfico and its collections were the rightful domain of professional science, and yet they lay within the legitimate purview of a broader public, defined by more elastic forms of social, academic, and cultural belonging.

Antequeda's letter also highlights an important medium through which these inside-outside dialogues were conducted: museum objects. The Museo Etnográfico received object donations, requests, and offers of exchange from a wide variety of sources, including other museums and universities, as well as schoolteachers such as Antequeda, landowners, prominent public figures, military engineers, travelers, businessmen, artifact dealers, and other outside actors. Museum objects—access to them and rights of ownership and interpretation over them—served as the bargaining chips in these exchanges. As such, they became a contested form of currency or capital, to which different actors assigned distinct kinds and varying amounts of value. Outside actors had significant impact on the Museo Etnográfico's valuation of museum objects, introducing a suite of nonscientific variables, such as aesthetics and popular interest, that could transform scientifically ordinary objects into displayed treasures and keep other scientifically fascinating but aesthetically unappealing objects hidden away in storage drawers. In return, museum-centered scientific notions of object value also changed the way in which outside actors thought of archaeological artifacts and other museum objects, transforming them from curious commodities into national patrimony.

On Museums, Objects, and Authority

During the late nineteenth and early twentieth centuries, museums exhibited objects—fine art, natural scientific specimens, and anthropological artifacts—not as visual aids or examples requiring supplementary texts, but rather as physical embodiments of knowledge. Museum objects were perceived as direct vessels of knowledge, the contemplation of which offered the viewer direct access to understanding, in contrast to textual sources, which required the obligatory mediation of an author. Steven Conn has described this alignment between objects and knowledge as an "object-based epistemology."[6] As carriers of meaning, objects were seen as comprehensible not only to scientific experts but to anyone with the patience to observe them thoroughly and directly, including the museum-visiting public. Other scholars have emphasized the deliberate creation of this epistemological orientation by museum scientists themselves, arguing that objects in late nineteenth- and early twentieth-century anthropological museums exerted "a power over their viewers—a power not simply inherent in the objects, but given to them by the museum as an institution within a particular historical sociocultural setting."[7] In this way, museums became not simply purveyors of object knowledge but creators of that knowledge and judges of what constituted knowledge itself. Objects collected and displayed by museums underwent (and still undergo in museums today) a transformative initiation through which they ceased to be mere things and became museum pieces. This induction involved a variety of processes, or even rites of passage, often including identification, selection, collection, cleaning, preserving, restoring, measuring, cataloguing, labeling, photographing, and ultimately study and display. In undergoing these processes, objects acquired a mantle of—or, perhaps, revealed their innate—scientific truth value, which in turn added to the prestige of the museum housing them.

Museums' authority to define and create knowledge through the deployment of objects invokes a Foucaultian connection between power and knowledge, through the concrete medium of physical objects. The difficulty faced by the Museo Etnográfico, and by museums internationally during the late nineteenth and early twentieth centuries, lay in maintaining control over the knowledge-power of objects. In fact, the tangibility and portability of objects made them remarkably difficult for museum scientists to control based on scientific authority alone, and scientists were often forced to negotiate with other actors over the kinds of value that such objects possessed and who might rightfully claim to possess and interpret them. Antequeda, for example, attempted to code his tablet as a sort of scientific favor or credit, for which he might expect other scientific specimens in exchange from the Museo Etnográfico. The scientific-epistemological value of the tablet in this case was joined by an exchange value independent of scientific value or knowledge-power. This exchange value connected scientific knowledge with cultural cachet and economic worth, illustrating the multiple layers of value attached to the object.[8] Bourdieu's notion of symbolic capital offers a useful framework for understanding the compound values attached to objects such as Antequeda's tablet. Museum objects certainly bore economic capital for collectors and for museum scientists, many of whom paid for various objects in their collections. They also carried symbolic capital, both social and cultural. They conveyed social capital as objects representing and creating networks of interpersonal prestige and power, and they represented cultural capital by embodying culturally valued ideas and theories.[9] Interactions between academic authority and public involvement in the Museo Etnográfico, through the medium of objects, often employed languages that combined invocations of knowledge-power with negotiations over different kinds of value attached to both object and owner, intensifying the meaning of indigenous artifacts and cultures within creole Argentine society.

Museum "Insiders" and Academic Archaeology

Between 1904 and 1930, the Museo Etnográfico occupied two very different spaces, which reflected the changing roles of inside and outside voices in the museum's mission. Its first home, in a series of long, narrow storerooms in the basement of the university's central administrative building, spatially reflected its original purpose as a closed academic cabinet. This space was intended for the education of professional anthropologists, for small groups of people who, it was believed, would be less interested in the aesthetics of display than in functional scientific laboratory space. The Museo Etnográfico's second home—a two-story baroque building south of the Plaza de Mayo on Calle Moreno (named after independence hero Mariano Moreno, not Francisco)—underscored the museum's shifting priorities by the time of its relocation in 1927. Museum scientists dedicated the largest spaces of this building to public exhibits on Argentine archaeology, Peruvian archaeology, American archaeology, Argentine and American ethnography, extra-American ethnography, physical anthropology and human paleontology, and photography, reserving smaller rooms for lectures, closed laboratories, and collections storage. Of course, it is easy to imagine that the museum's scientists may well have preferred the larger and better-lit spaces of the new building for their own research and education work. However, the language they used to campaign for this location and to celebrate its acquisition, as well as their use of the space after obtaining it, consistently prioritized public exhibition and public access, sentiments echoed by outside actors who approached the museum with a sense of claim and belonging.

The Museo Etnográfico's first institutional home in the basement rooms of the university's administrative building would have come as something of a shock to admirers of Francisco Moreno's airy marble, iron, and glass museum palace in La Plata. In this cramped space, the museum's first director, Juan B. Ambrosetti, strove to embody what he called "the university ideal," a balance between professional training and academic research, which imagined for itself no connection with popular education or crowds of Sunday visitors.[10] Ambrosetti, a self-taught naturalist born in Entre Ríos province, directed the museum in addition to his duties as an instructor of American archaeology at the university. The son of a prosperous Italian immigrant and businessman, he had cut his museological teeth as a zoologist in Paraná and later as head of archaeology under Florentino Ameghino at the Museo Nacional de Ciencias Naturales. In the decade before the Museo Etnográfico's foundation, Ambrosetti cultivated an international reputation as an aspiring anthropologist; when he assumed the directorship of the museum in 1904, he had already produced nearly forty publications on anthropological topics, from sketches of provincial folklore to indigenous linguistic studies.[11] Ambrosetti's interest increasingly focused on Argentine archaeology, and despite its titular emphasis on ethnography, the new museum concentrated the majority of its educational and research resources on archaeological work.[12] The Museo Etnográfico identified itself as the progenitor of scientific archaeology in Argentina and of professional, academic anthropology more broadly. Ambrosetti wrote in 1908 that the museum had "already *begun* . . . the systematic study of prehistoric cultures of the Argentine Republic," effectively casting all work that had gone before in a prescientific and therefore imprecise, inferior light—a carelessness that Ambrosetti and his students strove to remedy with carefully controlled modern methods of investigation.[13]

During the last decades of the nineteenth century, the anthropologists of the Museo de La Plata had focused much of their attention on physical anthropology and the study of human remains. While these studies remained prominent into the first decades of the twentieth century, especially in connection with burgeoning schools of eugenic thought and social improvement science across Latin America and the Atlantic world, anthropologists in the Museo Etnográfico increasingly focused their attention on material culture–oriented questions in connection with pre-Columbian archaeology.[14] As the Conquest of the Desert—and with it the opening of the pampas and Patagonia to settlement and development—began to recede from the national political forefront, anthropological investigations in these southern regions also seemed to slow. Archaeology, and a regional focus on the Argentine northwest, offered a rich new field of anthropological research and a landscape of fresh discoveries for national and scientific audiences. Ambrosetti and many of his contemporaries specialized in archaeological excavations in the sub-Andean landscapes of the northwest, where pre-Columbian civilizations had left their traces in stone monuments; elaborate and striking artifacts in ceramic, stone, and metal; pictographs; and stonework settlements.[15] These cultures acquired tremendous symbolic importance in early twentieth-century Argentina, and their archaeological study steadily gained scientific ground and cultural popularity during this period, reverberating with questions of national identity and history.[16] The nationalist importance of this archaeological past struck chords with symbolic appropriations of the stonework structures and monuments built by the Maya in Mexico and

Guatemala, the Inca in Peru, and the Pueblo and Anasazi in the United States.[17] The stonework fortresses and settlement sites that archaeologists discovered crowning Argentina's northwestern hilltops and climbing valley walls served to anchor the Argentine nation within physical space and ancient time, through the quantifiable medium of science. European scientific expeditions joined Argentine archaeological researchers in the study of the Calchaquí, Santa Maria, and other pre-Columbian cultures of the northwest, collecting artifacts by the thousands. Particularly valued (and consequently collected by museums, photographed for academic publications, and sold by artifact collectors) were the distinctive ceramic funerary urns, decorative bronze work, and stone carvings of these groups.

This vision of archaeology as a national science with specifically Argentine institutions and areas of study became especially appealing to the Museo Etnográfico's intended audiences in the early twentieth century, as denizens of Buenos Aires were feeling what many saw as the negative effects of Argentina's strongly Europhilic pro-immigration policies. Millions of European immigrants flooded Buenos Aires—Argentina's main international port and largest city—between the later nineteenth and early twentieth centuries, and many settled there permanently, having never left the city, or returned there seeking work after unsuccessfully looking to settle in rural areas of the country. (Ambrosetti and Debenedetti were themselves both the sons of Italian immigrants.) As a result of this massive influx, Buenos Aires's demographic matrix had changed significantly by the time the Museo Etnográfico opened in the early twentieth century. By 1914, European immigrants—largely from Italy and Spain—made up 30 percent of the national population, and the majority of them were in Buenos Aires. The national population had also increased dramatically, from 1.7 million people in 1869 to 7.9 million in 1914. The Sáenz Peña electoral law, passed in 1912, established "universal" male suffrage, opening the political arena to a wide swath of Argentines and making their allegiance an important goal of increasingly competitive political parties. The Sáenz Peña law did not, however, extend the vote to women or to unnaturalized immigrants, who represented a large part of the national population. Although it represented a significant step toward popular political participation in Argentina, then, the Sáenz Peña law simultaneously highlighted the continuing marginalization of immigrant communities. The early years of the century also witnessed the florescence of Argentina's Socialist, Communist, and Anarchist Parties, which were often associated with foreigners. The anarchist Federación Obrera Regional Argentina attracted significant worker support in Buenos Aires, staging mass protests that, by 1910, prompted reactionary legislation in the Argentine Congress, which allowed the government to deport nonnaturalized immigrants deemed to pose a threat to national security or public order and made it easier to arrest and prosecute labor organizers. These groups also came to be associated in nativist and conservative circles with rabble-rousing, clandestine organizing, and even violence.[18]

Ambrosetti and Debenedetti pursued their archaeological research in this atmosphere of rising xenophobia, both in scientific circles and in broader Argentine society.[19] In this light, it is less surprising that their program of Americanist, pre-Columbian archaeology attracted state funding, as well as public interest, even as official state rhetoric continued to espouse national whiteness and Europeanization. Indeed, the drive for Europeanization that has inspired scholars to examine the idea and history of a "white Argentina" was, paradoxically, the very process that fed an interest in Argentina's indigenous heritage. As creole Argentines considered the unintended consequences of European immigration, the Museo Etnográfico dedicated its efforts to the preservation and study of Argentina's indigenous cultures of the past and present, especially glorifying the deep indigenous past. In this ancient indigenous past, archaeologists and the general public alike found a national connection to the ancient history of Argentina's physical territory, as well as a wistfully remembered moment before the "invasion" of outside cultures, a sentiment expressed without a trace of irony by European-descended archaeologists excavating in the Andean northwest. In a 1927 public speech, when speaking of the history of Argentina's northwest, Debenedetti referred to "the new culture that attacked without previous warning" and the heroic resistance of the Calchaquí and other northwestern indigenous groups—who were, it is important to note, coded as the rightfully autochthonous inhabitants of the region and as nationally Argentine—against this cultural and military invasion. In this reference to an invading "new culture," Debenedetti meant not Spanish conquistadores but the Inca, who had moved into the region's "native valleys" hundreds of years previously.[20] Thus, museum anthropology served a dual purpose for creole Argentines' national identity. First, it allowed them to possess, cleanse, and appropriate indigenous cultures as footholds of national identity that granted them a sense of connection with what they saw as their own native soil, while also using science as a means of separating themselves from those indigenous people and bodies enough to maintain cultural distance and a sense of possession and inheritance rather than genealogical community. Second, museum anthropology proved a helpful tool in distancing creole Argentines from unexpectedly unwelcome floods of European "radicals" by identifying creoles as the national heirs of ancient indigenous civilizations and their legacies and by denying European immigrants access to this connection. This romantic/scientific narrative allowed creole Argentines to cast themselves as true "natives" of this land, a sentiment that—in the eyes of creole museum scientists and publics alike—recently arrived European immigrants neither understood nor were entitled to.

Argentine archaeology of the early twentieth century was a visually saturated discipline. Artifacts lay at the heart of archaeological research, and artifact analysis often centered on visual representation or tangible exhibition of the object as a single whole or in a series, supplemented by verbal description or statistical measurement. Archaeologists focused significant attention on the construction of typological and morphological studies, tracing similarities between physical form and material composition and arranging artifacts into cultural types and chronological stages. Ambrosetti and a cohort of other Argentine archaeologists developed ceramic typologies that focused on the changing form and decoration of ancient ceramic vessels, and they attempted to construct cultural movement and meaning through these object-based physical markers. Among the most important figures in early chronology building in northwestern Argentine archaeology were Ambrosetti, German archaeologist Max Uhle, and Swedish anthropologist Eric Boman. These three engaged in strident debates over the chronological depth of northwestern archaeological civilizations and their relationship to the Incan cultural complex. Uhle contended that northwestern civilizations had developed autochthonously and well before the Inca culture arose in Peru, while Boman maintained that the Inca were more or less contemporaneous with Argentine northwestern civilizations and strongly connected culturally. Boman argued, in fact, that evolutionary science had led to the exaggeration of the depth of archaeological chronologies and advocated for the collapsing of these "false" timelines. In effect, he saw all pre-Columbian civilizations as roughly contemporary, contending that human occupation of the Americas had not been of long duration. Most of these arguments were hazy on exact dates, largely because chronologies relied on relative dating techniques until the discovery of more absolute dating methodologies. Ambrosetti's chronological thinking vacillated between Uhle's and Boman's positions, though publicly he supported Boman. Although both theories continued to carry scientific weight in the early decades of the twentieth century, the notion of a culturally independent ancient Argentina steadily gained cultural popularity. The implications of ancient cultural identity reverberated deeply with early twentieth-century Argentine questions of nationalism. In the Museo Etnográfico, the social utility and scientific value of these sites was embodied in the portable objects collected for the museum and displayed in its galleries.[21]

The visual focus on archaeology in the Museo Etnográfico was reflected not only on the shelves of its exhibit halls but also in the paperwork created by the museum. Professional publications, research notes, and correspondence were filled with drawings and photographs of objects, sometimes in excavation or museum context, sometimes floating in space. In some of these images, context and caption clues provided scaffolding for the viewer to analyze the depicted objects, such as a stone monolith in situ in a northwestern valley or a photograph of a ceramic vessel accompanied by illustrative diagrams or markings. In other cases, the artifacts themselves constituted the entirety of the image. All of these images became, in effect, proxy objects, replicable as often as the photographic negative could be developed, the object traced onto another sheet of paper, or the lithographic plate reprinted. Images taken of archaeological artifacts constituted a second collection and became objects of exchange on a lesser but representatively powerful plane, similar to late nineteenth- and early twentieth-century *cartes de visites*, but with a sharper twist of scientific detachment and legitimacy.[22]

Consider, for example, two images from Ambrosetti's 1906 publication "Exploraciones arqueológicas en la Pampa Grande," detailing the museum's first archaeological expedition to Salta province in 1905. The first image (fig. 7) is a photograph, credited simply to "the Expedition." It depicts a hillside, in front of which a ceramic vessel and a man are posed side by side, sharing the viewer's central focus. The man is a *peón*, or fieldworker, hired by the expedition (led by Ambrosetti) to assist in the heavier work of excavation; his spade, rolled sleeves, and sun-shading hat all attest to the nature of his work in the excavation. He is not, however, the intended focus of the photograph. Ambrosetti's caption identifies the subject as the "excavation of a small urn, superficially buried. Number 253 in the Catalogue." The man beside the urn, perhaps the worker who unearthed it from the hillside (and then again, perhaps not), is placed in the photograph purely to provide scale. Human participation in the urn's discovery is detached from a specific actor by nominalizing "excavate" into "excavation," thus removing the need for an agent. In essence, "the expedition" is credited with the find, not the human being in the photograph.

The purpose of this photograph is to depict the object in situ, as it was found during the excavation. By including the peón, the hillside, the more immediate plane of dirt between the camera and the urn, and the distant line of hazy mountains in the background, the photograph established the urn's authenticity as a scientific archaeological find, as well as the Museo Etnográfico's claim to the object from this original moment of disinterment. Finally, Ambrosetti's caption reinforced the link between this object and the museum by providing the urn's catalogue number, which it would only have acquired weeks or even months later, after being excavated, transported to Buenos Aires, and subjected to the transformative processes of museum cataloguing. By photographing the object in situ and associating this moment with a catalogue number, Ambrosetti transformed the photograph into a proxy object, a stand-in for the object itself that conveyed something of its knowledge-power and did so through a specifically visual medium.

A second photograph from the same publication depicts a very different scene, also centered on a ceramic vessel (fig. 8). The urn in this photograph, significantly larger than the previous artifact and likewise identified by catalogue number, has been excavated, brought to the museum, and restored for exhibition. The heavily edited photograph shows the urn on display, with a human being offering perspective, this time to underscore the object's sheer enormity. The background of the photograph has been removed entirely, apart from a small pool of floor tiles beneath the urn's pedestal and the feet of the man beside it. The "habitat" of the museum is not important to the photograph's purposes, as opposed to the in situ context of the excavation site. This censoring technique, common in museum photography of collections and objects for typological analysis, removes the distraction of stands, curtains, or display cases in the background, accentuating the centrality of the object and of the utility of the photograph as a stand-in for the object's physical presence.

Note also the differences between the two men in these photographs. The peón in the first photograph leans substantially on a spade, poses in work clothes and a face-obscuring hat, under which his eyes cannot be seen, and sports a bushy gray beard. The man in the second image, by contrast, stands quite straight and rests his hand only slightly—and yet also possessively—on the railing of the urn's display stand. His face is clearly visible, and he directs his gaze deliberately away from the camera and in the general direction of the urn, turning the viewer's gaze in that direction as well. He poses in slacks and dress shoes; the rest of his attire is covered by a white laboratory coat

Fig. 7 Ceramic vessel in situ.
Juan B. Ambrosetti, "Exploraciones
arqueológicas en la Pampa Grande
(Provincia de Salta)," *Publicaciones
del Seccion Antropológica* 1 (1906): 64.

that marks his scientific status and underscores the equally scientific nature of
his relationship with the urn and of the photograph itself. His hair and mous-
tache are pomaded and carefully combed. This scientific-type man is just as
much a prop in this photograph as is the peón in the first photograph, but his
physical form is deployed in a very different way. We might think of these
two men as symbolic inhabitants "of the field" and "of the museum," respec-
tively. Their physical presence and typological traits convey certain kinds of
object power to the urns beside which they stand.

Over the first twenty-six years of the Museo Etnográfico's existence, Ambrosetti and Debenedetti cultivated its collections through a network of "proper"
academic channels—expeditions, museum exchanges, and high-profile donations. These collecting practices were essential to the museum's authority, as
they facilitated its entry as a participant into international networks of professional exchange and conduct. The museum amassed the majority of its collections through museum-organized archaeological expeditions. Beginning in
1905, annual expeditions formed an essential part of Ambrosetti's educational
program, during which students of archaeology observed and practiced the
craft of excavation. These expeditions, which took Ambrosetti and his students to Salta, Jujuy, Catamarca, Tucumán, Entre Ríos, San Luis, and Tierra

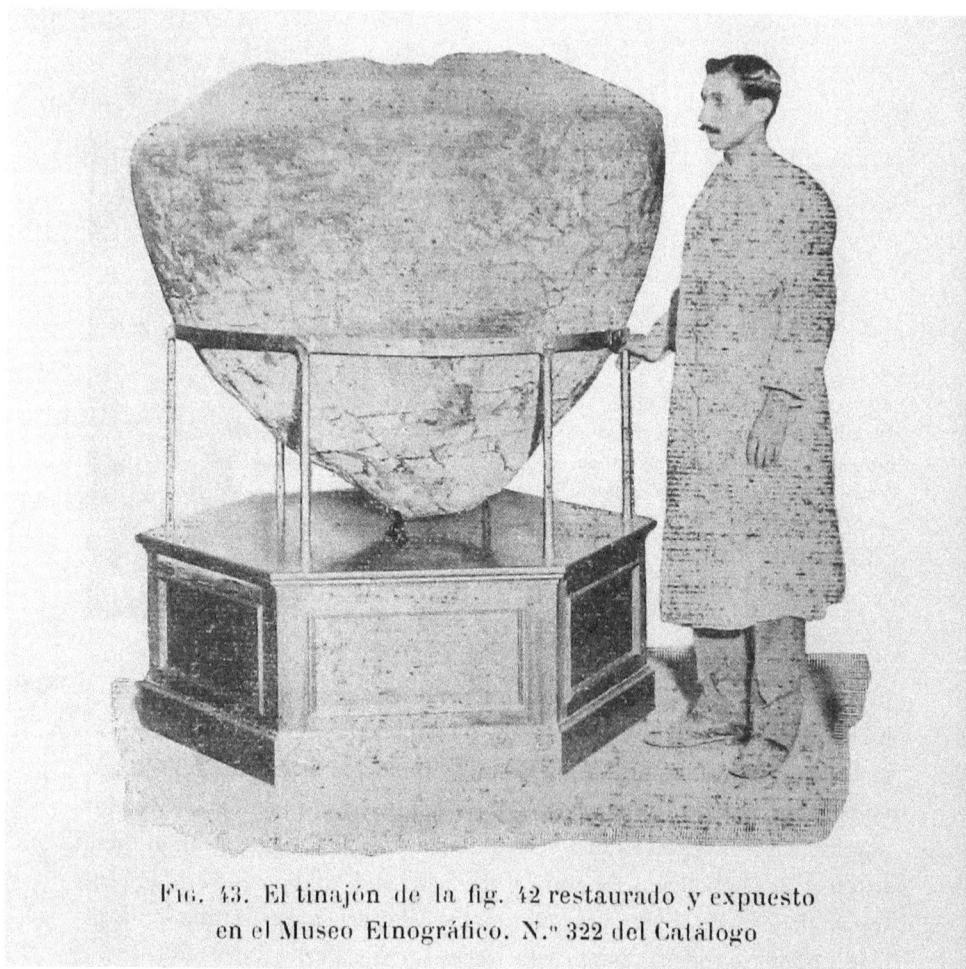

Fɪɢ. 43. El tinajón de la fig. 42 restaurado y expuesto
en el Museo Etnográfico. N.º 322 del Catálogo

Fig. 8 Ceramic vessel in the Museo Etnográfico. Juan B. Ambrosetti, "Exploraciones arqueológicas en la Pampa Grande (Provincia de Salta)," *Publicaciones del Seccion Antropológica* I (1906): 51.

del Fuego, facilitated the collection of thousands of pieces, all of which Ambrosetti demanded be diligently "numbered and catalogued, being therefore able to lend service to science or the education corresponding to it."[23] Ambrosetti's emphasis on the scientific nature of these expeditions legitimized the collected objects as proper scientific specimens and devalued other objects collected by amateurs and outsiders. (See chapter 3 for more discussion of archaeological fieldwork.)

Based on its sizeable collections from field expeditions, the Museo Etno-gráfico organized a series of exchanges with museums around the world, forming professional networks and international ethnographic collections that reinforced its global—not only regional—scientific consequence. These exchanges extended transnational arteries of object movement back and forth between Buenos Aires and other cities in Argentina (including Mendoza, San Miguel de Tucumán, Cuyo, Córdoba, and Paraná), Latin America (including Montevideo, Lima, Rio de Janeiro, and Mexico City), North America (including New York, Washington, D.C., and Toronto), Europe (including Leyden, St. Petersburg, Frankfurt, and Stockholm), and beyond (including Sydney; Tokyo; Canterbury, New Zealand; and Falmouth, Tasmania). Correspondence in Spanish, English, and French connected anthropologists at the museum with colleagues in dozens of different institutions and countries in a global scientific scavenger hunt for the most complete, comparative ethnographic and archaeological collections.[24]

The Museo Etnográfico was able to exchange, in many cases, duplicates and examples of common artifact types from its own collections—particularly archaeological ceramics from the northwestern expeditions—for objects that would have been prohibitively expensive to acquire commercially. Thus, the scientific value of these pieces was dramatically intensified via museum exchange. Ceramic shards, which due to their abundance seemed redundant to the archaeologists in the Museo Etnográfico, became precious holdings to museums in other parts of the world and yielded exotic treasures through their exchange. In 1908, Clark Wissler, curator of anthropology at the American Museum of Natural History in New York City, wrote to Ambrosetti seeking just such an exchange. The Museo Etnográfico shipped a collection of Calchaquí ceramics to Wissler that year, including a variety of painted urns, bowls, and jars that represented redundant types in its collections. Wissler acknowledged receipt of these objects in a letter glowing with the professional satisfaction of a scientist, liberally blended with the personal pleasure of a collector. "I need not tell you," he wrote to Ambrosetti, "that we are greatly pleased with the collection, for you will know that already. Before their arrival, we had not a single specimen from that part of the world."[25] In exchange, Wissler sent Ambrosetti ethnographic specimens from the Philippines, "twenty plaster busts of American Indians," and plaster casts of several "archaeological specimens from North America."[26] In 1913, this exchange was followed by another, in which Wissler requested more Calchaquí ceramics, by far the Museo Etnográfico's most plentiful object type, in return for a collection of ethnographic objects from the Fiji islands, from which the museum had nothing whatsoever. Intermuseum trades thus illustrated the changeable and lopsided scientific value of museum objects, which depended on such economically identifiable qualities as commonness and geographical distance from the site of their origin.[27]

The Museo Etnográfico also engaged in exchanges with other museums in Argentina. For example, it maintained close ties with the Museo de La Plata and often shared personnel. Salvador Debenedetti served as the Museo de La Plata's secretary and librarian between February 1912 and November 1913, as well as adjunct professor of archaeology at the Universidad Nacional de La Plata between March 1912 and April 1918, when his transition to director of the Museo Etnográfico required him to relinquish his post. Debenedetti maintained close ties to La Plata throughout his career and was one of many scientists and university men who frequented the commuter trains between Buenos Aires and La Plata.[28] The Museo de La Plata positioned itself, especially after its absorption into the Universidad Nacional de La Plata in 1906, as a sort of mentor institution to the younger Museo Etnográfico. In that year, for example, Samuel Lafone Quevado, an Argentine anthropologist who succeeded Moreno to the directorship of the Museo de La Plata, sent to the Museo Etnográfico "thirty-five plaster molds of objects pertaining to the ancient inhabitants of the Argentine Republic and Chile" to enhance its collections.[29] This donation was followed by another in 1908, this time of a plaster cast of a stone monolith, or menhir, from the Tafí Valley in Tucumán.[30] Over time, the two museums developed a more reciprocal balance of exchange, as the Museo Etnográfico's archaeological expertise distinguished it from the Museo de La Plata's broader, natural scientific research base. In 1914, Ambrosetti sent Lafone Quevado a "plaster cast of the 'tablet' discovered in Tiahuanaco by Dr. Max Uhle, and the original of which is found in the Museum für Völkerkunde in Berlin,"[31] and in 1922 the Museo de La Plata requested Debenedetti's help with preliminary questions for an archaeological survey that it planned to conduct in Tucumán province, an area in which the Museo Etnográfico had greater expertise.[32]

This sort of intermuseum collaboration, however, had its limits. Debenedetti seems to have overstepped the bounds of institutional independence on at least one occasion. He received a note from the secretary of the Museo de La Plata in May 1921, three years after relinquishing his post as adjunct professor in La Plata and accepting the directorship of the Museo Etnográfico, carefully reminding him of his separation from the former institution. "Keeping in mind that during Saturday afternoons and holidays, the Museo [de La Plata] is closed and there are thus no employees in it," the secretary painstakingly explained, "I beg the Señor Profesor that, whenever he wishes to visit the Museum, alone or accompanied on the given days, he would advise this Secretary in advance in order that service personnel might not be lacking who can be at the orders of the Señor Profesor should he require [assistance]."[33] No specific incident is mentioned, but it seems very likely that such an unannounced visit *did* take place, prompting this courteous but firm reminder that while Debenedetti was recognized as a fellow scientist, he no longer belonged to the inner sanctum of museum staff. He had become a visitor; he might readily demand the special privileges of a special guest (asking a member of the museum staff to report to the museum during its normal closed hours to tend to his needs, for example), but he could no longer expect free, unaccompanied access to the museum or its collections.

The Museo Etnográfico engaged in correspondence and exchange with less prominent Argentine museums as well. Hierarchy and its observance were constant fixtures in these exchanges, locating the Museo Etnográfico in a position to offer patronage to smaller museums. In 1923, Cristian Nelson, then director of the Museo Provincial in Salta, informed Debenedetti of the existence of this museum, which was dedicated to the collection and exposition of specifically salteño materials. In pursuit of this aim, Nelson hoped to appeal to the Museo Etnográfico for aid. "We do not attempt to compete with the Museo Etnográfico," he carefully explained, "but only to place ourselves in a position to be able to acquaint our visitors with what Salta has been, without needing to send them to visit Museums in Europe." For these reasons, "we would be grateful to enter into relations with the Museo Etnográfico, with the purpose of tending to shared interests. . . . I do not doubt that the señor Director will find my proposal of common work between both Museums reasonable, to make possible in that way work more beneficial to the country."[34] Like cordobese schoolteacher Antequeda, and with even firmer footing on the museum ladder, Nelson identified the Museo Provincial as occupying a lower rung of museum authority, demanding his recognition of Debenedetti's authority and allowing him to claim connection to the Museo Etnográfico as part of a network of museums, large and small. Nelson also suggested that Debenedetti see collaboration between their museums as a patriotic duty, facilitating "work more beneficial to the country." Through collaboration, both museums stood to contribute more effectively to the field of Argentine anthropology, which in turn served the nation as a whole.

Nelson also allied his museum to Debenedetti's through a shared opposition to nonscientific collecting, and specifically an ongoing struggle against artifact dealers and the sale of archaeological objects, activities that involved high-volume traffic in pre-Columbian indigenous artifacts. Nelson identified this struggle at the heart of his museum's mission, which he described as "saving where possible the remains of ancient and historical objects from the speculation of the merchants." In Salta, he explained, "private individuals are continually doing excavations for commercial ends," defrauding science of its rightful custodianship of artifacts and robbing Salta of its provincial heritage through the export and sale of these objects to collectors elsewhere. Nelson framed the Museo Provincial and Museo Etnográfico as compatriot institutions, linked by natural ties of scientific and national sympathy and defense and united in protecting archaeological objects and sites against the claims of private collectors and commercially motivated pothunters.

Finally, Ambrosetti and Debenedetti accepted private donations to the Museo Etnográfico, emphasizing several of them in the museum's publications as especially beneficial to its image and work. Between 1906 and 1912, Ambrosetti counted seventy-five individual donors to the museum, though he highlighted a far smaller fraction in his *memoria* to the college. There, he presented an assortment of carefully selected, prominent donations as proof that "from its foundation this Museum received the favor of the enlightened persons who have understood the transcendental importance of anthropological studies in the development of university high culture."[35] Among these high-profile donors, he identified government minister Dr. Indalecio Gómez, who donated Calchaquí bronzes; Minister of Justice and Public Instruction Juan M. Garro, who donated plaster casts and original stone artifacts from Egypt, Assyria, Asia, and Africa; his own father, Tomás Ambrosetti, who made an extravagant donation of a Japanese Buddhist shrine; and the Museo de Bellas Artes, which donated a collection of Calchaquí ceramics.[36] Such donations connected the Museo Etnográfico to the heart of porteño high society, both culturally and monetarily. Perhaps fearing that his point might yet be lost on his readers, Ambrosetti underscored that these donors, who "foresaw the great progress that this Museum would have in the future, called upon to be one of the most important, special, and interesting [museums] of this Capital, have not failed to give it their generous support, offering it valuable objects and collections that, united with those obtained in the various explorations, exchanges, and purchases, have allowed [the Museum] to achieve unforeseen progress in a short time."[37] With such support, the Museo

Etnográfico grew even faster than Ambrosetti had envisioned. Since its inception in 1904, its holdings had expanded from some half-dozen artifacts to encompass 12,156 objects by 1912—an explosive growth rate at which, Ambrosetti wrote frankly, "I personally confess, I am the first to feel surprise."[38]

The Museo Etnográfico also enthusiastically received private donations of individual objects with more peripheral scientific relevance to its aims, especially when those donations were extraordinary. Tomás Le Breton offered perhaps the most singularly sensational donation in the museum's early history. Le Breton, an Argentine lawyer, politician, and diplomat, traveled to Egypt in 1926, where he met British archaeologist Howard Carter, who had achieved sudden international renown four years earlier by uncovering the pharaoh Tutankhamun's tomb. Carter brought Le Breton to the Valley of the Kings and gave him a tour of the tomb, which he was still in the process of studying and cataloguing from a field laboratory nearby. Le Breton's traveling companion, Alfredo González Garaño, later wrote of the experience, "We could admire in the immense laboratory beside the crypt, a great part of the treasure that very few specialists have yet contemplated, the prodigious jewels, the imperial crown, the objects that were in the third chamber, and the sarcophagus of gilded wood and decorated with multicolored glass."[39] In his laboratory, Carter removed a small piece of dried incense from the outer casing of Tutankhamun's sarcophagus to show to Le Breton and González Garaño. Carter heated the incense, and the air "was perfumed with an aroma that was the same that filled that space 25,000 years ago." He then gave the piece of incense to Le Breton as a gift. Upon his return to Buenos Aires the following year, Le Breton donated the fragment to the Museo Etnográfico with a terse note: "On the advice of Señor A. González Garaño I send you a portion of the paste [incense] that covered the casket of TUT-ANKAMON [*sic*] and which was presented by Mr. Carter in February of 1926 in his laboratory in the Valley of the Kings."[40] The incense was accepted directly and catalogued.

Le Breton's donation, despite having little connection with the museum's stated dedication to hemispheric American archaeology or its extensive collections in this area, caused an immediate stir. Buenos Aires newspaper readers of the 1920s had been swept up in the global fever for all things ancient Egyptian. The prominent porteño newspaper *La Prensa*, for example, catered to its readers with photograph-punctuated pieces on Tutankhamun and other pharaohs, as well as ancient Egyptian culture and its mysteries. Readers pored over stories such as "The Tomb of Tut-Ankh-Amon" and "The Religious

Revolution and Its Sexual Aspect. Defects of Aj-en-Aton [Akhenaton]."[41] Egyptian archaeology captured Argentine imaginations through its invocations of exotic sensuality and Oriental beauty, coupled with the thrill of modern adventure and discovery.

Possessing the incense fragment, in short, connected the Museo Etnográfico with one of the most recognizable and alluring civilizations of the ancient world. Debenedetti expertly used the fragment to underscore this connection and to highlight the museum's national prominence at the inauguration of its new facility, barely two weeks after the donation itself was made. "The history of the Museo etnográfico," he declared in September 1927, "links in this moment, closing what we may call a cycle, two famous valleys in history, two valleys of legend, on two distant continents: the Valley of the Kings of Egypt and the Calchaquí Valley, in [northwestern] Argentina." Debenedetti drew a fateful line between these two sites of ancient civilization that passed directly through the Museo Etnográfico. The first pieces collected by the museum, he explained, were "taken from the Calchaquí lands" of northwestern Argentina, "exhumed from the sepulcher of one of those valiant warriors who defended the quebradas" against the advance of the Inca. He went on to state that "the last piece, accessioned yesterday . . . is a fragment of perfumed resin that the illustrious archeologist Carter removed from the sarcophagus of Tutankamón. Thus, through time, distance, and the succession of civilizations renewed, combined, or displaced, the material products of unknown and unsuspected peoples come to be found here, in the mystery of this reliquary, where things appear to be dead, and after millennia of shadows recover their lost life under our sun."[42] Le Breton's donation brought to the Museo Etnográfico the romance of ancient Egypt and the prestige of possessing even a fragment of the most captivating archaeological find of the century, personally given to Le Breton by Carter himself. Moreover, in drawing an equivalence between the Egyptian Valley of the Kings and the Argentine Calchaquí Valley, Debenedetti underscored Argentines' ability to grasp intuitively the gravity of this important discovery, because they too possessed an ancient and glorious past, of equal importance and merit to the Egyptian past. In other words, Egypt's ancient past, while internationally celebrated, was no more worthy than Argentina's own, which was on proud—as well as selective and possessive—display in the Museo Etnográfico. Notably, however, the incense's symbolic value was far greater in the abstract than in a physical or visual sense. The fragment was not pictured in the museum's many well-illustrated publications from the period, nor did its image appear in newspapers or magazines. The mystery and romance of ancient Egypt carried by the incense could not, in the end, transform it into a compelling display piece. Rather, it became a symbolic trophy of the collections, carefully guarded in storage rooms and hidden away from public view.

These exchanges, expeditions, and donations brought scientifically valuable and appreciably exotic objects to the Museo Etnográfico through the proper channels of museum work, without the messy materialism of purchase. Rules of professional conduct guided the propriety of these exchanges, a code perhaps most effectively demonstrated in its breach. German geographer and Buenos Aires resident Franz Kühn wrote a curt letter to the museum in October 1916, calling Ambrosetti's attention to a "stone head" that Kühn had given to him "more than two years ago" for the museum's collections. The purpose of this highly unusual letter was to request that the head be returned to him. Kühn argued that the stone head had not been "gifted to the Museum, but given in exchange for another object," an arrangement that Kühn felt had been agreed upon and subsequently ignored by Ambrosetti. "It has already been some time since I sent a letter in which I requested that you indicate a day on which I might come to find some object that you would approve in exchange for the stone head," Kühn complained. Not having received a reply in that time, Kühn stiffly wrote that "it seems to me now more opportune, if you cannot keep your promise, to reclaim this head." The letter is accompanied in the archive by Kühn's calling card, delivered to the museum a few days later with a handwritten note: "[Dr. Franz Kühn, Professor] salutes the Director of the Museo Etnográfico, J. B. Ambrosetti, and requests that he deliver the stone head to the bearer of this [card]. B. Aires, October 17, 1916."

Kühn's indignation prompts two observations. First, his status as a member of the European academy, who had come to Argentina by invitation to teach courses at the Instituto Nacional del Profesorado Secundario in Buenos Aires, positioned him very differently than Manuel Antequeda or even Cristian Nelson along spectrums of academic and social inclusion. Kühn invoked Ambrosetti's honor as a brother scientist, recalling their exchange agreement in terms of respect between equals, and without the deference that Antequeda or Nelson demonstrated. As a member of an international academic stratum, Kühn demonstrated a sense of affront at having been ignored by a fellow scholar. We might also speculate that Kühn, coming on special invitation from Europe, perhaps understood himself to be not equal but superior to the Argentine scientific setting around him. The Argentine Republic's habit of

importing European scientists to fill educational and research positions, perhaps even compounded by Ambrosetti's lack of formal training, may have
contributed to Kühn's indignation at what he perceived as a professional and
personal slight.

Second, the mental image of Kühn selecting an object from among the
museum's collections is reminiscent, more than anything else, of a visit to a
store. Kühn proposed to treat the museum as a sort of private antiquities
market, purchasing "credit" with a donated object and then browsing for
his new acquisition, with Ambrosetti trailing him to set the limits of what
his stone head could "buy." The manner in which Kühn proposed to conduct
this exchange deviated considerably from the contemporary norms of intermuseum exchange, in which specific objects or types were proposed in
exchange for others, and negotiations were carried out between museums
through correspondence and detailed object lists to establish the parameters of
the exchange before any actual object was sent. Instead, Kühn sought an open-
ended and more manifestly economic exchange. This exchange also differed
from the one suggested by Antequeda, who conceded control over any future
(and hypothetical) exchange of objects to the Museo Etnográfico's discretion.
Kühn's actions violated the limits of academic privilege and professional propriety and demonstrated that academic authority—the disembodied social
capital of Bourdieu's symbolic capital matrix—depended not only on status
and title but on conduct as well. It seems that Kühn's head was returned to
him and its number stricken from the catalogue.[43]

Museum "Outsiders" and National Patrimony

While bad professional behavior such as Kühn's helped define the peripheries
of "proper" or inside behavior, the museum faced an equally pressing wave of
potentially challenging input from outside actors who sought access to it. The
Museo Etnográfico's carefully constructed network of professional and scientific belonging was jarred by these outside actors, whose volume increasingly
affected the museum's form and function by the 1920s.

Ambrosetti was actively campaigning for a larger home for his museum by
1912, having encountered in its first location the same problem that had
plagued Hermann Burmeister and his successors at the Museo Público (later
the Museo Nacional de Ciencias Naturales): the Museo Etnográfico needed
more space.[44] After a long campaign that outlived Ambrosetti and occupied

the first ten years of Debenedetti's directorship, in September 1927 the Museo Etnográfico relocated to new facilities two blocks south of Buenos Aires's central Plaza de Mayo. The two-story Baroque-style building it occupied was originally designed for the Universidad de Buenos Aires in 1874 by architect Pedro Benoit, who also designed La Plata's civic spaces. The relocation offered the museum more storage space, better-lit (aboveground) laboratories, and an opportunity to expand its research and educational focus toward exhibition for public audiences.[45]

The inauguration ceremony was open to the public and attended by a crowd of people who squeezed in, shoulder to shoulder, among the museum's plaster-cast statuary in the central atrium to hear the opening addresses. On that chilly spring morning, Debenedetti addressed an assembly that included Argentine president Marcelo T. de Alvear, university rector Ricardo Rojas, former university administrators, and more than one hundred other people. Debenedetti's address highlighted the transformation signified by that moment: the Museo Etnográfico was officially becoming a public museum. As of the moment of relocation, he proclaimed, "the Museo Etnográfico opens its doors to all, in a building that is spacious, luminous, and full of tradition in the history of the porteño university. Thus is realized the hope that inspired Ambrosetti, when he sensed the crisis of location, the tightness of environment, in the gloomy catacombs of calle Viamonte." In its new incarnation, the museum would be oriented "more to the life of the city, an institution that will be, without doubt, [a place] of tranquility and of meditation, that will move the spirit of the people and will lead them from epoch to epoch, from region to region, from culture to culture." Debenedetti cloaked the new public visitors in a mantle of "patriotic conjunction, inspired by the desire for scientific progress, the love of truth, the desire to know better and penetrate in its essence the thought of our native ancestors in the land of América."[46]

Debenedetti's conscious acknowledgment of public visitors as part of the Museo Etnográfico's mission in 1927, however, responded to rather than created public interest in the museum. The volume of this public interest was forcibly demonstrated by the press coverage of the inauguration ceremony itself. Before the actual event, at least five prominent newspapers in Buenos Aires—*La Nación*, *La Prensa*, *La Libertad*, *La Razón*, and *La Época*—ran announcements of the upcoming inauguration, providing the address, day, and time of the ceremony. One such announcement in *La Prensa* two days before the inauguration optimistically anticipated the "better use of the museum" as a result of its relocation, in addition to "free public access." Another announcement in *La Época* described the Museo Etnográfico as "the leading [museum] of its specialization in South America."[47] The inauguration was even more lavishly publicized after the fact, in photograph spreads and reproductions of the speeches given by Debenedetti, Alvear, and others, accompanied by commentary from correspondents from fourteen separate newspapers, some of which ran stories on the event for days afterward.[48] Unanimous approval for the museum's scientific mission filled these reports, blended with the mystically tinged enthusiasm exemplified by *Crítica*, which printed an article entitled "The Ashes of Our Ancestors Are Found in the Museo Etnográfico, Inaugurated Today":

> The seven halls of the Museo Etnográfico contain the ashes of our ancestors. Urns of Uazca, huacos and utensils from the Incaic period, mummies from the altiplano, funerary art pieces from the Indians of the quebrada of Humahuaca and from the Calchaquí valleys, discs with zoological representations, childlike drawings where the primitives experimented with representation of their myths and their beliefs, sleep in the cases and on the shelves of the Museo. The past lives and governs the present by means of the ashes of the dead. The millenarian civilizations sleep until today in the quiet peace of the Museo Etnográfico of Moreno 350, before the absorbed eyes of the studious and researchers.

In such reports, outside interest in the museum revealed itself to be characterized not purely by a scientific or "tranquil meditation" or the "love of truth," as Debenedetti would have had it. Rather, it also entailed a sense of possessive romance and a search for the deep national past, made visible and tangible in the "ancestral ashes" on display in the Museo Etnográfico.

Outside actors made their voices heard in the museum through a number of channels. Popular actors addressing the Museum Etnográfico combined conciliatory recognition of museum authority with determined assertions of their own rights to demand time and resources from museum scientists, and they centered their inquiries, offers, and demands on the circulation and meaning of tangible museum objects. Just as archaeology had risen to the forefront of professional anthropological research, it also captured the imagination of Argentine society more broadly. Many archaeological artifacts—ceramics, bronze objects, carved stone, funerary goods, ruins—were aesthetically appealing, personally or sentimentally precious, and economically valuable, as well as scientifically interesting. Outside actors interpreted the value of these objects in different ways, placing highly variable emphasis on different kinds of value.

Nothing demonstrated the growing social and national significance of the Museo Etnográfico better than the flood of packages that the museum received from outside actors, containing objects that their owners had decided to donate to the museum. In principle, both Ambrosetti and Debenedetti distrusted such privately collected or purchased materials. Most private collectors, Ambrosetti explained, "never concerned themselves with collecting provenance data [*data de yacimiento*], but only with collecting the greatest number of well-conserved objects possible with the sole end of selling" them. Other collectors, he complained, fancied themselves archaeologists, but their excavations were dilettantish and unscientific.[49] Despite these reservations, however, Ambrosetti and Debenedetti each accepted private donations to the Museo Etnográfico on a regular basis, from a variety of sources both well and ill defined. These donations demonstrate an active engagement with the nationalist narrative of the museum itself—the idea that indigenous cultures belonged to national patrimony and that artifacts pertaining to indigenous cultures belonged in the museum—as well as a sense of personal ownership over the museum. As a rule, objects were donated without any question as to the museum's need for them; a donation was made because of the *donor's* desires, or his or her sense of connection to the museum, and conveyed an expectation that the object would be accepted.

In 1914, for example, Clemente Zamora sent the museum two *boleadoras*, along with a brief note explaining that he had found them "in the town of 'De la Serna,' Buenos Aires Province" and was donating them, "it being my desire that they become part of the archaeological collection of the museum that you worthily direct." Zamora was not connected to the museum by profession or social prominence, and his donation was identified only by his proper name, which lacked, significantly, any honorific title such as "don" or "señor." Moreover, his donation lacked provenance data, being linked only with the "town of 'De la Serna'" and not with any more specific site within those parameters. Despite these limitations, Zamora's unsolicited donation of two extremely common stone *boleadora* weights, made specifically to the Museo Etnográfico and even more specifically to its "archaeological collection," suggests the identification of the museum as a center for Argentine archaeological interest and as the proper home for such incidentally discovered anthropological and archaeological objects.[50] Rather than keep the bolas as curiosities or keepsakes for himself, Zamora turned them over to the museum, effectively presenting them not as curiosities but as scientific objects and museum pieces.

Zamora was far from alone in mentally linking his find with the scientific work of the Museo Etnográfico. The museum's archives attest to the fact that when Argentines stumbled across indigenous artifacts, they often associated those objects with scientific anthropology and with museums. Interestingly, this also held true—as the museum gained institutional footing in the early years of the twentieth century—for long-possessed artifacts that began to gain new meaning in their owners' eyes. Arturo Frutos, a lawyer in Buenos Aires and a personal friend to Ambrosetti, sent the latter a stone artifact in 1906, explaining that "with the present [letter] I am pleased to send you the stone from Misiones about which I have spoken and which I donate to the Museum of the Faculty of Philosophy and Letters, convinced that there it will be more necessary and will offer greater service, than that of paperweight in my study." Frutos had obtained the stone some ten years earlier when it was sent to him by an acquaintance in Misiones as a curiosity for his personal collection, "with the explanation that [such objects] were abundant there and that they were used in other times by Indians as a weapon of combat." Although Frutos knew Ambrosetti personally, this acquaintance alone had not compelled Frutos to think of the stone as a scientific specimen. With the establishment of the Museo Etnográfico, however, Frutos evidently came to feel that his study was no longer the proper place for this object. What had once been merely a curio and perhaps a conversation-starting paperweight had transformed in Frutos's eyes, through the lens of the museum, into an anthropological artifact.[51]

Private donations to the Museo Etnográfico often carried an explicit overtone of patriotism that linked anthropological science and the museum to nationalism and patrimony. In donating the cranium of an indigenous man, which he had collected in 1911, Carlos Brackibux of Mendoza province felt himself to be complying with his national duty. He closed his letter to Ambrosetti by "expressing my great pleasure as a son of the Argentine republic at being able to enrich our national anthropological collections" with the donation.[52] Another donor, Héctor Nuñez, underscored the national mission and collective importance of the Museo Etnográfico in his careful execution of his brother Carlos Alberto's will. Carlos Alberto Nuñez had charged his brother with donating two pieces of column capitals that he had collected in Jerusalem; Héctor explained, "It was his expressed wish before his death that they might be given to the Museo Etnográfico Argentino."[53] Nuñez's retitling of the museum is especially revealing; the Museo Etnográfico did not have the word "Argentino" in its name, but to Nuñez's mind, consciously or subconsciously, it may as well have. Such donations illustrated both a rising social interest in anthropological and archaeological collecting and the coalescence of anthropological authority in museum settings. Private collectors such as Nuñez, Brackibux, Frutos, and Zamora willingly donated their modest collections to the Museo Etnográfico in what they identified as the consolidated and authoritative interests of science and the nation.

The gathering strength of the museum's ties to an imagined national mission not only inspired outpourings of public support in the form of object donations, however. It also spurred increasing public demands on the museum, most notably demands for visiting privileges and access to museum collections. During the 1910s and early 1920s, the Museo Etnográfico received a rising tide of requests for special visiting hours, accommodations for large groups, and additional educational resources from schoolteachers and event coordinators for scientific societies and social organizations. Among the dozens of school requests surviving in the museum's archives, for example, is a series of requests submitted each year during the early 1920s by the Escuela Normal No. 3 de Maestras in Buenos Aires; it asked permission to bring its fourth-year students to the museum for an afternoon visit, accompanied by their history instructor, Dorotea Ana Rosa.[54] These visits—for students at the Escuela Normal No. 3 and other schools in Buenos Aires—evidently became part of an annual curriculum, an addendum to students' instruction that the museum offered freely and according to the requirements of outside teachers.

Workers' unions, political parties, and social associations also arranged special visits to the museum, broadening its utility to the Argentine people as well as its profile in Buenos Aires's circle of cultural institutions. The popular library "La Comuna," an extension of the Municipal Workers' Union Society, wrote to Debenedetti in January 1923 requesting that the museum host an informative lecture for its members, a group estimated at around seventy people, "on the collections in the possession of the important Museum under your direction." Members of Buenos Aires's German Scientific Society and the Socialist Party–affiliated Sociedad "Luz" likewise requested and received special visiting privileges, guided tours, and dedicated lectures from museum personnel. Such examples are representative of a growing flood of public educational and social aid groups whose interactions with the museum pivoted around requests for access to collections, instruction, and assistance.

The Social Aid Commission of the National Women's Council offers a particularly striking example of the Museo Etnográfico's interaction with outside groups seeking this kind of access and privilege, as well as the balance of power between the museum and outside petitioners. In May 1920, Debenedetti received a form letter from the Social Aid Commission, addressed generically to the "Director of the Museo Etnográfico" (in fact, the form letter's stock greeting, "Señor Don . . . ," had been haphazardly overwritten in pen to say "Señor Director . . ."). The letter announced that "the Commission of Social Aid of the National Women's Council, in organizing for the current year a series of instructive visits to museums, public buildings, industrial establishments, estancias, factories, refrigeration plants, etc., asks that you allow us to visit the [handwritten:] *Museo Etnográfico* that you direct, and if you grant us the necessary authorization, we would appreciate permission to make the aforesaid visit on Thursday, [handwritten:] *June 10 at 3 PM*." A handwritten note below the text of the form letter added, "We would also appreciate perhaps a small lecture that would very much interest the visitors."[55] Within the Social Aid Commission's broad schema of instructional tours, the Museo Etnográfico offered a notable—but by no means isolated or unique—stop. This visit, the letter implied, would be dictated by the schedule and terms of the commission and offered an opportunity for the museum to participate in something larger than itself.

Evidently, the museum agreed to take part in the Social Aid Commission's program, because Debenedetti received a second letter, this time handwritten, on May 3, 1920, modifying the arrangement. The letter informed Debenedetti that the commission needed to "change the day of [its] visit to the Museo Etnográfico to the 15th of June," because it had received a conflicting invitation from a private collector in Buenos Aires, "to show us her magnificent Collection of Antiquities."[56] The commission's willingness to reschedule its visit to the museum in favor of another opportunity may have simply reflected the more rigid schedule of a private collector, as opposed to an institution such as the Museo Etnográfico. It also highlighted, however, the transformation of the Museo Etnográfico into a tool of instruction, to which the commission confidently believed it could gain access and with which it might successfully negotiate and renegotiate access for a group tour and lecture, even when its reason for rescheduling was a less-than-tactfully phrased visit to someone else's "magnificent Collection." In 1920, it must be remembered, the museum had not yet announced any mission toward public exhibition or access and remained an explicitly academic institution in its original location in the Universidad de Buenos Aires's administrative basement. Nonetheless, the Social Aid Commission and other porteño groups clearly interpreted the Museo Etnográfico as a public resource rather than an isolated academic stronghold, and access to the museum's halls and collections was interpreted by outside actors such as those at the commission as lying well within their grasp, not held exclusively by anthropologists in their ivory basement.

Perhaps some of the most conflicted, and the most insistent, outside actors clamoring for access to the Museo Etnográfico's resources were professional artifact dealers and others seeking to sell objects to the museum. Archaeology lent itself naturally to private collection and generated a booming market in antiquities sales in Argentina and beyond, much more so than had earlier interests in physical anthropology. The ancient and contemporary skulls that had formed the nexus of physical anthropological collections in La Plata and elsewhere were difficult to obtain or recreate, especially in the case of diagnostic or famous skulls taken from well-known contemporary figures or celebrated ancient sites (for example, the Neander skulls of France or the remains of famous caciques such as Cipriano Catriel). Archaeological artifacts, on the other hand, were easier to find or forge, and highly collectible. Ceramic vessels, stone implements, and even metallic objects were discovered quite accidentally by hacendados on their estates, by military engineers in their surveys and works, and by what might be described as "recreational archaeologists" or even pothunters, who deliberately sought out and excavated ancient sites in search of artifacts for their own collections or for sale. The economic motivations behind artifact dealers' collections struck Ambrosetti and his museum contemporaries as deeply contradictory to the aims of science and dangerous to the purity of its pursuit. He wrote in 1908 that "it is always necessary to mistrust those [materials] connected to antiquities merchants" because the objects in their care gained and lost value according to their own accounts of objects' origins and provenance. An artifact dealer wishing to make a greater profit might be tempted to manipulate an unsuspecting collector into paying a higher price for a ceramic urn, for example, by claiming that it came from a famous archaeological site such as Tiahuanaco, when in fact it came from a lesser-known site, an unassociated culture, or even a forgery workshop. This sort of duplicity certainly did occur among artifact dealers internationally, and Ambrosetti attempted to safeguard his institution against the corruptive influence of such inaccuracies and the damage they could do to the museum's academic and scientific reputation.[57]

The Museo Etnográfico's rejection of artifact dealers as crass commodifiers of scientific treasures, however, did not stop professional artifact merchants and private collectors from approaching the museum with offers of sale. Nor did its rejection of such overtures in principle stop Ambrosetti or Debenedetti from capitalizing on offers that suited their designs for the museum. For example, Ambrosetti arranged in 1909 for a man named Juan Paglia to send the museum four indigenous skeletons, exhumed from cemeteries in the Andean northwest. Paglia's correspondence with Ambrosetti detailed the difficulty of the work, which he hired local laborers to do, in order to justify the high price of fifty pesos per skeleton. Paglia explained that his workers had to "work at night and secretly from the Indians"; this secrecy was necessary partly because the skeletons they were excavating were not ancient, but extremely recent. "The [skeletons] I send you have been buried for two years," Paglia wrote. "Older [skeletons] are not possible to find, without the bones being completely decayed." This frank confession of grave robbing, reminiscent of the type of "specimen collecting" that had typified anthropological exploration south of the frontier before and during the Conquest of the Desert a generation earlier (see chapter 1), exposed the lingering contradictions and even hypocrisies within anthropological museum science. Ambrosetti, who is often credited with transforming Argentine archaeological excavation from a hobby into a science, and who played a significant role in reenvisioning archaeological remains as part of Argentina's national patrimony rather than as commercial or private property, seems to have been largely unconcerned with Paglia's methods in 1909 and fulfilled the contract. Paglia also offered to orchestrate the exhumation and shipment of additional indigenous skeletons to the museum from cemeteries in the same area, where he assured Ambrosetti that he could find "other skeletons, of tobas, chaguan, chulupi, and masajo Indians."[58]

Ambrosetti dealt not only with incidental agents such as Paglia, but also with a circle of established antiquities merchants of precisely the type he decried in print. The museum's archives preserve a number of artifact catalogues from dealers in France, Germany, Egypt, and South America, as well as correspondence with dealers regarding specific purchases. Ambrosetti dealt over a period of years with a London-based artifact dealer named W. O. Oldman, for example. Oldman, whose letterhead identified him as a dealer in "Ethnological Specimens, Eastern Arms, &c." wrote to Ambrosetti in September 1910, "I shall at any time have great pleasure in sending you special lists of objects obviating duplicates of any specimens already sent you, and forming a collection up to any amount you may intimate."[59] Oldman's offer not only expressed his estimation of Ambrosetti as a potentially valuable future client, meriting the detailed work of compiling individualized lists from his catalogue that might suit Ambrosetti's needs, but also revealed that Ambrosetti had already purchased objects from Oldman, which his records would allow him to omit from future lists of suggested purchases. During the early 1910s, Ambrosetti and Oldman exchanged information, payments, catalogues, photographs and sketches, and, of course, objects.

Oldman's success in winning Ambrosetti's confidence, and accordingly his business, may have lain in his ability to convey a sense of professional reliability and quasi-scientific accuracy. "You may rest assured," he wrote to Ambrosetti in 1910, "that at all times your orders and wishes shall be carried out to the best of my ability and the specimens as described and genuine."[60] Oldman's style of listing objects from his catalogue in letters to Ambrosetti revealed an awareness of museum style and an ability to imitate the careful yet not overly artistic sketching, the specific measurements and details, and the noncommercial flavor of exchanges. Oldman did not send glossy catalogues or polished business cards. Rather, he sent sheets of his personal stationery, closely covered in handwritten lists and descriptions, as well as drawings, that contrasted sharply with the materials distributed by many other artifact dealers.

Consider, for example, Oldman's sketches of two wooden figures from Dutch New Guinea, which he described as "idols" (fig. 9). The two idols are drawn from scientific, Bertillon-inspired angles—one in profile and one directly facing the viewer. Both are accompanied by vertical legends bearing the specimens' height and by a series of marginal notes on provenance, material, and condition. The note below the left-hand idol reads, "Idol from Lake Santani, carved from heavy wood colored orange and black and a little white." The right-hand idol's head plumage is identified as "cassowary feather fastened in like a brush," and text in the bottom margin notes, "Nose chipped, wood handle fastened on, painted design, black and red and white." Oldman has also portrayed this idol in profile from above, showing it to be a curved plaque rather than a full effigy. Finally, there is a fracture at the bottom right corner of the idol, noted accordingly. A list of Polynesian oil bowls (fig. 10) demonstrates a more condensed dedication to measurement and description. Each item on the list is identified by its material, physical dimensions, and

Oldman's rather vague approximations of age ("very old," "not so old"). Many items are also accompanied by small sketches of shape and markings. These sketches and rough descriptions are much more reminiscent of archaeological field notes than commercial catalogues, and Oldman may well have employed this approach in an attempt to access and redeploy scientific authority in his own service.

Law 9080: Transforming Archaeological Objects into National Patrimony

Ambrosetti and Debenedetti were both acutely aware of the commodification of archaeological objects in an international market and feared that this trend could threaten Argentina's archaeological patrimony. Internationally, ethno-graphic and archaeological objects were being exported in vast quantities to Europe for display in public museums and purchase by private collectors. This export trade was largely uncontrolled through the nineteenth century and revealed dynamics of economic and cultural inequality that character-ized informal imperial control in Latin America and beyond.[61] An early wave of legislation regulating artifact exports in countries ranging from Peru and Mexico to Egypt illustrated the volume of exportation and the concern it occasioned. These early efforts at regulation, however, were largely unen-forced and ineffectual. Egypt, among the countries most highly exploited by artifact dealers and private collectors, was forced to relegislate in 1912 to stem the enormous flow of artifacts to Europe and North America.[62] Latin Ameri-can countries followed suit in the early twentieth century with renewed attempts to stem the mass exportation of artifacts, which were increasingly described as national property, treasures, and patrimony. Archaeology gained social importance in Argentine society within this turn-of-the-century inter-national context, and museums such as the Museo Etnográfico, the Museo de La Plata, and the Museo Nacional de Ciencias Naturales allowed for the expression of archaeological interest through official channels that transformed individual and social interest into national pride. In 1913, creole Argentine state makers concretely expressed this vision of their nation as possessing a precious and self-defining archaeological past through the passage of law 9080, which nationalized archaeological and paleontological remains and legislated the retention of these materials within national boundaries.[63]

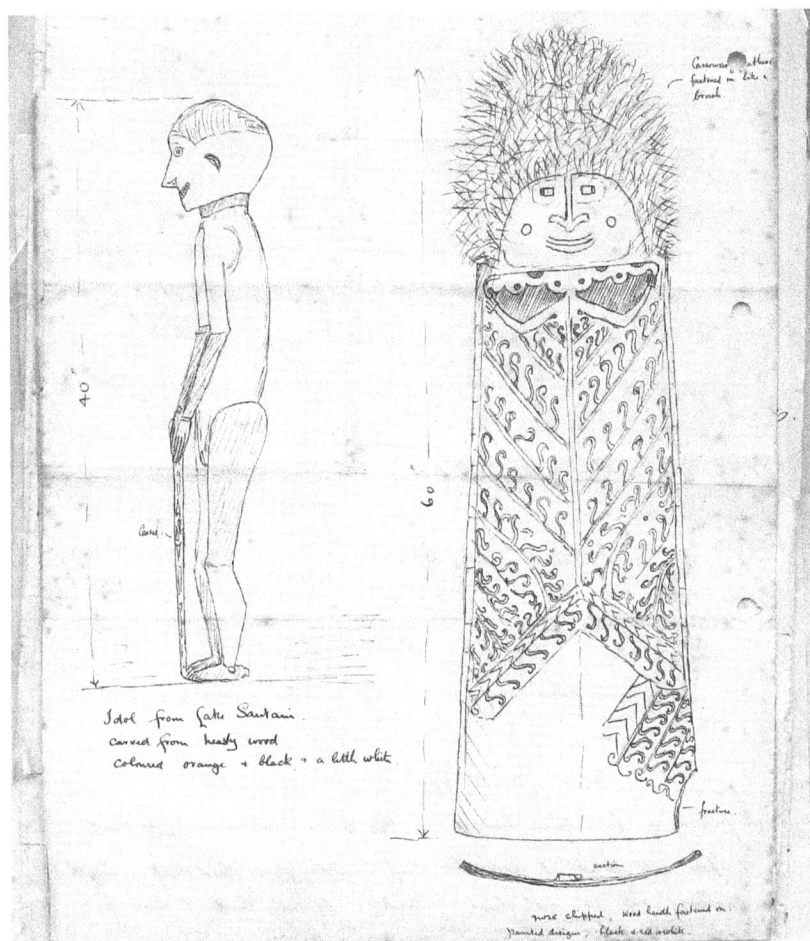

Fig. 9   Idol drawings by W. O. Oldman. Caja 3.30, Archivo Fotográfico y Documental del Museo Etnográfico "Juan B. Ambrosetti," FFyL, UBA.

Representative Manuel Gonnet, speaking for Buenos Aires in the Cámara de Diputados, proposed the law in 1912, arguing that archaeological and pale-ontological remains constituted as essential an element of national wealth as did other natural resources that were economically measured more directly. "The riches that are found in the depths of the earth, the mines, the deposits, the mineral oils, the petroleum deposits, are of the public domain," Gonnet reminded the House, "and the State has always claimed them." He went on to argue that "apart from these material riches, which can easily be transformed

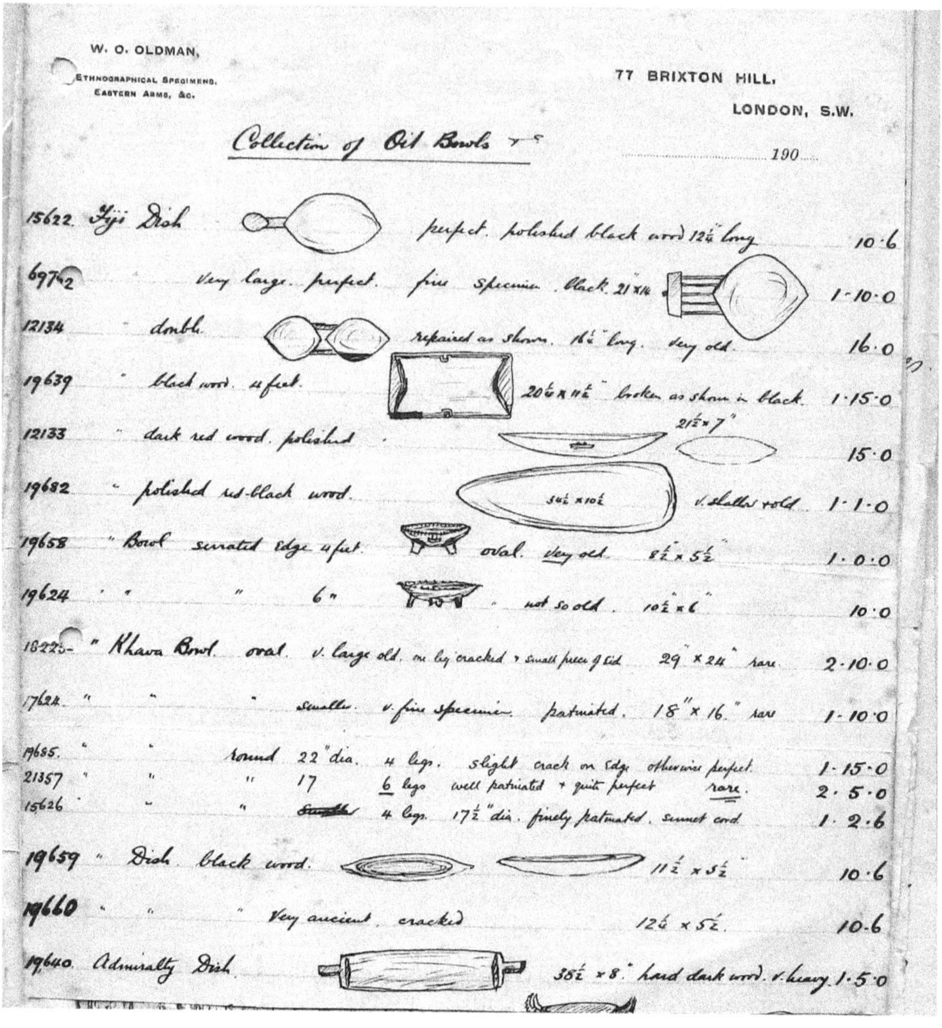
W. O. OLDMAN,
ETHNOGRAPHICAL SPECIMENS,
EASTERN ARMS, &C.

77 BRIXTON HILL,
LONDON, S.W.

Collection of Oil Bowls &c

190....

15622. Fiji Dish — perfect. polished black wood 12¼ long — 10·6
6972 " very large. perfect. fine specimen. black. 21 x 14 — 1·10·0
12134 " double — repaired as shown. 16½ long. very old. — 16·0
19639 " black wood. 4 feet. — 20¼ x 11½ broken as shown in black. — 1·15·0
12133 " dark red wood. polished. — 21½ x 7 — 15·0
19682 " polished red-black wood. — 34½ x 10½ — v. shallow + old. — 1·1·0
19658 " Bowl serrated edge 4 feet. — oval. very old. 8½ x 5½ — 1·0·0
19624 " " " 6 " — not so old. 10½ x 6 — 10·0
18225 " Khava Bowl. oval v. large old. one leg cracked + small piece of lid 29 x 24 rare — 2·10·0
17624 " " " smaller. v. fine specimen. patinated. 18" x 16" rare — 1·10·0
19655 " " round 22" dia. 4 legs. slight crack on edge otherwise perfect. — 1·15·0
21357 " " " 17 6 legs well patinated + quite perfect rare. — 2·5·0
15626 " " " ~~smaller~~ 4 legs. 17½" dia. finely patinated. sennet cord — 1·2·6
19659 " Dish. black wood. — 11½ x 5½ — 10·6
19660 " " " very ancient. cracked — 12¼ x 5½ — 10·6
19640. Admiralty Dish. — 38½ x 8" hard dark wood. v. heavy — 1·5·0

Fig. 10 Oil bowl drawings and descriptions by W. O. Oldman. Caja 3.30, Archivo Fotográfico y Documental del Museo Etnográfico "Juan B. Ambrosetti," FFyL, UBA.

into exploitable material and have a fluctuating price in global commerce, there exist other riches with a priceless value to science." Gonnet described archaeological remains in particular as "necessary to the study and reconstitution of history, so essential for resolving the problems of humanity, many of which directly affect the development of contemporary societies," and emphasized that "these goods, these riches, do not belong to the owner of the land; they belong and should belong to the State."[64] Such resources required the state's intervention to regulate and protect them, in the interests of national wealth and the irreplaceable reservoir of national patrimony. Gonnet invoked the specter of looting and extortion as an incentive for protective legislation along the models presented by Egypt, Peru, and Mexico. "I need not tell the House," he declared, that in the past "the lack of a special law on this subject authorized certain explorers to ask exorbitant prices for the collections that they had amassed and that ought to belong to the Nation, with the result that those collections left the country and went to the European museums. There are constantly occurring serious leaks of fossils, elements perfectly useful to science, and that ought to reside in the museums of the country."[65]

According to Gonnet, European nations had already gained an advantage over countries such as Argentina in two ways. First, scientific institutions in Europe and North America "send commissions of exploration to open and free territories like ours for exploitation and exploration," exporting the specimens they gathered to their own museums to be studied by foreign scientists, to the detriment of Argentine national scientific institutions. Second, European countries had passed laws protecting themselves against similar exportation of scientific and artistic objects, "and it is for that reason that the entire world marches to Florence, to Rome, to Naples, leaving behind massive amounts of gold, to admire the hundred thousand statues of Greek and Roman art, the inimitable paintings of the galleries of Florence." By retaining their own historic and scientific resources, Gonnet argued, European countries attracted visitors and bolstered their own economies, at the same time cultivating international reputations for national cultural richness. "I hope," he concluded, despite "the maelstrom that rules us and that directs our best energies toward purely material interests, that this initiative may permit us to collect and classify these riches, so that the entire world might come tomorrow to our national museums and recognize that we were worthy of our heritage, that we knew to collect it in the same spirit that showed the scientific world the immortal genius of Darwin!" Gonnet's final, impassioned flourish was greeted by applause and cries of "Muy bien! Muy bien!" in the House.[66]

Gonnet's proposal revealed a multilayered appreciation for the importance of archaeology. First, he recognized and sought to legislate archaeological artifacts' economic value. Rather than focusing on the short-term profits to be gained by selling archaeological artifacts and paleontological remains, Gonnet argued that Argentina needed to look to the future and to conserve its ownership of what was not a market commodity but a national resource,

in order to attract long-term economic profit in the form of corollary indus-
tries such as tourism. His proposal also illustrated the extent to which archaeological science had become entangled with national meaning and cultural
value, beyond the realm of professional science. Gonnet did not directly
invoke any specific scientific institutions during his congressional addresses,
nor did he rely on the support of any scientific experts. He connected science
to the nation directly, framing scientific awareness as a measure of national
progress. Porteño newspapers followed the congressional debate and passage
of law 9080, reproducing excerpts from Gonnet's addresses, as well as additional commentary. *La Nación* argued in a report published just days after
Gonnet's proposal that the legislative project "affirms the personality of
the country in the scientific world." The archaeological remains of pre-
Columbian civilizations, the report contended, "have an undoubted importance for the study of our prehistory"; "if in many ways these [archaeological]
sites cannot be compared with the ruins of Egypt, for example, it cannot be
denied, nevertheless, that their intrinsic value is comparable and that from
our American point of view it is absolutely equal."[67]

The Sites Commission (Comisión de Yacimientos) was formed as a result
of law 9080 to consider requests from individuals and institutions in Argentina and abroad to excavate and collect objects from paleontological and
archaeological sites. Composed by late 1913 of the Museo Nacional de Ciencias Naturales, the Museo de La Plata, and the Museo Etnográfico, the commission reviewed these requests during jointly held meetings. Its presidency
rotated among the member museums, as did the official trappings of organi-
zational power—blocks of letterhead-bearing paper and envelopes, document
files and *copiadores*, two rubber stamps bearing the commission's seal, and a
bronze plaque inscribed with the words "Sección Yacimientos Secretaría."[68]
The Sites Commission served both to reflect museums' centrality to scientific
authority in Argentina by the 1910s and 1920s and to amplify it through the
museums' ability to deploy state power on their own terms.

Surviving archival materials reveal that the Sites Commission operated into
the 1940s, though its functions were evidently interrupted shortly thereafter,
during the Perón administration, perhaps due to changes in state interest in
scientific patrimony and museum science after World War II.[69] Despite its
institutional decline, however, law 9080 had done the official work of transforming archaeological objects into national patrimony; this deeply emotional
nation-science tie was fostered in and survived through the operations of the

commission's constituent museums. The Museo de La Plata still displays a plaque in its archaeological gallery, addressed to its visitors, that reads,

> The Direction of the Museo de La Plata reminds the public that, in virtue of Law 9080, all the paleontological and archaeological sites uncovered in the Argentine territory are property of the Nation, and it is a civic duty to report their discovery and facilitate the exhibition of their contents in the National Museums. . . .
>
> Every Argentine who loves his country, and every foreigner who wishes to show his gratitude to the nation that receives him hospitably, may contribute in this way to the progress of Argentine science.[70]

Historians María Endere and Irina Podgorny have couched law 9080 in an "alliance between science and nation" that recoded scientific knowledge and institutions as focal points of "national spirit and tradition." They contend that "history, archaeology, and even paleontology acquired a central function, as inspiring sources for the construction of nationality." Within this broad alliance between knowledge and nation building, Endere and Podgorny furthermore argue, "archaeological remains formed an integral part of the national territory and of the emotion of its landscape. From this point of view, the necessity of saving them from commercial rapacity was equivalent to the defense of the national territory itself."[71] Thus, law 9080 effectively became a measure of national security that protected not just Argentina but *argentinidad* and absorbed scientific objects and knowledge into the rubric of national property and utility to the state.

This crucial insight can, however, begin to blur the line between scientific utility to and alliance with Argentine nation making, on one hand, and scientific subordination to the state, on the other. Podgorny has also argued that "law 9080 consecrated the co-optation by the State of scientists, of collectors, and of scientific societies that, by this law, must now be subordinated to the control of the Nation." I contend that describing the Museo Nacional de Ciencias Naturales and the Museo Etnográfico as the "institutional arm" of the state overlooks tensions between scientists' often genuine nationalism and more strategic invocations of nationalist rhetoric prompted by other motivations—a dynamic that had characterized Argentine museum science since Hermann Burmeister's masterful control over the Museo Público in the late nineteenth century.[72] The Museo Etnográfico and the Museo Nacional without doubt enthusiastically embraced their role as national arbiters of scientific authority—in fact, the Museo de La Plata soon joined their ranks on the Sites Commission after an outraged appeal from then-director Luís María Torres protesting its exclusion, certainly illustrating the desirability of inclusion in the commission[73]—but their scientists' motivations were as much professional as patriotic. Controlling access to Argentina's paleontological and archaeological sites and exportation rites meant professional leverage for commission members, as they were the ones who answered requests from scientists domestically and abroad to conduct research in Argentina. The relationship between state and science, even as it functioned through explicitly state-sanctioned channels such as the legal authority of law 9080, was more complex than one of state patronage and scientific clientelism.

Law 9080 had captured a climate of scientific nationalism and codified it into legislation, helping the Museo Etnográfico, the Museo de La Plata, and the Museo Nacional cement their authority and wield the power of the state as their own. The law sanctioned museum authority in a way that did not simply underscore ties between science and the state, but gave museum scientists an upper hand as recognized experts holding power over other scientists domestically and abroad, with the express permission and recognized authority of the state. These museums became guardians of national patrimony, rescuing it from exportation and exploitation and defining Argentina once again as a member of the "civilized nations" of the world, on par not only with its South American neighbors but with the European and Atlantic nation-states it saw as its true counterparts.

Conclusion: Museum Archaeology as National Rescue Project

In 1928, the Museo Etnográfico had occasion to turn national enthusiasm for archaeological patrimony to its own advantage through the purchase of a collection of Peruvian ceramics from artifact dealer Mauro Pando. Pando offered the Nasca Collection, consisting of some five hundred pre-Columbian ceramic pieces, to Debenedetti at the sizeable price of 50,000 pesos, an amount well beyond the museum's customary budget for acquisitions and collections growth.[74] However, Debenedetti deemed the collection to be of extraordinary value and set about fundraising to facilitate its acquisition, framing it as a patriotic crusade to keep so valuable a collection of South American antiquities from being sold to an outside collector or museum.

Debenedetti, who only the previous year had inaugurated the museum's new facilities and officially thrown open its doors to public visitors, now appealed to the public to help fund the purchase of the Nasca Collection. The museum issued and supported independent newspaper appeals for donation, such as the column that appeared in *La Libertad*, a daily paper published in Debenedetti's hometown of Avellaneda, in August 1928. The column informed readers that "the said collection, once acquired, would pass to the Museo Etnográfico directed by doctor Salvador Debenedetti, one of the most distinguished figures of the science of archaeology, who honors the country and the City of Avellaneda, the place of his birth." The museum also circulated direct requests to wealthy and prominent figures, attempting to secure larger donations from likely candidates within its network of porteño and broader Argentine social connections.[75]

The response was prolific. The museum received a series of large donations from prominent citizens and companies, including 500 pesos from the Buenos Aires newspaper *La Prensa*, 1,000 pesos from porteño financier Ernesto Tornquist, and 500 pesos from Colegio Internacional president Francisco Chelia. The Banco Hipotecario Nacional donated 1,000 pesos, Caledonio Pereda 5,000 pesos, and porteño doctor Carlos Madariaga a staggering 10,000 pesos.[76] Smaller donations also came in from a variety of sources. Notably, for example, chocolate baron Carlos Noel and kitchenware mogul Oscar Schnaith each donated 100 pesos. Many addressees of Debenedetti's letter-writing campaign felt compelled to respond even when they were unable or unwilling to contribute, to explain their refusal. The board of directors at the tobacco manufacturing firm Piccardo y Companía offered the following vague regrets: "Our board of directors has always had singular satisfaction in lending its support to all work of cultural character; but today, circumstantial reasons do not permit the Directors to demonstrate practically the special attention that your request merits, for which reason it is my disagreeable duty to express to you, that in this opportunity it is not possible for them to contribute to the patriotic end that the Museo Etnográfico pursues and that you present in the aforementioned note."[77] Despite the regrets of some hopeful sources of corporate and individual funding, by October 1928 the museum was only 1,089 pesos short of its goal. Debenedetti himself supplied this amount through a personal donation, cementing the museum's successful acquisition of the Nasca Collection.[78]

The Museo Etnográfico's success in fundraising for the collection reveals the tangible social and national importance commanded by pre-Columbian archaeology, as well as the museum's ability to channel this national and social interest in archaeological science and objects through its institutional housing. Individuals contributing to the purchase of the collection clearly invoked a swirling nexus between nation, science, and heritage and used the museum's public appeal as an avenue for claiming their own authoritative positioning as interpreters and possessors of this nexus. However, other interpretations of Argentina's national anthropological heritage were emerging—connected in no small part to the northwestern focus of the Museo Etnográfico—that envisioned Argentina's true anthropological heart not in the coastal plains and pampas of Buenos Aires and its southward expanses but in the sub-Andean slopes of the northwest.

3

El Alma del Norte: Northwestern Regionalism and Anthropology, 1900–1940

Introduction

In August 1936, the Museo Nacional de Ciencias Naturales attempted to remove a menhir from the Tafí del Valle in Tucumán, one of the most iconic archaeological sites in Argentina's northwest. Menhirs, stone monoliths associated with the pre-Columbian Calchaquí culture, had attracted archaeologists' attention since the late nineteenth century. When the Museo Nacional sought to relocate this menhir from the Tafí del Valle to Buenos Aires, the Universidad Nacional de Tucumán appealed to the provincial government for support in halting the process. The tucumano provincial government in turn addressed a telegram to the national Ministry of Public Instruction, demanding both the cancellation of the menhir's removal and the Universidad Nacional de Tucumán's immediate addition to the Sites Commission, which controlled the enforcement of law 9080 (see chapter 2). The San Miguel de Tucumán newspaper *La Gaceta* reported on this exchange on August 28, citing the provincial government's argument for "the necessity of conserving those artifacts as a regional archaeological asset and the importance of not removing them from the place where they exist as a living reminder of the civilization of our forebears."[1]

At this moment, the Museo Nacional de Ciencias Naturales was one of the most influential museums in Argentina. It housed the Sites Commission, which oversaw rights of excavation and artifact removal throughout the country and was also closely connected with the federal government, to which the tucumano provincial government was petitioning. By all rights, this appeal had very little chance of succeeding. And yet, as *La Gaceta* triumphantly reported, the provincial government's demands met with "complete success." The paper reproduced a telegram from Minister of Public Instruction Jorge de la Torre, in which the removal of the menhir was officially halted by the director of the Museo Nacional and de la Torre agreed to forward the tucumanos' request for inclusion in the Sites Commission to the director of that commission.[2] Although the tucumanos were never granted membership, the menhir remained resolutely in place.

This story raises a number of questions. First, why did people in the northwest—including members of universities, provincial government representatives, and a much broader body of newspaper readers, based on this example alone—care about objects such as the menhir? Second, why was there such a strong reaction against this attempted removal on the part of scientists from Buenos Aires? This incident reveals a palpable divide between a "we" in the northwest and a "them" in Buenos Aires. Where was that line, and of what did it consist? Finally, how was the Universidad Nacional de Tucumán—a relatively small, young provincial university—able to overcome a powerful institution like the Museo Nacional? What tools did it use to lay claim to the menhirs that were ultimately effective not only within a regional sphere but also on a national level? The answers to these questions offer insights into regional tensions between Buenos Aires and the northwest in the early twentieth century, as well as the emergence of a regionalist identity movement in the northwest that coalesced around defining and preserving the "spirit of the north." This regionalist movement employed anthropology as a key to identity building and regional differentiation, which created in the northwest an alternative national project to the cosmopolitan liberalism of Buenos Aires. Northwestern regionalism and its engagement with anthropology and indigenous cultures also reflected larger currents of romantic identity landscapes in twentieth-century Latin America, and especially antipositivist and *indigenista* imaginings of "nuestra América" that reverberated from Mexico to Argentina and virtually everywhere in between. These connections make this both a uniquely Argentine case and one that lends applicable insight into the rest of Latin America, for questions of ethnicity and identity, science and romanticism.

When compared to the alluvial flatlands of the pampas, on which both Buenos Aires and La Plata stand, the Argentine northwest feels like a different world (see map 1). The northwest, a regional umbrella that includes the provinces of La Rioja, Catamarca, Tucumán, Jujuy, and Salta, is not flat but mountainous, delving into the eastern heart of the Andes.[3] It contains both semitropical and semiarid ecosystems, as it ascends from lowland valley into highland puna. In lieu of the wheat fields and grassy pasturelands of the

Map 1   Northwestern Argentina. Created by the author.

bonaerense plains, the northwest presents the eye with sugarcane fields, citrus trees, cacti, and hardy scrub vegetation. Population density in these provinces throughout the national period has been lower than in the littoral provinces (Misiones, Corrientes, Entre Ríos, Chaco, Formosa, and Santa Fe) or in Buenos Aires province, where larger urban centers and more developed networks of rail and river transportation led to greater economic opportunities and denser settlement patterns.

The northwest's difference and isolation—geographic, economic, and social—from the pampean center of national power played a crucial role in the region's identity. During the colonial period, it enjoyed economic prosperity as a supplier of mules, wine, and other staple commodities for the Andean silver mines to the north. This position was strengthened in the later colonial period after Buenos Aires was officially opened as a Spanish port, allowing a second route of trade to flow through the northwest, between the Andes and the Atlantic port.[4] However, after playing a formative role in the early nineteenth-century independence movement of the Río de la Plata region, the northwest's fortunes shifted dramatically. First, newly drawn national boundaries severed the region's traditional economic ties to the Andean silver economy, which was, in any event, in near total collapse in the years following independence. Second, the northwest was swept up in the political and military struggles over provincial rights and alliance building associated with *federalismo* during the nineteenth century—struggles that often took heavy tolls on human life and economic production and widened the gap between the port and province of Buenos Aires and other regions of the country, while bonaerense politicians maneuvered themselves into a position of primacy.[5] As the Argentine Republic consolidated national state power in Buenos Aires after 1862, and as Republican state makers institutionalized their own image of the nation according to European-inspired progressive models, with Buenos Aires as the national metropolitan center, the northwest stagnated economically and was deemed peripheral to coastally defined visions of national civilization.

During the tumultuous years of the early twentieth century, however, the northwest's isolation underwent a transformation in meaning that reshaped the region's identity. This transformation emerged, first, as a result of increasing resentment in the northwest toward Buenos Aires's control over Argentina's economic resources and the political sphere, as well as its claim to domination over the nation's cultural realm. Northwestern frustration arose in combination with a sense of nostalgia for what had been. Regional memory of the northwest's distinguished past and illustrious heritage was both widely felt and seen as closely connected to present concerns. This transformation in the meaning of northwestern regional identity was also connected to the changes then occurring in the region's sugar industry. Sugarcane agriculture made possible by the northwest's semitropical pockets was undergoing mechanization during the late nineteenth and early twentieth centuries, with resulting leaps in production and profitability. The region's sugar elites, in turn, were emerging as an increasingly powerful sector of regional society, with greater social, economic, and political power in the northwest and with an eye on the national stage as well. Attempts to rehabilitate and revitalize the northwest's reputation as a region were doubly useful to regional elites seeking power on a national level, as a means of promoting the northwest's regional image to others and as a means of instilling pride in northwesterners in an attempt to stem a demographic drain, as laborers were being lured away to Buenos Aires to seek work. Moreover, much of the labor force in regional sugar mills was drawn from the region's indigenous populations. Thus, controlling representations of indigenous regional culture had multiple implications for regional sugar elites, who supported regionalist projects, including anthropology. These projects captured an interest in exploring regional cultural identity and its economic and political utility. Anthropology allowed sugar elites to portray themselves as enlightened leaders and provided them with potential tools for culturally tuned labor control.[6]

While many coastal observers continued to see the northwest as peripheral, backward, and isolated, the region's remoteness from the vortex of economic and political power in Buenos Aires was politically and intellectually reinterpreted by northwesterners as a strength and even a blessing, and its landlocked location in the core of the continent was recoded as central rather than peripheral. This difference in interpretation often turned the landscapes and cultures of the northwest into a symbolic battleground, upon which coastal and northwestern observers projected conflicting understandings of the nation. Anthropology played a key role in both visions of the northwest— as an empty and peripheral landscape and as an alternative national center. In keeping with the spatial vision of a Buenos Aires–centered nation, coastal archaeologists saw the northwest as a field site for their research—a peripheral space or landscape in need of their metropolitan, scientific attention to give it coherent meaning in relationship to the nation's urban, coastal core. Tropes of colonial hierarchy, travel and adventure writing, and scientific authority played out in their field journals and publications along well-worn lines, deployed not by an imperial power against a colonized landscape but by one part of the Argentine nation-state against another. Coastal archaeologists saw themselves as leaving their scientific institutions in the urban heart of national civilization and progress and traveling to conduct fieldwork in a space dominated by backwardness and empty Nature. To provide a single example, porteño archaeologist Salvador Debenedetti often described the northwest as a remote and unknown space, untouched by the hand of modern Argentine civilization, which he explicitly located in Buenos Aires. In January 1918, while encamped in a valley near Tilcara, Jujuy, Debenedetti commented in his personal field journal on the "solitude of this distant valley that seems like the edge of the world and the end of life"; he described a primordial and deeply private experience, shared only between himself and the landscape, without the interference of other human beings. "I adore you, solitude," he wrote, "because you seem like a piece of my soul. Only here do we understand one another because here we are in unison, we vibrate in the same way."[7] Although he was surrounded by members of his own expedition and was visited almost daily—as his field journals attest—by local residents and other travelers, Debenedetti felt himself to be utterly alone in the uncharted spaces of northwestern nature, far from the metropole of Buenos Aires and his institutional center in the Museo Etnográfico.

Northwestern regionalists of the early twentieth century, however, saw these valleys not as isolated or uninhabited wilderness but as the geographical and human heart of the continent. Juan B. Terán, a member of Tucumán's sugar elite and first rector of the Universidad Nacional de Tucumán, described the northwest in 1921 as a "geographical frontier," not because it constituted the outermost edge of civilization but because here "the mountain comes from the center of América and in Tucumán it smoothes itself out and [to the] south, the earth unfolding itself endlessly in the pampa. . . . The torrents lead into rivers and majestically soothe themselves; the brilliant sky of the tropics is profoundly chilled as it progresses; nature is less imperious, simpler the appearance of things and beings." From its position at this geographical crossroads, Terán argued that the northwest occupied the crux of the continent and the true seat of national "race and destiny," of argentinidad itself.[8]

The northwest and Tucumán, as a self-crafted and recognized center for regionalist study, constructed an alternative vision of national character during the early twentieth century that differed from the porteño vision, which cast them in a peripheral role. Creating an alternative northwestern regional identity involved—and perhaps required—critiquing and even rejecting certain aspects of porteño nationalism. Regionalists argued that the porteño model of Argentine identity, which relied on European cultural modeling, urbanization, and immigration, would ultimately change Argentina into something different, a self-declared "civilized" nation that would nonetheless have lost its essential self. In the northwest, by contrast, argentinidad was strongly linked not only to present and future change but to the preservation of the colonial and indigenous past. Alfredo Coviello, a prominent regionalist thinker in Tucumán during the early twentieth century, described the "spirit of the North" as markedly different from that of Buenos Aires, whose natural character had been woefully eroded by waves of immigration, leaving the port city culturally transient and overly materialistic, lacking an identity rooted in its own heritage. Regionalists such as Coviello contended that in contrast to the over-cosmopolitanization of Buenos Aires, which resulted from its overexposure to the vicissitudes of the Atlantic world, the northwest was insulated from such influences. As Terán described it, the region was "equidistant from two oceans, protected from each by high mountains," and this distance from the coast had protected the northwest from the corruptive influences of immigration and cultural drain. Consequently, northwestern intellectuals saw their region as retaining "a strong historical tradition" with deeply rooted ties to the cultural and artistic legacies of the indigenous and Spanish colonial past, as well as the great deeds of independence. Largely as a result, the northwest's present looked very different from the coast. Coviello cited the region's "singular meteorology," its "social makeup, very distinct from Buenos Aires," and the regionally focused and prominent Universidad Nacional de Tucumán as markers of regional society that differentiated the northwest from the coast and "characterize[d] the North as a region"; its unique identity bound its inhabitants together within a regionally oriented vision of the past, present, and future, beyond the orbit of Buenos Aires. Regionalist speeches and events often appeared in northwestern newspapers, celebrating these regionalist strengths and weaving indigenous cultures into broader civic notions of regional identity.[9]

Between the 1910s and 1940s, northwestern intellectuals, educators, politicians, and others took up the task of exploring regional culture and fortifying northwestern identity through the celebration of its unique heritage. This project combined cultural renaissance with the more pragmatic aims of strengthening the region's economy and stemming demographic drain from the northwest to the coast. Historians have identified Terán and Coviello as belonging to a generational group called the Generación del Centenario, which aimed, after the centennial of Argentina's independence statement, drafted in San Miguel de Tucumán in 1816, to revitalize northwestern cultural identity and power within the nation. In their explorations of northwestern heritage, these thinkers located the region's unique cultural font in the union between Spanish and creole colonial culture, which linked the northwest to Spain's Golden Age and to indigenous cultures past and present. The two parts of this double heritage could be strategically deployed together or separately to highlight different elements of the northwest's distinctive regional character. The idealized cultural identity thus created was flexible and yet resilient, and it took a different direction than coastal Argentines' more selective and conflicted embrace of indigenous cultures in spaces such as the Museo de La Plata and the Museo Etnográfico.[10]

This is not to say that indigenous cultures were universally embraced in the northwest or that all regionalist projects recognized them as a part of northwestern heritage and culture. In his study of folklore in this region, Oscar Chamosa shows that northwestern folklorists during the early twentieth century focused on "the mestizo-criollo rural workers from the country's interior" as the central subjects of their studies, "recasting rural workers' culture as the authentic national culture." Chamosa underscores the "Eurocentric agenda" of folklore study, looking at indigenous communities primarily as they appeared in the context of that narrative and arguing that folklorists "usually lumped all villagers [under study] into a single ethnic category. Furthermore, for the folklorists, the villagers' rituals and customs were just tokens of bygone civilizations preserved as exotic 'atavism.'" While folklorists channeled their efforts toward celebrating the region's criollo heritage as "the authentic Argentina," northwestern anthropologists were likewise envisioning the region as the cradle of argentinidad, but not as an essentially criollo region.[11] Anthropologists imagined the northwest as a cultural palimpsest, in which indigenous cultures were a foundational, ancient presence and also played a critical and complementary role in the present, and were instrumental in the creation of northwestern regionalism as a cultural and political identity project during the early twentieth century. It was the combination of these two pieces—indigenous and criollo heritage—that gave northwestern regionalism its strength and its uniqueness. Northwestern regionalists deliberately played up the union between criollo and indigenous cultural practices, even as they conserved the right to refer to each side of this regional legacy independently. They did not see the northwest as entirely culturally blended or as a mestizo region in this sense, but rather as a constantly shifting cultural mosaic, and they embraced this cultural combination as a source of strength and identity worthy of study in the past and the present.

Anthropology played a crucial role in cultivating regionalist consciousness, and northwesterners appropriated the scientific weight of anthropological study for their own purposes. While anthropologists traveling to the northwest from Buenos Aires and La Plata most often came as archaeologists to excavate the pre-Columbian ruins of the region's ancient past, northwestern anthropologists focused much of their energy on contemporary ethnography. Regionalist anthropologists identified indigenous culture not as an ancient heritage disconnected by time or disappearance, but as a continuing, living tradition and an element of the shared cultural identity of all northwesterners. Although indigenous culture and heritage were strategically deployed tools within the arsenal of regionalism and thus were sometimes pushed to the background in favor of Spanish or criollo heritage when it served the purposes of the moment, indigenous cultures remained an important component of regionalists' identity tool kit, readily put to use and no less central to regional identity than Spanish or creole heritage.

Northwest as Space: Coastal Archaeologists in the Field

Cultural geographers, historians, and other scholars have used notions of space and place to great effect in understanding human interpretations of the physical world. Yi-Fu Tuan defines these two notions, crucially, in dependent relation to each other. "Place is security, space is freedom," he writes. "From the security and stability of place we are aware of the openness, freedom, and threat of space, and vice versa."[12] Moreover, space is neither passive nor timeless, but constantly (de/re)constructed by human agency, and in that battle over meaning, humans imprint notions of time and history onto the landscapes around them. The power of this sense of history, embedded in place, can impact human actions and even the course of history. Visions of a place as having a significant past or not, as adapting to a changing present or not, have important ramifications for how these places are understood and used by human beings. Space and place can offer compelling theoretical lenses through which to understand humans' interactions with their surroundings, not least because these terms enter so often into everyday life and thus present scholars with myriad openings into how humans in the past and present have understood their world.

Space and place provide a very natural and analytically fruitful entry point into historical understanding of the Argentine northwest, as both coastal and northwestern observers most often characterized the region through meaningful descriptions of its landscape. Northwestern landscapes were alternately identified as empty spaces, lacking in coherent identity and awaiting the action of human interpreters to give them significance, or as richly meaning-laden places, whose true and intrinsic significance was already recognizable to qualified observers, "qualification" itself becoming a relative and highly contested term. Coastally built narratives of a northwest with a splendid ancient prehistory hidden beneath a stagnant present clashed against regionalist histories of continuous northwestern cultural florescence—conflicting narratives imposed simultaneously by different actors on the same physical landscape.

Coastal archaeologists traveling in the northwest generally favored narratives of meaning building in empty spaces and cast themselves—perhaps unsurprisingly—as the proper interpreters of the region's hidden significance or place-ness. They described the region via two main channels: scientific notations of their excavations and personal responses to their experiences in the field. In field journals and photographs, coastal archaeologists coded themselves as scientific pioneers in an empty wilderness. Their descriptions of landscape often revealed feelings of connection with and possession of the land, detached from its human inhabitants. Indeed, coastal archaeologists presented largely pessimistic accounts of their interactions with contemporary northwesterners, whom they saw in clear contradistinction to the region's ancient inhabitants.

Science was the most deliberate language through which coastal archaeologists sought to build their understanding of northwestern landscapes. To them, the region was a field of forgotten history, of burial and settlement sites lying unheeded and abandoned in remote ravines and along stream beds, waiting for science to reveal their hidden meaning. Locals—including middle- and working-class people, typically of mixed indigenous and Spanish descent, who were employed as field guides or informants—were often aware of the existence of these archaeological ruins, and coastal archaeologists relied on their knowledge to find new sites to excavate. Knowing where to find ruins, however, did not place northwesterners on a plane of equality with coastal archaeologists. Local informants pointed archaeologists toward new sites, but archaeologists did not believe that locals recognized these sites' true value or potential to produce knowledge of the region's ancient past. Only through scientific exploration could this knowledge be recovered and given its proper place within the scope of Argentina's national heritage. Fieldwork constituted, in this way, a necessary component of knowledge building, a means of distancing coastal archaeologists from the present communities living in the region, and an act of appropriation as coastal archaeologists claimed possession over the landscape in which they traveled and excavated, effectively dispossessing the people who actually inhabited the land of their rights to it as well as any connection to the ancient cultures under study.

At the turn of the twentieth century, modern scientific fieldwork was beginning to emerge from earlier practices of collecting, which a new generation of scientists now lamented had been more concerned with the accumulation of beautiful and display-worthy specimens than with the collection of scientific information about each object or site. Archaeologists in the field were shifting their priorities from the ends—namely, amassing exotic or rare objects—toward the means—refining provenance information and collecting methodologies. This change spurred a transformation from specimen collecting, which might be outsourced to secondary actors, to fieldwork, which required the special training and expertise of a professional scientist. Archaeology in the Argentine northwest obeyed this pattern, transitioning from a field dominated by general naturalists and untrained enthusiasts to one increasingly led by professional archaeologists, who mounted expeditions to conduct sustained excavations at single or multiple sites, decrying the efforts of their predecessors as lamentably unscientific and destructive. Salvador Debenedetti, a student of Juan B. Ambrosetti and his successor as director of the Museo Etnográfico in Buenos Aires (1917–30), was a constant fixture of northwestern archaeology from the beginning of the 1900s through the 1920s. Debenedetti's numerous excavations in the region represented the cutting edge of Argentine archaeological methodologies and produced some of the most influential studies and discoveries of his generation.

Debenedetti was born in Avellaneda, a flourishing urban center south of Buenos Aires, in 1884. After attending the San José Academy, he enrolled at the Universidad de Buenos Aires, where he studied under Ambrosetti. He received his doctorate in 1909, and before succeeding Ambrosetti as director of the Museo Etnográfico in 1917, he held faculty posts at both the Universidad de La Plata and the Universidad de Buenos Aires. Debenedetti had a reputation among his colleagues as an impressive archaeologist and a soulful poet, a dichotomy that his field journals certainly capture. On the second anniversary of Debenedetti's death, his fellow archaeologist Eduardo Casanova explained that "in [his] field journals, beside meticulous observations of strictly scientific character, appear beautiful descriptions of landscapes that spoke to his soul and delicate verses that express a faint hope or painful memory."[13] Debenedetti died unexpectedly at the age of forty-six, as the result of a sudden illness while traveling in Europe. His field journals, as Casanova suggested, provide a rich record of archaeological fieldwork and method, coupled with emotional and even poetic responses to northwestern landscapes and people that capture rich evidence of the region's multilayered place- and space-ness, although Debenedetti most often seemed to view the northwest as an empty landscape, disconnected from the progressive present.

As Debenedetti's journals illustrate, archaeological fieldwork created distance between the museum and the field through lopsided power dynamics of observation and collection. Museum archaeologists traveling in the field saw theirs as a mission of collection, not regional collaboration or reciprocity. They amassed objects and information for their research and display in the museum, and they imposed their own scientific interpretation on the landscape, often in contrast to the perspectives of people living there. Most often, fieldwork offered a reciprocal exchange only insofar as anthropological expeditions purchased supplies in nearby cities or towns and offered some short-term, limited employment for local laborers hired as expedition servants, fieldworkers, or assistants. The Museo Etnográfico employed local fieldworkers in its expeditions to the northwest, but they were relatively few in number— generally speaking, a dozen or less—and archaeologists such as Ambrosetti and Debenedetti tended to rehire the same workers year after year. So limited and desired was this seasonal employment that archaeologists arriving in regional city centers such as San Miguel de Tucumán and Salta were approached in their hotels by potential and past employees seeking positions on the expeditions' crews. On Christmas Day in 1923, Debenedetti's lodgings in Andalgalá, Catamarca province, were visited by Harold Blamez, who provided the expedition with mules; by Don Pedro Moreno, "the old baqueano [field guide and outdoorsman] and servant on various previous voyages," who successfully negotiated for renewed employment by describing "his poverty and his miseries"; and by José Quiroga, whom Debenedetti described with satisfaction as "a good boy, already familiar from previous trips."[14] Four years later, another expedition to Catamarca rehired both Moreno and Quiroga.[15] The availability of these men year after year for weeks-long stints of travel and hard labor in the field, away from their home communities over the Christmas holidays (a significant time to be absent in a predominantly Catholic society), suggests the preciousness of the limited employment offered by archaeological fieldwork. The Museo Etnográfico's archaeologists, in turn, could rely on these experienced local field hands whenever their research agenda took them to Catamarca. In other years, the museum conducted its fieldwork elsewhere—in Jujuy or Tucumán, Salta or Santiago del Estero—a change of regional venue that certainly would have had a different impact on laborers such as Moreno and Quiroga than on the traveling archaeologists, who took their funding with them. Such uneven relationships of limited reciprocity ensured that archaeologists maintained considerable control over what happened in the field and how they ultimately interpreted it.

Archaeological excavations during the early twentieth century did not greatly resemble, in many respects, what archaeologists in the field do today. Trench or pit excavations, in which fieldworkers dug out considerable areas quickly with shovels and even pickaxes, were a common approach, punctuated by the slower and more careful excavation of interesting features uncovered by this comparatively rough method. Excavations generally favored burial sites and high-profile settlement sites, which were likely to produce noteworthy artifacts for collection and display. Burial sites were particularly tempting because they were often contained within small, stone-built chambers that preserved the original placement of bodies and grave goods inside a relatively well-protected capsule. Archaeologists had but to break open the burial chamber like a geode to discover its treasures readily displayed before them, without the painstaking work of unearthing each artifact individually. Debenedetti recorded the orientation of the preserved artifacts and remains he uncovered in such burial sites in detailed sketches in his field journals (see fig. 11). The work of excavation itself was conducted, for the most part, by crews of locally hired fieldworkers who did not have formal archaeological training, augmented by archaeology students. Lead archaeologists on these expeditions did not participate in most of the actual digging. In 1917, the year in which he assumed the directorship of the Museo Etnográfico, Debenedetti wrote with nostalgia of earlier excavations "in which, full of enthusiasm, I dedicated myself to the work of excavating remains with my own hands."[16] By this time, he had transitioned to the work of a lead archaeologist, which was to analyze the finds of his crew and to supervise the excavation of particularly noteworthy features that his students and crew called to his attention. A photograph from an archaeological excavation mounted by the Museo Nacional de Ciencias Naturales shows a fieldworker sitting near the left edge of the image and an archaeologist standing on the right (see fig. 12). The fieldworker has paused in his work to allow the archaeologist to note or sketch the ceramic vessel he has unearthed from the center of the frame, his spade stuck into the ground beside him. The division between physical and intellectual labor in this image serves as a diagnostic representation of much archaeological field-work during these decades.

Although scientific work formed the keystone of archaeologists' time in the field, the experience of fieldwork was not measured simply by the summa-tion of objects and information collected during excavation. This scientific work was colored and complemented by archaeologists' personal experiences of daily life in the field. Fieldwork involved, by necessity, removing archae-ologists from their museums and transporting them to a space beyond the generally urban sphere of their normal lives, where they underwent transfor-mations in wardrobe, diet, occupation, and lifestyle. These changes were symbolic of the geographical and even chronological distance between museum and field, and personally experiencing them became integral to fieldwork itself. Many archaeologists, including Debenedetti, saw the rustic lifestyle of the field as an adventure and viewed themselves as explorers of untamed, primitive landscapes. This adventurous tenor, which was expressed in emo-tional and personal rather than scientific terms, underscored coastal archae-ologists' visions of the northwest as an unexplored terrain or empty space that their own experiences endowed with meaning and place-ness. The flavor of adventure that saturated daily life in the field also served to legitimize the scientific work of excavation, which relied in part on an understanding of the field site as an unknown space. Archaeological expeditions to the northwest proved team members' dedication to their craft through their willingness to endure hardships and to brave wild spaces in order to pursue knowledge of the ancient past.

Expedition cameras recorded many images of daily life in camp, which tended to revolve around a handful of central themes crucial to this adventur-ous ethos. These images, which fall into a different category from the photo-graphs taken of excavations and artifacts in situ, depict field life rather than fieldwork and demonstrate the importance that these nonscientific elements held for the expedition members directing the camera and for subsequent record keepers selecting photographic exposures to retain in museum archives. Such images illustrate the domestic, material accoutrements of fieldwork. In fig. 13, two figures in the middle ground sit on folding chairs at a folding table. These are clearly the archaeologists, based on their physical situation at the center of the campsite and use of what appears to be its best furniture, their occupation (the man in the white coat is writing, while the man across

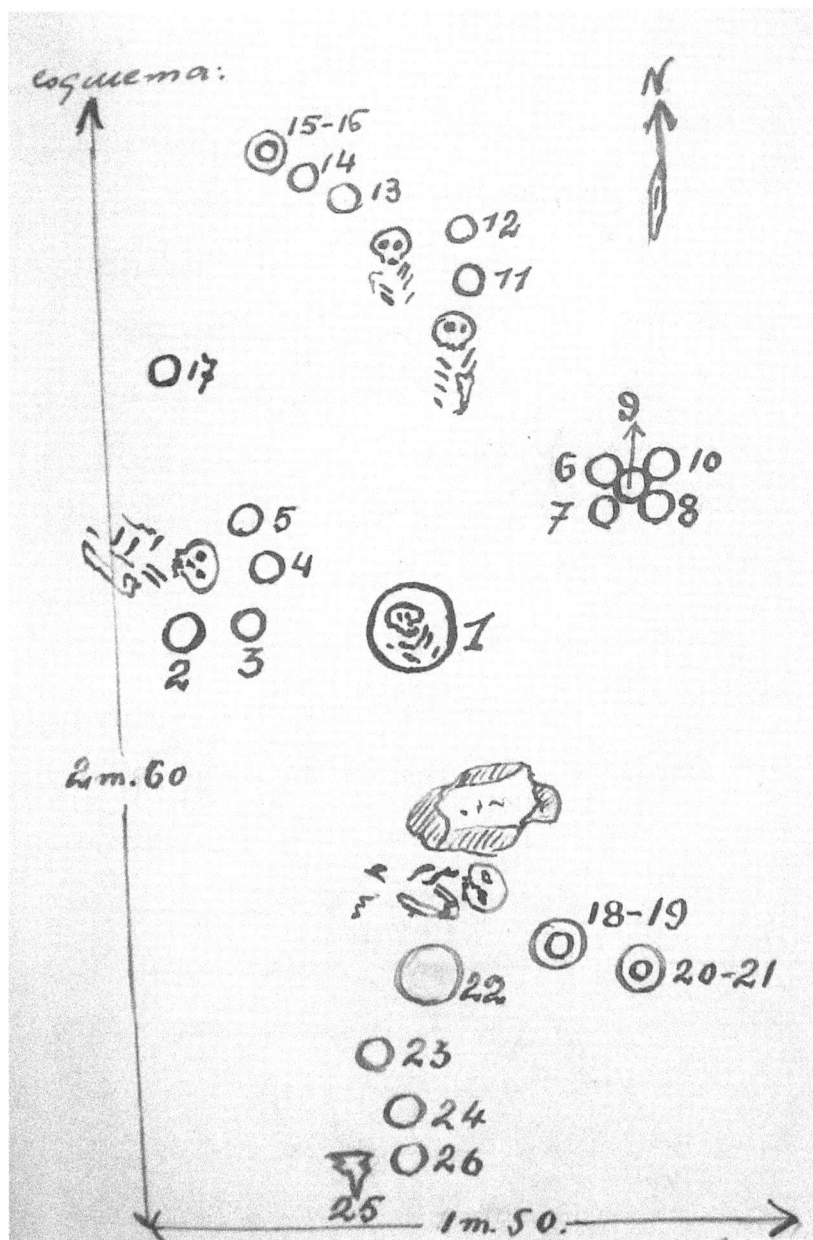

Fig. 11a–c Sketches from Salvador Debenedetti's 1927 field journal, La Ciénaga, Catamarca. Numbers correspond to notes on separate pages regarding artifacts found in association with the remains. Archivo Fotográfico y Documental del Museo Etnográfico "Juan B. Ambrosetti," FFyL, UBA.

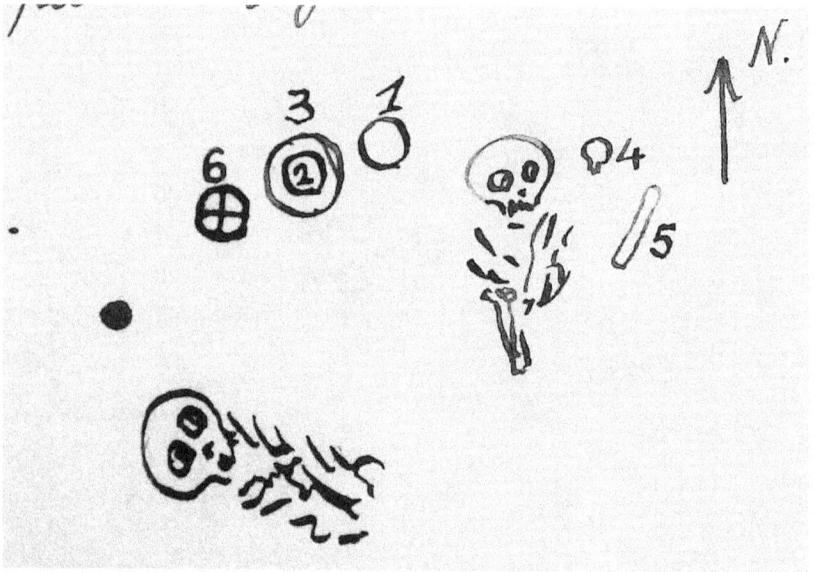

Fig. 11b

Fig. 11c

145

Fig. 12   Excavation photograph illustrating the archaeological
division of labor, or the intersection/distance between manual and
intellectual work. Caja 336–62, Archivo Fotográfico y Documental
del Museo Etnográfico "Juan B. Ambrosetti," FFyL, UBA.

from him is watching him work), and their clothing, which reveals an individuality of style indicative of comparative financial wealth. The two men in
the background are field hands or servants. They stand in the camp's kitchen
(note the pots and ladle hanging behind them) and wear simpler clothing,
which at this distance appears to be virtually identical. Images like this, of
archaeologists and other expedition members in camp, project a conscious
pride in the time spent in the field; they stand, in fact, as a deliberate record
of that time. The incursions of nature into such images—in this case the trees
and bushes that surround the campsite and even invade the foreground of the

Fig. 13   Field camp life. Caja 342-a3, Archivo Fotográfico y Documental del Museo Etnográfico "Juan B. Ambrosetti," FFyL, UBA.

photograph, standing between the viewer and the human subjects—serve as a reminder that this image was taken in "the field," a space of untamed nature where original information and objects were gathered from their primal sources and where folding chairs became the best seats in the house.

Other images of field life emphasize the adventurous lifestyle of the archaeologist as a kind of scientific frontier hero and display the trophy-like qualities of archaeological artifacts. In fig. 14, for example, ceramic vessels are spread across the foreground, some standing upright, some laid on their sides, in a haphazard way that makes it clear that analysis or comparison is not the intention of the photograph. This is not a diagnostic record; it is a trophy shot. Rather than examining one vessel or a series of vessels in scientific profile, this image encourages the viewer to marvel at the sheer volume of artifacts collected. Note how casually the man on the left is holding one of the vessels—by its rim, without supporting the bottom or sides. This careless

Fig. 14   Ceramics as trophies. Caja 342-a6, Archivo Fotográfico y Documental del Museo Etnográfico "Juan B. Ambrosetti," FFyL, UBA.

posture suggests a moment not of cautious preservation but of personal possession. Note also the differences between the two individuals in this photograph: the man on the left stands forward confidently and his face is visible, while the man on the right slouches backward, his face obscured by the shade of his hat. Moreover, the right-hand figure, who is likely a hired field hand based on his dress and staging in the photograph, is not holding any of the ceramics. If he is indeed a northwesterner, this image represents a tangible— if perhaps subconscious—moment of dispossession, as the region's archaeological patrimony quite literally passed into the hands of coastal archaeologists.

Archaeologists' responses to the landscapes surrounding them helped construct geographical distance between field and museum and effectively reinforced the daringness of their own scientific missions far afield. Once again, Debenedetti's personal field journals offer a window onto the emotional relationship between coastal archaeologists and the landscapes of the northwest, not least because he wrote so often and so readily about his personal feelings while living in the field. Debenedetti described the northwest as a landscape of solitude, where the grand scale of nature in its unknown and unexplored form enveloped the lone traveler in the enormity of space. He referred variously to being a "solitary traveler," to "the solitude of the mountains," and to "the august solitude of my camp."[17] Despite being surrounded day and night by his fellow expedition members, living together in the cramped quarters of camp tents, Debenedetti felt himself to be alone and even adrift within the enormous emptiness of northwestern nature. In October 1914, he and his expedition camped after dark in an unknown spot. The following morning, Debenedetti considered his surroundings: "With the first light of day we can see the Zonda valley. We are at the foot of the peak of Zonda, in a wide and tree-filled space. The ranch that has offered [its] hospitality is of poor aspect. Upon asking a boy for the name of the finca where we are, he replies that he does not know."[18] Bounded by what he saw as the untouched emptiness of the natural landscape, the ranch where Debenedetti and his expedition pitched their tents seemed ephemeral or even unreal; not even the local boy knew its name.

Northwestern nature was also viewed as hostile, adding to its emptiness a feeling of hardship and impending danger. The heat and dryness of the environment were frequent complaints. "Santiago del Estero and Tucumán as always seem like two unbearable ovens," Debenedetti wrote in December 1917, subsequently noting that "the fields are sad, and the forests withered. There is no water to give life to this agonized landscape."[19] Archaeologists also faced the attacks of persistent insect life, especially biting vinchucas, fleas, and bedbugs. "I believe," Debenedetti wrote in his journal in January 1917, "that I no longer have a free spot on my body for stings and bites. If to this we add the filth that surrounds us, filth that is sticky in the mornings and choked with sand in the afternoons, you will have an approximate idea of our situation."[20] Nighttime presented another array of challenges, notably the nocturnal storms that shook camp tents and robbed the expedition members of sleep. These storms were at times so violent that they threatened to uproot the tenuous network of communication and transportation utilities that connected the northwest to coastal civilization. The Museo Etnográfico's 1923 expedition was impeded by a thunderstorm that "destroyed all the telegraphic and telephonic instruments," as well as a subsequent flash flood that covered the railroad tracks leading toward their destination in "stones and mud . . . accumulated to a meter in depth."[21] Such accounts paint the northwestern landscape as wild and hostile to human control, barely controlled even in a loose sense by the technologies of civilization.

On the other hand, the isolation and harshness of northwestern space as it was seen by coastal archaeologists could cast a spiritual and introspective light on their time in this landscape. The northwest presented archaeologists with breathtaking vistas, and the hardships endured to reach these remote horizons in some cases accentuated the significance of being there and seeing them firsthand. Debenedetti's personal connection to northwestern landscapes filled the pages of his field journals, outweighing his scientific notes by a comfortable margin in many cases. In December 1918, he wrote a passage characteristic of his feelings of wonder and deep affinity for northwestern nature:

> I arose early this morning because I felt a vehement desire to see this valley under the first light of the morning. Long before the dawn I felt that inquietude with which one awaits a new day and the birth of an emotion. . . . What a splendid morning! A sweetly cold air ran over the quebrada, illuminated by the first light of dawn. . . . The fresh air of the morning fortifies me. I feel a desire to be an eagle, to soar into the void to distant and unknown peaks, and if it were possible to infinity.[22]

Debenedetti's personal connection with the landscape was distinctly transcendental, drawing a strong line between northwestern nature and himself, without any desire for intermediaries or companions. In fact, in this affinity between himself and the landscape, Debenedetti declared not only his strong connection to but also his unique understanding and even his possession of the landscapes he surveyed. He underscored this possessive appreciation even more clearly in 1927 when he recorded his expedition's arrival at a place called Chañaral, where he had conducted excavations in past seasons. Intending to set up camp in the same location, Debenedetti was pleased to discover that "our old algarrobo tree, in whose shade we have passed so many days in other times, is deserted. It seems to be waiting for us. Three years ago we were here, for the last time. Since then many of its branches have dried out and, therefore, its shade is less dense. No matter. It will always be loving with us. Of that I am certain."[23] Communion between archaeologist and the landscape of the field was personal, profound, and based implicitly on the idea that his eyes were uniquely able to see and appreciate the true value of this place. Northwestern nature itself recognized Debenedetti as a kindred spirit, it seemed, expressing that here through the constant friendship of an algarrobo tree.

Despite their sometimes romantic and often possessive connection to northwestern landscapes, archaeologists such as Debenedetti often viewed the modern human inhabitants of the northwest, especially the rural landscapes that surrounded their excavation sites, as backward and stagnant, oblivious to the ancient heritage and powerful natural beauty around them. If, in the eyes of coastal archaeologists, the landscape was imbued with a rich past and the timelessness of untamed nature, the largely mixed-descent Spanish and indigenous rural communities inhabiting the region during the early twentieth century seemed unaware of that past and unwilling or unable to join in the progressive march of Argentina's national present. As a result, coastal archaeologists often described northwestern society as hovering between past and present, at best offering material aid to their excavations and at worst detracting from or even destroying the region's precious past and potential for a progressive future. The contrast that these archaeologists drew between a glorious northwestern past and its bedraggled present constructed a sense of northwestern time/space in which the past was more valuable than the present, and it contended that that value was only visible to the objective gaze of outside scientists gathering data in the field. Urban, elite regionalists such as Terán and Coviello conspicuously failed to appear in coastal anthropologists' records of fieldwork in the region; if their travels took them to urban centers such as San Miguel de Tucumán, Debenedetti and his contemporaries did not record meetings with fellow anthropologists, politicians, poets, or regionalist thinkers in their field journals.

In decrying what they saw as the degeneration of northwestern society, coastal archaeologists joined the international ranks of colonial and postcolonial travelers who articulated hierarchy through constructions of difference and who often enhanced their scientific authority through racial typecasting and the devaluing of local knowledge. Notably, however, coastal archaeologists' descriptions of the northwest's present inhabitants were lacking conspicuously in ethnographic definition. While archaeologists focused their excavations on specific cultural groups in clear and deliberate distinction to other groups, they most often identified modern-day inhabitants of the same region simply as "locals," a convention that allied their descriptions with the rhetorical practices of contemporary travel writing. Debenedetti drew largely uncomplimentary pictures of the people he encountered during his fieldwork expeditions. In his journals, he described most northwesterners as lazy, backward, and superstitious. He complained, for example, that the locally hired laborers on whom he depended in his excavations were unreliable and lacked a proper work ethic. As he began excavations in December 1917, he wrote with frustration that "of the seven men that should have left for work I have seen only one. The chronic laziness of these people is unpardonable."[24] He also derided what he saw as their pathological overindulgence in alcohol, shaking an unmistakably pedantic finger and observing, "Poor people! I feel sorry for them. My admonitions against vice have come to nothing, especially [my warnings] against alcohol. When will the consciousness of these unfortunate people change? Nothing is done here to resolve the grave social problems that have undermined [them]."[25]

When his warnings against alcohol went unheeded, Debenedetti assumed the cause to be a lack of consciousness among his northwestern companions. If social change were to come to the northwest, he implied, it would come not from their own action but from the guidance of others, almost certainly from metropolitan Buenos Aires. Debenedetti commented routinely on the chronic backwardness of local visitors to his field camps, mostly women and children who came out of curiosity or in search of food or medicine. Of the three women who visited his camp near Tilcara in 1917, who offered him a cheese and asked for sugar, Debenedetti wrote that "the poor [things] were extremely filthy. . . . I gave them wine and sweets which they gobbled up gluttonously. They said they will return but who can believe in these people, as false as [they are] distrustful?"[26]

Debenedetti also used the northwesterners he encountered in the field as place markers to construct his own position as a civilized observer. He occasionally made jokes at their expense, commenting in disbelief, itself redolent with progressive condescension, on northwesterners' reluctance to embrace new Western technologies, as well as their perversion of those that did make their way to the region. For example, automobiles had made an appearance in northwestern cities by the late 1920s, but Debenedetti explained with a mixture of curiosity and humor that their influence was being felt in a way unintended by their original manufacturers:

> I have noted the first manifestation of the civilizing influence of the automobile on the poor people of La Ciénaga in the[ir] sandals. They have substituted the millenarian, traditional leather sandal with those fabricated from the rubber tires of automobiles. It cannot be denied that in these times of tennis and shoes with rubber soles, the inhabitants of La Ciénaga have placed themselves at the height of sporting, which is the culminating point of current culture. I have not yet asked

what advantage the rubber sandal has over the leather [one] but it is certain that it begins a new era in this valley, the era of rubber, which, without doubt, with the passage of time will acquire the corresponding cortege of myths, legends, extraordinary and, perhaps, divine personages. A new Manco Cápac or Viracocha will be born, new civilizers of the era, whose dawn I have the honor to witness and whose effects I have seen with my own eyes.[27]

Debenedetti's sardonic tone hints at disdain for the blending of modern technology and ancient culture. The wearers of these rubber sandals, he seemed to suggest, willingly corrupted their ties to a "millenarian, traditional" past, yet failed to use the technology of automobiles and tire rubber in a proper, civilized way. The sandals, rather than being the harbingers of "a new era," symbolized for him the simultaneous dislocation of the northwest from the past and from the present, as it stood with one foot in each but truly engaged with neither. Debenedetti's comments on the rubber sandals of La Ciénaga offer an emblematic example of coastal archaeologists' construction of distance—geographical, temporal, and cultural—between the coast and the northwest, as well as their construction of scientific authority, as they sought scientific footing for their work in a region hundreds of miles from their own museums, in the landscape of "the field."

Northwest as Place: Regionalist Anthropology in Tucumán

Coastal archaeologists' attempts to take representational control of the northwest and to monopolize the languages of science, civilization, and nation in connection with the region implicitly framed the northwest as a dependent periphery within the orbit of Buenos Aires's metropole, denying regional actors access to these languages. From the 1910s through the 1940s, however, regionalist thinkers strove to position the northwest at the center of an alternate model of Argentine nationalism that rejected what they framed as the relentlessly materialistic, cosmopolitan dissipation of Buenos Aires. The regionalists of the Generación del Centenario "imagined a country structured territorially by regions," rather than a nation dichotomized between Buenos Aires and a group of peripheral provinces.[28] Regionalism's focus on a search for identity somewhere between the traditions of the past and the present— on cultural heritage, historical events, and timeless traditions rather than progress toward a civilized, European-focused future—responded in part to an international crisis in modernist models following World War I and the Bolshevik Revolution, as the comfortable institutions of Western Europe collapsed into crisis. The 1920s and 1930s witnessed an international surge of antipositivism, whose adherents searched for alternatives to explain the darkened horizons of modernism's promise. Surrealist and cubist artists willfully transcended the "real" and explored internal worlds and truths; psychoanalysis and generational theory delved into the individual and collective human mind for the sources of human behavior and passions; and political and social utopias attempted to escape the tainted institutions of Western modernity in favor of alternative models.[29] Northwestern regionalists belonged to this international trend of antipositivism and criticized Buenos Aires's national vision as too embedded within tarnished modernist practices, too dependent on the clearly shaky foundations of Western progress. Regionalists instead looked to the past and to non-Western cultural traditions for a strength that did not rely on current European fashions but on the geography, history, and culture of the northwest.

Juan B. Terán outlined the northwest's geographic and demographic strength in defiant opposition to coastal visions of the region. He described Tucumán in 1921 as "the center of an extensive zone populated by approximately one fourth of the total [national] population. It is not only a topographic center, but also a center of natural attraction. . . . The Argentine north is not a desert, nor is Tucumán a hamlet: the provinces of Santiago, Salta, Catamarca, and Jujuy, with Tucumán, represent more than one million inhabitants and the [regional] seat city today has more than 70,000." The northwest was not, Terán argued in implicit response to the marginalizing narrative of coastal observations, an uninhabited backwater or a remote desert. It was a dynamic and meaningful place, rather than an undifferentiated space. Regionalists contended that the northwest's spatial centrality coincided with a unique shared history. Terán described the region as "a historic unity" with "Tucumán [at] its center," and Alfredo Coviello confirmed this sentiment twenty years later, in 1941, when he wrote that the northwest "possesses a strong historical tradition" filled with deeds and symbols "important to our sense of argentinidad"—from the independence-era Battle of Tucumán, fought in September 1812 near San Miguel de Tucumán, to the Casa Historica, the site of Argentina's declaration of independence and a symbol that figured prominently in national iconography. Through this litany of nationally formative events, in addition to a rich repository of colonial culture, architecture, and symbols redolent of Argentine identity on a national level, the northwest demonstrated its centrality to national history and a coherent regional identity based on a shared and proud past. Within this regional sphere, moreover, regionalists such as Terán and Coviello argued that Tucumán formed the natural center for regionalist study and identity.[30]

Most significantly, regionalists argued that the northwest's geographic and historical unity had nurtured its unique culture and heritage, which represented Argentina's truest national stock. Terán drew this connecting line very clearly, contending that "history obeys nature and over the centuries this land of Tucumán was the line of encounter of two civilizations, the theater of their struggles, cradle of their union."[31] According to regionalists, the combination of Spanish colonial heritage with indigenous cultures created a unique northwestern folk tradition and cultural blend. Regionalists argued, in fact, that the northwest displayed a purer form of "true" Argentine heritage than did the coast, in its preservation of this union in isolation from the corrupting influences of European immigration.

This invocation of true national character calls to mind other early twentieth-century ideas about national culture and ethnicity. Northwestern regionalism employed language drawn from eugenic science to argue a very different point; rather than defining national cultural strength in terms of European purity, regionalists presented Argentina's authentic self as racially intermixed stock that was made stronger by this unique combination. The northwest was, in this view, a gestalt of racial and cultural traits that made the region not just indigenous, not just Spanish, but Argentine. In their vision of the blended cultural makeup of the "real" Argentina, regionalists of the northwest invoked contemporary ideas about national *mestizaje* across Latin America, such as the *raza cósmica* of postrevolutionary Mexico.[32] If the *raza cósmica* sought to valorize *mestizaje* within an international atmosphere of burgeoning biological racism and eugenics and to identify Mexico as a nation of universal destiny, northwestern regionalism in Argentina used the combination of criollo and indigenous cultural elements to accomplish a similar goal. Regionalists sidestepped the positivism of Buenos Aires and its fixation on a European-oriented future by locating the nation's true future in connection with the past and linking the traditions of the criollo and indigenous past with national spirit and identity. Taking up the same languages of spiritualism manifested in José Vasconcelos's famous essay "La raza cósmica," northwestern regionalists in Argentina recast Buenos Aires as a hub of materialist decay and corruption—a symbol of the old nationalism, not the new—

obsessed with the quixotic pursuit of a future that no longer reflected Argentina's (or Latin America's) true nature.

At the same time, however, northwestern regionalism did not promote a truly mestizo identity, in the sense of a new, thoroughly blended third identity that left the original groups behind. Rather, regionalists saw criollo and indigenous cultures as mutually strengthening—but also distinct—elements of northwestern identity. Critically, the survival of criollo and indigenous identities within northwestern regionalism allowed each of them to be used strategically, whether separately or in tandem. Thus, northwestern regionalists—and especially the Generación del Centenario, deliberate thinkers who cultivated this ideology with careful attention to its utility to their careers as politicians, businessmen, educators, lawyers, and so forth—could strategically employ anthropology, its imagery, and its languages in ways that suited their regionalist interests. These interests at times aligned with those of state makers in Buenos Aires and at times ran counter to them, as regionalists sought to valorize their distance from the porteño metropole and promote regional autonomy for themselves. The utility of anthropology to regionalists in and beyond the Instituto de Etnología at the Universidad Nacional de Tucumán shows that indigenous cultures played a role in regional identity politics that resonated strongly with many and thus lent themselves easily to scientific and cultural promotion and popularization.

Anthropology served a critical role in exploring the northwest's cultural identity and gave the northwest the ability to control scientific language about regional cultures and traditions, wresting this control away from the exclusive custody of coastal scientists. Regionalist anthropologists framed their work as a project of regional self-discovery rather than salvage science by outsiders. They insisted that anthropology in the northwest should not focus exclusively on the ancient past (thereby implying or even directly asserting the degeneracy and lesser interest of the present) but rather must incorporate studies of contemporary northwestern ethnography and folklore, as part of the modern regional cultural tapestry. Northwesterners' interest in modern ethnography reflected a unique relationship between indigenous cultures and contemporary Argentine national culture. Whereas the Conquest of the Desert in the pampas and Patagonia had aimed at emptying those landscapes of native peoples during the late nineteenth century, the approximately contemporaneous military conquest of indigenous peoples in the northwest and the northern Chaco had resulted in the forced assimilation of many of these groups into creole Argentine economic structures en masse as day laborers. As a result, indigenous communities of the northwest remained in closer every-day contact with other sectors of northwestern society and were impossible to simply ignore or erase.[33] The rolling advance of modernity, now seen during the 1920s and 1930s in an increasingly sinister light, led northwestern anthropologists to focus their energies on those elements of regional culture that differentiated the northwest from the decadence of the capital. The folktales, songs, and artisanal crafts of traditional northwestern indigenous and criollo cultures were embraced by regionalist anthropologists as treasures threatened by the advance of a materialistic porteño homogeneity.

The Instituto de Etnología, established in 1928 by the Universidad Nacional de Tucumán, embodied these regionalist concerns with contemporary and ancient indigenous cultures and provided regionalists with a scientific tool kit for the ongoing celebration of northwestern uniqueness and cultural purity. The institute's research program—and especially the career of its first director, Swiss anthropologist Alfred Metraux (1928–34)—captured the broader interests of regionalism and focused them in new directions. Regionalists in San Miguel de Tucumán capitalized on the international scientific prominence and regional utility of the institute's research and sought to popularize anthropological knowledge and interest through public museum displays, the popular press, educational curricula, and government action. The Instituto de Etnología thus became a prism through which northwestern identity could be scientifically examined and fanned out into its constituent elements in the past and present. The institute is also a powerful case study for understanding northwestern identity building within the region and in dialogue with Buenos Aires.

There is a danger, in constructing a contrast between coastal and regional visions of the northwest, that the first perspective will take on the somewhat villainous character traits of an overbearing elite metropole, while the second will adopt its opposite, the persona of the heroically resistant subaltern periphery. It is important to recognize, then, that the regionalists who embraced anthropology as a means of defining and exploring their own cultural heritage and regional uniqueness in the northwest were *not* popular actors. They were not the same northwesterners who appear in Debenedetti's journals—the everyday visitors to his camp or the workers he derided for their "chronic laziness." Nor did they claim to be. Regionalism was a distinctly urban, creole, elite movement, led by intellectuals, educators, and politicians who saw themselves as a vanguard of regional identity. In their own way, northwestern regionalists sought to educate and change the region's population just as much as coastal anthropologists did, although the model on which they hoped to mold northwestern society differed in significant ways. Whereas coastal archaeologists hoped that northwesterners would adopt their own vision of Argentine modernity, willingly taking their place as productive citizens whose labor and energy would support the prosperity of a Buenos Aires–centered politics and economy, northwestern regionalists sought to train the population to take pride in their own region's potential and identity, thus stemming the tide of labor flight to the coast and laying the groundwork for a northwest with the political power, economic might, and cultural solidarity to oppose the dictates of the porteño state.

Regionalist anthropologists focused their attention on indigenous ethnography and archaeology, but they themselves almost entirely self-identified as Argentine-born and European-descended creole, urban elites, and not often as directly criollo or belonging to peasant folk cultures. Similarly, the regionalist embrace of indigenous cultures, while integral to the regionalist program of cultural uniqueness and heritage, was strategic and flexible. These progressive creole elites' celebration of a combined and flexible criollo-indigenous heritage did not stop regionalist politicians or sugar barons, for example, from exploiting a largely indigenous labor force or attempting to confine indigenous communities within a modernized system of *reducciones* evocative of the colonial era. Regionalism and its embrace of indigenous culture and heritage had a profound impact on northwestern identity, but in many cases did not transcend contemporary practices of racism or exploitation in the region.[34]

The Instituto de Etnología was created through the initiative of the Universidad Nacional de Tucumán, itself established in 1914 and dedicated from its inception to regionalist study and improvement. "Founded to meet the needs of a vast region," the university "occupied itself from an early moment with the historical and sociological investigation of the Argentine Northwest."[35] Within its regional orbit, rector Juan B. Terán declared, the university had "the mission of revealing . . . [the northwest's] unity in the past in order to build its strength and consciousness" in the present.[36] Between 1915 and 1928, anthropology constituted one section of the university's natural history museum. In the latter year, the university moved to create a separate body dedicated exclusively to anthropological studies. In search of a lead scientist for this organization, Terán wrote to renowned French anthropologist Paul Rivet for recommendations. Rivet nominated his student, twenty-six-year-old Alfred Metraux, for the post. "Metraux is my best student and also of [Swedish anthropologist] Erland Nordenskiöld," Rivet wrote.

If he were French, I would keep him here, but he is Swiss and you know that French law does not permit foreign employees. I give you a jewel and if you accept him, I can tell you that Tucumán will have *the best ethnologist in all Latin America* .... Metraux speaks Spanish as if it were his maternal tongue, French, German, reads English perfectly and Danish, and also speaks Swedish. I repeat that we are speaking of a man *of the first order.* Take him with every confidence. After a short time you will thank me.[37]

Based on Rivet's unequivocally glowing recommendation, the university promptly offered Metraux the directorship of an ethnological institute of his own design and a two-year renewable contract with a salary of eight hundred pesos monthly.[38]

Metraux's design for what he originally called an ethnographic museum revealed his stratospheric ambitions for Tucumán and the northwest in Argentine anthropology. "I would like the Museo de Tucumán," he wrote, "to be representative of all the ancient indigenous cultures of the Argentine Republic, and especially of the *Province of Tucumán* (ancient and modern). In my sense, this museum must be a 'Museum for the Argentine Indian' like the Museum 'for American Indians' of the United States. This is to say that I will attempt to unite sufficient ethnographic and archaeological collections to illustrate the indigenous civilization of the distinct geographic regions of the Argentine Republic." Metraux hoped to create in Tucumán the foremost center of Argentine anthropology, superseding even the museums of Buenos Aires and La Plata and building anthropological authority in the northwest. He also contended that the vital importance of this kind of museum and the research it would foster transcended regional and national interests. The disappearance of indigenous peoples throughout the Americas, he argued, made Tucumán's potential as a stage for salvage ethnographic work an opportunity of value for all humankind.[39]

Alfred Metraux's claim to an interest in Argentine anthropology stemmed from his youth. Born in Lausanne, Switzerland, Metraux moved with his family to Mendoza, Argentina, shortly after his birth and spent several years of his childhood in that country. In his autobiography, Metraux remembered having "an Argentine childhood, and the cordillera and the dry pampa formed a part of my memories. I believe that that marked inclination that from a very young age I felt for the Argentine landscape signaled the origin of my career."[40] This personal attachment to Argentina, compounded by his ability to connect northwestern anthropology with an international promi-nence hitherto largely limited to the prominent museums of Buenos Aires and La Plata, rapidly transformed Metraux into a symbolic champion for regionalist studies. Regionalists' willingness to employ Metraux's European connections in their program of antipositivist identity building, which openly rejected Buenos Aires's tendency to rely on European models and approval in measuring national progress, was somewhat ironic. On the other hand, how-ever, Metraux openly agreed with regionalist concerns about the dissipation of Western mores and much preferred the northwest to the metropolitan confines of Buenos Aires. During a trip to Buenos Aires in 1932, he rejected the hustle and bustle of porteño life as meaningless busyness, lacking in sub-stance and overladen with frivolous form. As he wrote in frustration to a tucumano colleague, "I live a dog's life [in Buenos Aires], to which I am not accustomed. A tea here, another one there, ministers to visit, people to invite, and thus the day and night pass and one is exhausted and after all in the end one accomplishes nothing." Buenos Aires's cosmopolitan crush seemed to Metraux to reflect dissipation rather than sophistication, as well as a distrac-tion from Argentina's true nature. Argentina's most authentic self, he con-tended alongside northwestern regionalists, was to be found in the countryside beyond the port city. Whereas residents of Buenos Aires lived overcrowded and hectic lives, constantly worrying about "catastrophe, the fall of the peso, revolution, and the silliness of fashion," northwesterners lived free from such cloying conventions and in greater communion with Argentina's cul-tural roots.[41]

Metraux framed himself as belonging to this authentic Argentina, more so than did the urbanites of porteño society. "I know the country better than they do," he wrote to a friend. "Who among them in Buenos Aires knows Catamarca, the Calchaquí Valleys, the Quebrada del Toro, the deserts of the puna, Aconquija? My taste for the truth makes it difficult to believe in their sentiments, which seem to me artificial. How can one love the pampa if one sees it only from the train, en route to Mar del Plata? Who among them, my friends, have slept beneath an algarrobo or a quebracho [tree]?"[42] Thus, despite being a European scholar, which traditionally would have allied him with Buenos Aires's vision of national progress, Metraux favored the regionalist approach of northwestern anthropology and invoked his Argentine upbring-ing and personal experiences in the northwest to link himself with this brand of regional and national authenticity. Unlike Debenedetti, who saw no contra-diction between identifying strongly with Buenos Aires's porteño ethos and connecting strongly with the northwestern landscapes through which he traveled, Metraux argued that to truly know and understand northwestern landscapes, it was necessary to escape and even to reject the hustle and bustle of coastal life.

Metraux's approach to anthropological research in the northwest also aligned with regionalist thinking. Contrary to the coastal tendency to celebrate the remote indigenous past while detaching it from the indigenous present, Metraux insisted that deep continuities existed between the past and the present and that these continuities demanded that the past and present be studied in connection with each other. Metraux believed that the indigenous peoples of the modern northwest were the descendants of the region's ancient inhabitants and not degenerate invaders, and therefore ethnographic and archaeological research in the northwest offered complementary and necessary insights into each other. He called this approach "modern ethnography" and underscored its moral component of recording the traditional cultural practices of contemporary northwestern indigenous societies before they melted away.[43] Metraux focused his own ethnographic work in the Argentine Chaco and the Bolivian altiplano, conducting studies of groups such as the Chiriguano, Matako, and Pilagá, who had not yet been studied systematically by cultural anthropologists and were relatively unknown to science. Metraux also initiated the publication of the *Revista del Instituto de Etnología*, which acquired an international reputation for excellence in regional studies and brought the Instituto de Etnología to the attention of the international anthropological world. In the *Revista*, Metraux aimed to embody his larger anthropological goal, which he described as "a work of salvation, publishing documents, photographs of objects, myths and dictionaries of the primitive races of South America, above all those that are on their way to extinction."[44]

Metraux's work made an enormous impact on Tucumán's anthropological practices and reputation, but his stay was not of long duration. Six years after being hired by the Universidad Nacional de Tucumán to organize the Instituto de Etnología, Metraux requested a leave of absence to lead a French-organized expedition to Easter Island. A year later, he tendered his official resignation without returning to Tucumán, citing a lack of funding and the volatility of political maneuverings in San Miguel de Tucumán as insurmountable obstacles to his work; he accepted a position with a joint French and Belgian anthropological expedition in the Pacific.[45] Metraux went on to a prolific anthropological career in hemispheric American and Pacific ethnography and also became an advocate for the importance of anthropological participation in human rights and relief work, collaborating with the United Nations and UNESCO. In his wake, the Instituto de Etnología struggled to find a stable institutional path, but it always retained the image and model of Metraux as a guiding ideal.

Metraux left lasting legacies in the northwest, among them helping establish the Instituto de Etnología's prominent place within a regional sphere of influence. Regionalists combated the northwest's marginalization on the national stage by framing the northwest as a dynamic social and geographical unit, operating beneath the umbrella of vibrant regional universities and institutions, most notably the Universidad Nacional de Tucumán. A 1948 map from the university's annual *memoria* illustrates this spatial imagining concretely, showing not only the cohesion of the northwest as a region but also the tucumano vision of Tucumán as the region's anchor (fig. 15). In this map, Tucumán's "zone of influence" extends beyond the northwest into the littoral provinces of Misiones and Corrientes, broadening northwestern regionalism into an even larger territory. Arrows connect the capitals of Argentina's northern provinces with Tucumán, suggesting by their directionality a sort of pilgrimage to the northwest's "First House of Studies" in San Miguel de Tucumán, represented on the map by a Grecian-style portico at the bristling center of a nest of arrowheads. The map's caption explains that "the Universidad de Tucumán must attend to the scientific, technical, and cultural needs of a population that amounts to one-quarter of the inhabitants of the country." By midcentury, the northwest had acquired a strong sense of its own regional identity and of that identity's independence from the porteño model; Buenos Aires is not even marked on the map. Within the Universidad Nacional de Tucumán, the Instituto de Etnología occupied an important position among a pantheon of regional studies departments and institutes. By the end of the 1930s, the Instituto de Etnología (which was renamed the Instituto de Antropología in 1937) was joined by the Institute of Regional Medicine, the Institute of History, Linguistics, and Folklore, the Institute of Mineralogy and Geology, the Institute of Zoology, the Institute of Technical-Industrial Research, the Institute of Economic and Sociological Research, the Photography and Drawing Studio, and the Miguel Lillo Institute of Botany, all branches of the university dedicated to a specifically regional focus.[46]

Within this vibrant regionalist university culture, the Instituto de Etnología contributed crucially to the development of northwestern cultural identity and to the Universidad Nacional de Tucumán's regional sphere of influence

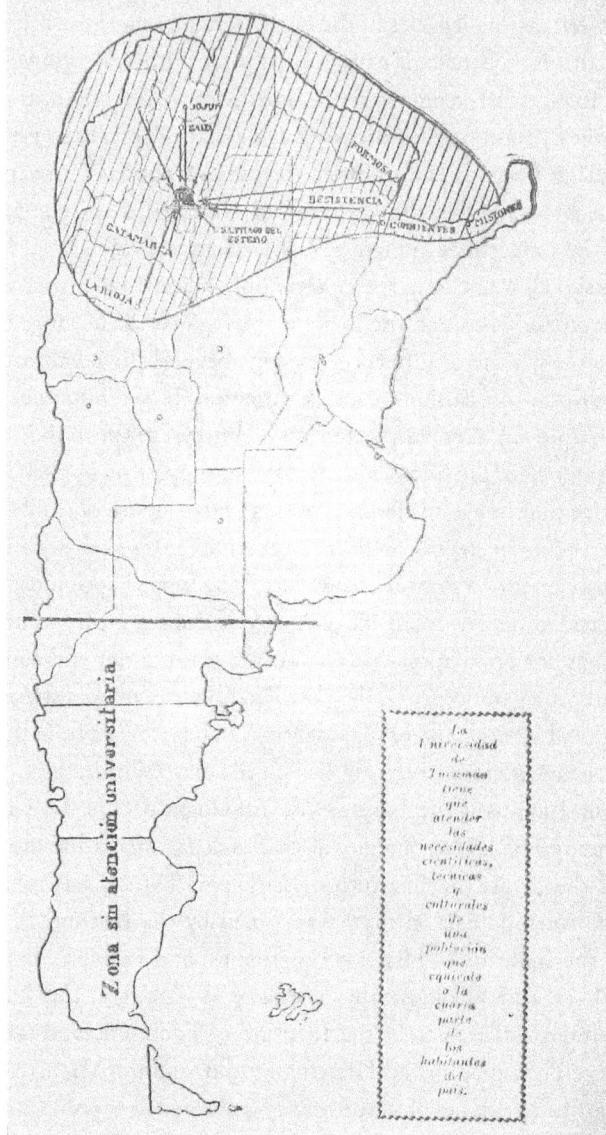

Fig. 15 The northwestern zone of influence. *Universidad Nacional de Tucumán, memoria año 1948* (Tucumán: Universidad Nacional de Tucumán), 17.

through the cultivation of international anthropological and scientific renown and especially through the regional and international exchange of publications. The institute's surviving correspondence archives do not begin until 1948, but the wealth and pattern of archived materials from this late date suggest long-standing publications exchanges based on the international prominence of the institute's publications. The *Revista del Instituto de Etnología*, its most prominent and long-lasting publication, began under Metraux's directorship in 1929 and boasted an impressive list of European and North American institutional subscribers, including the Smithsonian Institution, the American Museum of Natural History, Columbia University, Harvard University, Cambridge University, the British Library, Universiteit Leiden, and other European institutions. In addition to its European and North American contacts, and well exceeding these connections in volume, were the institute's publications exchanges within and bordering on its regional sphere of influence. In 1948 alone, the Instituto de Etnología recorded publications exchanges and requests from educational institutions and interested individuals throughout the northwestern umbrella, in Tucumán, Chaco, Santiago del Estero, Mendoza, Catamarca, and Salta. In the same year, the institute responded to publications requests from a wide array of universities and museums in other Latin American countries, including Peru, Uruguay, Chile, Mexico, Brazil, Ecuador, Bolivia, Colombia, and Cuba.[47]

The institute's geographical focus on its own regional sphere and on Latin America as a more dominant circle of professional collaboration than Europe offered a striking contrast to museums in Buenos Aires and La Plata, which built their scientific reputations on connections with European and North American institutions. By the mid-twentieth century, northwestern anthropologists and anthropological enthusiasts found their interests better served by collaboration with fellow specialists in Americanist anthropology. Since European anthropologists were focusing a good deal of their attention at midcentury on African and Asian studies, the colleagues most important for tucumanos were now more likely to be found in La Paz and Montevideo, rather than London or Munich. This is not to say that the Instituto de Etnología did not interact with European or North American institutions; Tucumán cultivated ties with a number of such museums and universities. The institute's focus, however, was not on this arena but on South America, Argentina, and especially the northwestern region, the heart of the South American continent.

The Instituto de Etnología maintained close professional ties with the museums of La Plata and Buenos Aires. For example, Metraux orchestrated a collections exchange with the Museo Nacional de Ciencias Naturales in 1931 in order to obtain from it ethnographic materials from Tierra del Fuego and Patagonia, in exchange for ethnographic collections from the Chipaya and Chiriguano, groups that Metraux had studied and of whose material culture he resultantly held unique and otherwise difficult-to-obtain examples.[48] The two museums conducted another exchange in 1934, when the Museo Nacional traded eight ceramic vessels from its archaeological collections for four large stone heads from Tiahuanaco in the institute's collections.[49] The Museo Etnográfico, with its emphasis on northwestern archaeology, became a particularly important partner in the institute's complementary work of ethnography coupled with archaeology. The institute focused its own work, during Metraux's inaugural tenure and afterward, primarily on ethnographic studies, but Metraux's call to "modern ethnography" required that this research be supplemented by archaeological work. The Museo Etnográfico, whose specialization had led it down the opposite path, served as an ideal trading partner. Metraux cultivated a regular correspondence with Félix Outes, who became director of the Museo Etnográfico after Salvador Debenedetti's death in 1930, and the two often exchanged objects, photographs, and information. In the inaugural year of his directorship of the Museo Etnográfico—the second year of Metraux's directorship in Tucumán—Outes named Metraux *encargado ad honorem* of the Museo Etnográfico's ethnographic section, placing the Instituto de Etnología on collegial footing with one of the nation's most well-funded and internationally recognized anthropological museums and conceding to Tucumán a certain measure of scientific autonomy, all precious victories for the cultivation of regionalist scientific identity and strength.[50]

By 1939, four years after Metraux's official resignation and eleven years after its founding, the Instituto de Etnología, now the Instituto de Antropología, had established itself as a scientifically legitimate, regionally oriented center of cultural research. Its collections had grown to an impressive size, described in the university's annual *memoria*, in passionate if imprecise terms, as containing "several thousand archaeological, ethnographic, and anthropological pieces, which makes its Museum truly unique in the Central, Andean, and Northern regions of the country." The institute published its visitor statistics as a demonstration of its broader public utility, boasting that "the exhibition Hall of the Institute is constantly visited by individuals, university students and professors, and secondary and primary [students]. During the year 1939 it was visited by some 1,600 upper-grade students from the provincial primary schools. Students from the secondary and superior schools of Tucumán and the littoral also attended the museum. The total number of visitors reached 2,500."⁵¹ The institute was thus not only an academic space but also a public one, and this dual role was highlighted by university anthropologists as one of its accomplishments. The regionalist project of cultivating cultural identity and pride found scientific expression in the exhibit halls of the Instituto de Etnología, making the institute and the anthropological science it cultivated variously and flexibly useful to scientists, regional thinkers, regional elites, and other northwesterners in their constructions of region and nation.

Conclusion

During the decades following Argentina's centenary, the sub-Andean valleys of the northwest became a symbolic battleground as opposing factions engaged in struggles over the meanings of northwestern space and culture and who would define those meanings within a regional and national context. Although coastal and regionalist observers touted very different interpretations of the region's landscape and cultures, the two groups were also linked by their use of shared languages and symbols in this debate. Both sides employed anthropological language and science as a legitimizing medium to claim interpretive rights over northwestern landscapes and cultures, and did so from different and even mutually exclusive positions of authority. Both coastal and regional observers saw identity in the northwest as embedded in landscape and used anthropology as a tool to construct space or place and to either give power or attempt to take it away. In essence, then, the battle over identity was a battle over space and place. It was also a battle over authority and power. Who really knew the northwest as a landscape and as a culture? Both northwesterners and coastal archaeologists claimed to wield a powerful combination of scientific observation and personal experience and thereby positioned themselves as authoritative voices. Both groups also excluded the indigenous cultures living in the present-day northwest as contenders in this debate; as in Buenos Aires and La Plata, indigenous cultures were the object of creole discussions about identity and heritage, but not active participants in the interpretation of northwestern landscapes. However, the regionalist program offered an alternative to Buenos Aires's coastally and progressively

oriented national model. It promoted a new look at the strategic incorporation of indigenous culture within twentieth-century creole Argentine nation-
alisms, and it interpreted anthropology not only as scientific but also as a
vibrant cultural signifier of Argentina beyond the official bounds of museum
anthropology.

4

Sensational Discoveries: Heroes, Scandals, and the Popularization of Anthropology

Introduction

In July 1913, the Buenos Aires newspaper *La Nación* printed a story entitled "The Triumphs of Ameghino," outlining the scientific theories of Argentine paleontologist Florentino Ameghino, who had died two years earlier. Ameghino had argued, in brief, that the oldest human remains on earth could be found on Argentine soil and that humankind had, in fact, originally evolved there. In the article, the contention that "man was originally of our soil, that he has followed this ascendant line to become what he is today, without ever having been a monkey," was entangled with national pride, both in Argentina's extreme antiquity as the cradle of humankind and in Ameghino's audacity in defying scientific convention to make this claim. The article dismissed the ancient remains then being uncovered in Europe, Oceania, and Africa, claiming that they were clearly not ancestors of modern humankind but rather "a remote branch of this [species], which became separated from the trunk following a direct path to bestialization."[1]

This article captures an important crossroads in the social life of anthropological science in twentieth-century Argentina. In the early years of the twentieth century, scientists debated the merits of Ameghino's theories in an international forum abuzz with discoveries and theories regarding human-kind's origins. The 1880s and 1890s had set the stage for strong scientific and social interest in these origins, thanks to a wave of provocative discoveries that were published and republished in scientific journals and the popular press. As scientists around the world searched for answers to the riddle of human origins, Ameghino's theories presented a new and at times unwelcome New World spin on largely Old World–centered theories. Many Argentines, however, saw in Ameghino's theories an ideal entry point into the sanctum sanctorum of civilized nations. What better way to demonstrate their nation's pedigree than to prove scientifically that Argentine soil was the cradle of humanity itself? Ameghino's theories, as one newspaper commentator wrote while the debate raged in 1915, "ran through the scientific world like a destructive ray," drawing passionate responses from scientific and popular voices alike.[2]

By the time *La Nación* printed its article on Ameghino's "triumphs" in 1913, his theories of human antiquity and evolution in Argentina were already being debunked by professional scientists domestically and internationally. Despite this scientific rejection, however, Ameghino became a popular scientific hero in Argentina, championed from the 1910s through the 1930s in newspapers and magazines, public monuments and celebrations, in ways that became increasingly disconnected from professional science. Regardless of the voluble scientific objections to Ameghino's theories by 1913, *La Nación* contended that European scientists' new theories were, in fact, "the same as the old [words] of our illustrious Ameghino." In the Argentine popular press, Ameghino became a kind of irresistible force, his ideas so powerful that even those who initially rejected him ultimately agreed with him, much to the "honor of Argentine science."[3]

As earlier chapters of this book have shown, Argentine museum anthropologists of the nineteenth and twentieth centuries deliberately cultivated anthropology's cultural utility as a means of justifying their work to various state and public audiences. So effective was this mantra that, by degrees, anthropology's cultural utility escaped from professional anthropologists' control. Cultural utility, often expanded or contracted to fit the contours of civic, regional, or national culture, became something that museum anthropologists could no longer offer voluntarily in order to connect their work with society. Rather, it became something that was required of them by overlapping publics with their own conflicting agendas. When popular actors felt that museum scientists did not adequately or faithfully meet this social need, they began to look elsewhere and to reshape anthropology themselves in public spheres such as the popular press, public celebrations, antiquities markets, and monument building.

Professional museum anthropologists responded ambiguously to these appropriations, celebrating the evidence of anthropology's importance in Argentine society and yet also resisting their own inability to control these public expressions of anthropological enthusiasm. The oscillating tensions and alliances between professional science and popular engagement illustrate the changing social life of anthropology in early twentieth-century creole Argentine identities. Popular claims on anthropology and museums ranged from simple curiosity to political maneuverings, and they were pitched from polite requests to belligerent demands. This chapter follows the discussion of these outside voices beyond the walls of museums, exploring the creation of scientific celebrities in the popular press and the bifurcation of popular scientific enthusiasm and the "actual" work of professional science. This popularization of anthropological interest was often lamented by museum scientists; a growing divide emerged in the first decades of the twentieth century between those who applauded popular enthusiasm for anthropological science as a triumph of national culture and scientific interest and those who decried it as vulgar sensationalism, a violation of meaningful science in the name of jingoism and entertainment.

Debates over human antiquity in Argentina also significantly transformed the meaning of indigenous artifacts and human remains. Although by the early twentieth century it was generally acknowledged that such objects belonged to the precursors of modern indigenous cultures, these connections were rarely spoken of. Instead, these ancient artifacts and remains were discussed as belonging to "early man" or "proto-man," who was understood as universally human rather than indigenous.

Scientific Heroes

Through the popular retooling of anthropology in Argentina's early twentieth century, museum anthropologists found themselves at the center of public attention in new and important ways. A number of prominent anthropologists were singled out in the popular press and other public spaces as scientific heroes, and their ideas became the focus of public debate. Among the heroes created during this period, Florentino Ameghino (fig. 16) was especially renowned. His theories of human evolution captured imaginations and spurred scientific controversy. Bitter debates played out in professional scientific publications and in popular magazines and newspapers over the truth or untruth of Ameghino's theories, and such writings were often reprinted from one venue to the next with ironic and acrimonious commentary on the purportedly unsound tactics of his supporters or opponents. As a figure who, both in life and posthumously, seemed to have a talent for attracting controversy, Ameghino and his evolutionary theories highlight the struggle over scientific cultural utility that simultaneously divided professional museum anthropologists from a broader public and attracted their attention as the twentieth century progressed.

Ameghino's elevation to the center of public debate involved a distinctive and transformative process, in which he ceased to be simply a man or scientist and morphed into a symbolic, heroic version of himself, taking on characteristics that suited those who claimed the right to interpret his legacy. Especially since much of the more heated debate about Ameghino's theories on human evolution occurred after his death, his symbolic identity as an anthropological hero became highly malleable and perhaps more powerful than it might have been had he lived to participate directly in the controversy. In this sense, Ameghino's heroification calls to mind Emiliano Zapata, Che Guevara, and other twentieth-century heroes whose early deaths at what their supporters believed to be the peak of their accomplishments sparked posthumous careers of heroism and symbolic power that continue to command instant and meaningful recognition.[4] Ameghino's heroism as a scientist was, perhaps, more narrow than the heroism of a revolutionary; however, the highly selective and creative processes of reimagining Ameghino as a posthumous scientific hero bore a striking resemblance to those that created more familiar heroic figures such as Guevara and Zapata. Moreover, Ameghino's fractious appeal—he was admired by some, ridiculed or even despised by others—calls to mind Guevara's contested heroism in twentieth-century Latin America.

Máximo Farro and Irina Podgorny have described the modern heroification of scientists such as Ameghino as a kind of secular sanctification.[5] Argentine medical doctor and writer José Ingenieros, presiding over Ameghino's civil funeral in September 1911, accordingly asserted that "modern sainthood is in wisdom" and that in a modern world "saints do not know how to perform miracles, but they know how to search for truth. We learn from them and will be faithful to their teachings."[6] The notion of modern or secular sainthood captures effectively the potency of scientific heroes' renown in twentieth-century Argentine society, as well as the fierce loyalty

Fig. 16 Florentino Ameghino at his desk. Image 4743, Archivo General de la Nación, Departamento de Documentos Fotográficos, Buenos Aires.

that these figures often inspired in their followers. Ameghinistas—followers of Ameghino—were often accused by their detractors during the early twentieth century of defending Ameghino's scientific theories without actually understanding them. In some ways, however, "understanding" in a scientific sense became peripheral to the debate as the century progressed, and a lack of understanding, alleged or real, did not dampen Ameghinistas' enthusiasm in the slightest.

Many historians have seen Ameghino as an enigmatic and irascible exception within an otherwise milder-mannered procession of scientific public figures. This sort of characterization is certainly present in the many biographies of Ameghino written in the decades after his death, as well as in more recent scholarly treatments. While this scholarship provides useful insight into Ameghino's career and importance to Argentine culture, another result of the focus on his exceptionality has been scholarship that overlooks his significant continuity and connection with the context in which he—and his posthumous legacy—existed.[7] While it would be difficult to argue that Ameghino was not a controversial figure, revered and reviled for his stubbornness, his theoretical audacity, and his scientific bellicosity, he nonetheless fit within a broader trend in Argentine history that heroized and caricatured museum scientists as public heroes and secular saints. Such figures were, in fact, *often* highlighted for their personal peculiarities and quirks, a trend that began in the 1860s and continued well after Ameghino's death. Indeed, Ameghino's flawed heroism was scandalous and therefore engaging (or enraging) to both sides of the debate precisely because it struck a nerve within a long-standing and culturally familiar tradition in Argentine society. What made Ameghino's posthumous career so uniquely heated within this larger tradition was not simply the fact that he was himself a controversial figure, although his personality certainly added spice to the mix. Rather, the debate drew its force from the importance of Ameghino's ideas to the integrity of Argentina's already highly developed scientific social identity. Many of the people involved in the Ameghinista debates had little or no specific firsthand knowledge of Ameghino's writings or theories, but this did not diminish their passion. By the 1920s, the notion of debunking the theories of a scientific hero such as Ameghino seemed, to many Argentines, tantamount to cultural heresy—a belief connected with the long trajectory of scientific hero worship within which Ameghino must be understood. In the fever of enthusiasm that followed his death, to threaten Ameghino was to threaten the very foundations of Argentine anthropological science, which, after half a century of cultural utility building, constituted an important element of national pride and identity.

The image of Ameghino as a scientific "saint" prompts questions about the role of religion and the Catholic Church in debates over human evolution in Argentina. As elsewhere, Darwinism drew sharp critiques from Argentine church leaders and Christian thinkers, especially during the later nineteenth century. Scholars have explored the grievances of the "Catholic opposition" with regard to the effect of Darwinism on Argentines' worldview—intellectuals and church leaders such as José Manuel Estrada, who argued that Darwinian evolution distracted from science's truest purpose: the illustration of the Creator's universe. As historians of science have shown, however, these Catholic opposition leaders recognized that the secular and "naturalistic worldview" that they were protesting was the predominant view in Argentine society. They saw themselves as leading a vocal minority in favor of a more moral cosmology and approach to science. Given that most of Argentine society did not share the Catholic opposition's deep moral uneasiness with Darwinian evolution by the turn of the twentieth century, Ameghino's theories—even his theories of human evolution—met with a widely sympathetic audience on at least a basic philosophical level, even as the opposition continued to voice its concern. Newspaper stories and public addresses related to Ameghino's theories very rarely touched on these spiritual qualms, emphasizing instead his contributions to national science and to Argentina's international reputation.[8]

Ameghino's Posthumous Heroism

Florentino Ameghino died, after a slow decline, from diabetic complications on August 6, 1911. With his death began a spectacular transformation in which the self-taught paleontologist-anthropologist, who had been frankly unpopular among many of his contemporaries, was lavished with praise by those same scientists; in addition to tributes from journalists, politicians, schoolteachers, and poets, this praise facilitated Ameghino's canonization as an Argentine scientific hero, a cultural model that had been forming in Argentina for at least a generation but now reached new heights of intensity. At his civil funeral on September 18, José Ingenieros captured the incipient tide of Ameghinista fever when he declared that "glory and death lay in wait together to compete over the body of Florentino Ameghino. Few tombs have seen like his the cypress and the laurel blooming and intertwining at once, as if in the flickering twilight of his physical existence one would have lit an offering lamp to the eternal glorification of his genius."[9] Cypress and laurel, fin de siècle horticultural symbols of mourning and of victory or academic achievement, represented in Ingenieros's florid address the very specific nature of Ameghino's emerging celebrity. In death, he became symbolically malleable in a way that his forceful personality had prevented in life; this posthumous pliability shed new light on the details of his life and work, making him an ideal candidate for national scientific heroification. Ameghino, a self-taught naturalist and self-framed "outsider" to the traditional echelons of academic power, was held up as the champion of the Argentine everyman and a testament to what every single Argentine could achieve through individual hard work and dedication to the progress of human knowledge.

Ameghino's legacy, and his posthumous symbolism for Argentine science and society, revolved centrally around meaning-laden constructions of Ameghino as a *sabio*, a term that merits some consideration. The Spanish word *sabio* derives, literally, from the verb *saber*, to know, and translates most directly as "a learned person," "a wise person," or "one who knows." It is also sometimes translated as "sage," "expert," or even the French word "savant." None of these, however, fully captures the meaning of *sabio* in this context. In professional science, the term is distinguished from titles such as "doctor" or "maestro," insofar as it does not denote any specific formal training. Although he was granted an honorary doctorate by the Universidad de Córdoba early in his career, Ameghino was usually referred to by scientists before and after his death as Don Florentino Ameghino and as a sabio, rather than a doctor. This title is, however, a decidedly double-edged sword. On the one hand, it could be used as a term of differentiation and exclusion, leaving Ameghino outside of professional science's inner circle of officially titled, formally trained scholars. On the other hand, to be called a sabio could also denote great respect; it was in this sense that the term was increasingly used in connection to Ameghino after his death. Indeed, in his posthumous career, Ameghino's self-taught expertise, in isolation from the university classroom, was often interpreted as a strength rather than a shortcoming; his *doctor honoris causa* from the Universidad de Córdoba was forgone in favor of the title of sabio not in order to degrade him, but to elevate him as an intellectual of the people, whose wisdom came not from European or European-influenced universities, but from the direct inspiration of the Argentine soil itself.

To understand Ameghino as a scientific hero in early twentieth-century Argentina, it is critical to first understand the larger context in which he was imagined as a sabio of "the people." The year before Ameghino's death, Argentina celebrated the centennial of its declaration of independence from Spain. Grandiose public ceremonies and celebrations transformed Buenos Aires in May 1910, entailing parades and public speeches, main thorough-fares hung with banners and garlands, and monuments erected to Argentina's independence. Argentina sought to celebrate its coming of age as an independent and progressive nation with an identity and solidity of its own. Ameghino, alongside fellow Argentine museum scientists such as Francisco P. Moreno, Juan B. Ambrosetti, and the latter's cortege of youthful students (including his protégé Salvador Debenedetti), fit neatly into this image of a robust Argentine nation-state fulfilling its national mission and forging ahead along the path of national destiny. These festivities were juxtaposed eerily, however, against the violent police suppression of anarchist and union agitation taking place in the city. In response to a general strike on May 18, 1910, President Figueroa Alcorta declared a state of siege and unleashed a combined force of police and civilian militia against the strikers, resulting in a series of imprisonments and deportations, as well as the destruction of anarchist and union operational headquarters in the city. When angry anarchist agitators bombed Buenos Aires's prominent Teatro Colón in response, Congress quickly passed legislation banning anarchist associations and instituting six-year prison sentences for interfering with laborers willing to work during a strike. These events created a strange atmosphere of militaristic patriotism in the capital city, in which the celebration of heroes who symbolized national identity and unity became tangibly relevant. Ameghino presented a flexible and potentially useful figure, as he was an outsider to the traditional elites and oligarchy, against whom the rising Syndicalists, Anarchists, and Socialists rebelled politically, and yet also a member of respectable scientific circles with whom the upper classes of the city and provinces could connect. Ameghino, through the lens of centennial celebration, became an Argentine mediator; after his death, he served as a peacemaker in a way that his forceful personality would not likely have allowed in life.[10]

During the height of Ameghino's posthumous celebrity, from the 1910s through the 1930s, Argentine politics and national culture began to tilt away from the Europhilic progressivism of the early Republic and toward an increasingly pointed celebration of "authentic" argentinidad. The civilizing promise of European immigration became tarnished by urban overpopulation, immigrants' poverty, and the crisis of Europe's cultural superiority in the face of world war; national politics was opened to mass participation through the Sáenz Peña law of 1912, which established universal male suffrage; radicalism rose to national political power, shaking the ascendency of the traditional oligarchy; and the Argentine tango hit the global stage as an authentically Argentine musical form, eclipsing the popularity of other, foreign music in the *milongas* and dance academies of Buenos Aires. This atmosphere bred increasing distrust of foreigners and of an exclusivist European academia that did not resonate with the lives of everyday Argentines. Ameghino's celebrity as a self-taught sabio connected viscerally with this climate, and both his followers and critics overwhelmingly referred to him as a sabio when emotions ran highest in the Ameghinista debates of the 1910s through the 1930s.[11]

Ameghino's natural connection to Argentine soil by birth became a subject of controversy after his death, when writers in the popular press suggested that he was actually an Italian immigrant who had come to Argentina as a very small child with his parents. *La Razón* printed a report on this debate on September 8, 1916, along with interviews with a number of Ameghino's former colleagues, who denounced the allegation as unfounded and politically motivated. The author contended that a false Italian birth certificate had been produced by a priest in Luján (Ameghino's claimed Argentine birthplace) in defense against "the attacks of liberal elements who had adopted the name of the sabio like a flag." The article included an image of Ameghino's Argentine birth certificate and asserted that he was Argentine indeed and to suggest otherwise was slanderous politicking.[12] Ongoing controversy over Ameghino's place of birth, despite a shared acknowledgment that he had lived virtually his entire life in Argentina, revealed a jingoistic undertone to Argentine nationalism during these years; to be Italian by birth was less desirable than to be Argentine, and it would undermine Ameghino's ability to represent Argentina as a sabio of the people. Such debate had very little, if anything, to do with Ameghino's scientific work, and yet it shaped his image as a scientific celebrity in the public sphere.

Monuments to Ameghino, and calls to action made in his name, proliferated in the years immediately following his death. In September 1912, as the Argentine Congress debated the merits of law 9080, which would nationalize archaeological and paleontological remains, one supporter characterized it in the Buenos Aires newspaper *La Nación* as a "firm continuation of the work of Ameghino" that "affirms the personality of the country in the scientific world."[13] Others honored the sabio more concretely; a bust of Ameghino was constructed in Buenos Aires's zoological park, a fitting place, one newspaper article explained, as scientists generally preferred spaces conducive to quiet contemplation over the hustle and bustle of teeming metropolitan plazas (these sites, the author mused, were better suited to military heroes, who would enjoy marshaling the urban masses).[14] Such a general reflection on the preferences of scientists in itself suggests cultural engagement with the idea of scientific heroism in Argentina by the 1910s, as the author assumes that these categorical traits would be recognized and appreciated by newspaper readers at large. The city of Mar del Plata constructed an even more prominent memorial to the sabio (fig. 17). An enormous carving of Ameghino's face, shown in a photograph of an inauguration ceremony tentatively dated 1936 (placing this ceremony twenty-five years after his death), provides a sense for both the longevity and the intensity of feeling behind Ameghinista demonstrations.

Fig. 17   Effigy of Florentino Ameghino in Mar del Plata. Image 50530, Archivo General de la Nación, Departamento de Documentos Fotográficos, Buenos Aires. The back of the photograph reads, "The effigy of the great sabio, carved into the rock at mar del Plata, tribute that the said city paid him." And below, "The tribute to Ameghino, inaugurated in Mar del Plata . . . in the presence of the governor and high authorities. (1936?)"

Ameghinistas also celebrated the sabio with public galas and festivities, such as the "soiree" that, as *La Nación* announced on the second anniversary of Ameghino's death, "was held last night in the teatro Argentina, in La Plata," and attended by "a large crowd from that city and many persons from this capital." The newspaper's correspondent reported that the event's combination of scientific papers and musical performances, which lasted until after midnight, "proved very interesting" to its audience. Particularly noteworthy was Ernesto Nelson's "long lecture on the scientific work undertaken in his productive life by doctor Ameghino, which address was ably illustrated by close to one hundred illuminated projections."[15] The image of a public audience sitting through multiple scientific lectures, "ably illustrated" by scores of glass-plate slides, in the semidarkened baroque grotto of La Plata's Teatro Argentino illustrates the genuine intensity of Ameghinista enthusiasm as the 1910s progressed, as well as the transformative impact of posterity, as the scientist's accomplishments in life were cast in an ever brighter, gilded light.

Through the veneer of his posthumous heroism, even Ameghino's cantankerous personality quirks were remembered with a fondness bordering on reverence by friends and acquaintances and recorded in newspapers for a broad readership. Because Ameghino gave such an overwhelming proportion of his time to solitary professional pursuits, many of these personal reminiscences took place on the commuter trains that carried him daily between his work in Buenos Aires and his home in La Plata from 1902 to 1911. In these years, during which he was director of the Museo Nacional de Ciencias Naturales in Buenos Aires, Ameghino was known to take the same train in the morning and in the evening, and he was evidently surrounded by a faithful entourage of colleagues, for whom the daily commute constituted valuable social time with him, as recounted in later newspaper and biographical accounts. One such account, written by Rafael di Yorio for *El Hogar*, described these as precious moments and related stories that Ameghino had shared with the author, including a tale from his time in Paris that the newspaper embellished with an illustration for its readers (fig. 18). As di Yorio narrated it, upon leaving the opera one night, Ameghino discovered the city of Paris blanketed in snow. Passing a café as he walked, he decided to stop for an espresso. Ameghino had a strong aversion to changes in ambient temperature, believing that they had an adverse impact on one's physical constitution. Therefore, rather than entering the hot café from the snowy street, Ameghino opened the door and called to a waiter, asking for an espresso and remaining in the open doorway while the waiter prepared it. Naturally, di Yorio explained, the

Fig. 18   Florentino Ameghino drinking espresso in the snow in Paris. Rafael di Yorio, "A un paso de Ameghino," *El Hogar*, December 1, 1918.

other patrons of the café took objection to this, shouting "Close that door!" and mocking Ameghino's odd behavior. As soon as the espresso was ready, Ameghino took it out onto the snowy sidewalk, "where the waiter, slave to his duty, was forced to follow."[16]

Ameghino's defiance in the face of convention, even in a situation so trivial—and humorous—as the case of the wintry espresso in Paris, became a kind of testament to his individualistic heroism, a proof of his strength of character and his inherent argentinidad, which made him a worthy model and hero. This story had little to do with his scientific accomplishments and yet somehow added to his prestige as an eccentric scientific rogue. This kind of tale in particular, in which he appeared as the enigmatic outsider to academic and social conventions, sculpted a heroic Ameghino who constantly challenged accepted scientific and even social norms. In a speech given at the inauguration ceremony of Ameghino's bust at the zoological park on October 26, 1912, the park's director, Clemente Onelli, painted a similar picture of the sabio: "Few, very few, knew Ameghino; the sabio was not popular; popularity is not always glory. But Ameghino, this Argentine glory, at least after death should be known and his effigy popularized among the generations who follow and who, in waves of millions, happy and educated [will] parade and pass through this park."[17] It was precisely in bucking the conventions of genteel academic sociability, Onelli and others claimed, that Ameghino rose from unpopularity in life to unique prominence and heroism in death.

In casting him as a challenger to academic and social conventions, Ameghino's supporters united a number of familiar threads from Argentine nationalist lore and found an effective approach to mobilizing broad-based support for his theories and legacy long after professional science had turned away from them. Ameghino was not a gentrified member of the social aristocracy, nor was he a highly polished conversationalist. He was unpopular, uncouth, and eclectic. This kind of rugged individualism and nonconformism evoked comparisons with the gauchos and frontier heroes of Argentina's nineteenth century, which were especially apt in the first decades of the twentieth century, as the bloom was coming off the European rose in the crisis leading up to and following World War I and as socialist and anarchist political crisis rocked Argentine politics, prompting nostalgic calls for a return to traditional Argentine values, wherever they might be found.

Because his persona was so powerful and at the same time so flexible, Ameghino's symbolic life and lore were hotly contested by various parties during the early twentieth century. Some members of the professional Argentine scientific community saw Ameghino as symbolic of their country's readiness to throw over its dependence on European scientific conventions and personnel, touting him as a native son of a distinctly national Argentine science with its own methodologies and institutional forms. The Argentine

Socialist Party and especially its pedagogical institution, the Sociedad Luz, championed Ameghino as a figure embodying socialist virtues for the Argentine working classes (although Ameghino himself never openly espoused socialism). Argentine writers and intellectuals of diverse political affiliations and agendas battled over custody of Ameghino's legacy, with the result that "the dead man began to be affiliated with fights in which he had never participated," based largely, if not entirely, on the political and cultural force of his endorsement's appeal—authentic, inferred, or fabricated. So flexible and often stretched was Ameghino's legacy that one anthropologist-biographer, writing forty years after his death, lamented that the end result was, in fact, "an Ameghino who has never existed."[18]

Anthropological Heroes: Ameghino in Context

Ameghino's explosive posthumous celebrity seemed not to surprise his contemporaries. They expressed amazement at his qualities—his intellectual accomplishments, his work ethic, and his independence as a scholar—but the bare fact of his elevation to scientific sainthood and popular celebrity did not in itself raise any eyebrows in the popular press or even excite (much) jealousy among his still-living colleagues, despite the fact that many had nursed professional and personal quarrels with him before his death. This acceptance can be traced to the social practice of sanctifying scientists, well under way in Argentine society by the time of Ameghino's death in 1911. Placing Ameghino in a broader nineteenth- and twentieth-century context of scientific celebrities in Argentine society identifies him not as an anomaly but as a timely and impressive example of an Argentine scientific celebrity, produced by a society well practiced in constructing and recognizing the form.

Among the most prominent forerunners of Ameghino's scientific celebrity was Prussian naturalist Hermann Burmeister, who directed the Museo Público (later the Museo Nacional de Ciencias Naturales) in Buenos Aires between 1862 and 1892. Burmeister, a naturalist whose academic pursuits focused chiefly on paleontology and entomology, exercised direct and close control over the Museo Público during these decades, exemplifying an international trend of personalistic leadership in nineteenth-century museum science. Susan Sheets-Pyenson has used the term "museum masters" to describe a loosely bound group of scientists and administrators who "transformed their museums into world-class institutions" by means of their own ingenuity, political savvy, and forceful personalism, among other qualities.[19] Scholars have noted that Burmeister's command over the Museo Público was so strong in Argentine scientific circles that "more than the museum of this or that city or of this or that specialty . . . [the Museo Público was] only spoken of as Burmeister's museum."[20] In keeping with this, Burmeister's Museo Público was not a "public" museum as modern readers might imagine it, but rather a state-funded institution of research open to visitors at the director's discretion. While the museum listed itself as a public institution, more than one would-be visitor was turned away at the door.

Burmeister's personalistic control over the museum was sharpened by a famously aggressive and even unpleasant personality. As early as 1856, Juan María Gutierrez at the Universidad de Buenos Aires received a letter from Freiherr von Gülich, a German business envoy in Montevideo and Buenos Aires who had known Burmeister some years earlier; it cautioned Gutierrez against the Prussian scholar who was at that moment planning his first voyage to Argentina. Burmeister, von Gülich wrote, "is a very distinguished scholar, but as a man he has his failings, little friendliness and tact and too much appreciation of himself."[21] These personality traits proved to be hallmarks of Burmeister's career in Buenos Aires; biographers of the nineteenth and twentieth centuries called him "an obsessive of severe character, with a short fuse that inspired authority and fear," or alternately "a meticulous man, long-winded in the extreme."[22]

Burmeister's notoriously confrontational personality grew into a caricatured reputation even during his own lifetime, lending a sheen of celebrity to his directorship. Ameghino's ability to construct his own scientific reputation and celebrity was, in fact, directly connected with Burmeister's persona. Ameghino had first cut his scientific teeth in opposition to Burmeister, going to the director of the Museo Público with his earliest discoveries of fossil beds outside of Luján, Buenos Aires, where he was then serving as a schoolteacher. "Without doubt," Ameghino remembered thinking at the time, "Dr. Burmeister was the most competent person in the Republic to judge this question." When he presented himself at the Museo Público, however, he did not receive the treatment he had expected from a fellow devotee of science. "Here in a few words is what he said to me," Ameghino paraphrased: "Such discoveries do not inspire my confidence much; I do not believe in them; and even supposing that it was as you tell me, they are not very important and for me they lack interest." Ameghino's reaction reflected the size and strength of his own forceful personality and often explosive egotism: "How else could I have proceeded? What more could I have done? I knocked on the door of science not to deal in commercial questions or things that were strange [to science], not to forcefully assert my own personal opinions, but without pretension of any kind, asking only that science bring the truth to light, and its representative closed the door on me." Ameghino's feelings of rejection soon crystallized into lifelong rivalry. As he confided in Francisco P. Moreno years later, "This disgrace served a purpose; if, when I presented myself to Dr. Burmeister, he had examined the humble fruit of my amateur efforts, I would have been satisfied, and no longer occupied with such objects, and would be still today only a modest schoolteacher."[23]

Years after both Burmeister's and Ameghino's deaths, their rivalry still fed into the posthumous legend of each. Estanislao Zeballos, himself an important figure in Argentina's scientific world, wrote a celebratory reminiscence piece for *La Razón* in April 1920, in which he recalled this rivalry in vivid detail. In his youth, Zeballos had studied at the Museo Público under Burmeister's tutelage, in itself a marker of social status beyond Ameghino's reach. One day, while working in the museum, Zeballos asked Burmeister about Ameghino's theories on ancient man in Argentina and whether it might not be true that mankind had evolved in Patagonia. In response,

> Doctor Burmeister fixed his small green sparkling eyes upon me, and launched his favorite insult at me, with hoarse and punctuated voice:
> Ig . . . no . . . r . . . amus! . . .
> The discovery of Ameghino was, thus, discredited.[24]

Neither Ameghino's theories nor Burmeister's rebuttals are explored in the article; the anecdote stands alone, a glimpse into Burmeister's titanic personality and the lifelong antagonism between him and Ameghino.

Burmeister's reputation and notoriety attracted the kind of posthumous commemoration that Ameghino would garner almost two decades later. In May 1896, congressman Emilio Gouchón addressed the Cámara de Diputados regarding a proposal to construct a monument to Burmeister in the Museo Nacional de Ciencias Naturales, highlighting the cultural utility of his work as a scientist in service of the nation:

> I shall not hold back, señor president, from recalling to the honorable house the exceptional merits of Dr. Burmeister. He has been a sabio, in the full extension of the word, who has consecrated his life to science. . . .

The Argentine Republic has counted him among its greatest benefactors, seeing him during more than thirty years at the head of the museo nacional, which he has organized. He has studied its natural history, he has cooperated in the foundation of institutions [that are] extremely useful to the country, among others, the national academy of exact sciences, of Córdoba; in sum, he has helped all the institutions that have responded to the development of science in the Republic. Undoubtedly, Congress cannot proceed more correctly than in honoring the men who consecrate their lives to science; because science is the base of enlargement and of the well-being of a nation.[25]

The elements of Ameghino's later scientific celebrity—the utility of his work to Argentina's social development, his attributed selflessness as a researcher in the national interest, and the emblematic connections between science and nation—appear here in commemoration of a museum master who not only clashed with Ameghino on a regular basis but was not even of Argentine nationality. Burmeister, a Prussian who did not immigrate to Buenos Aires permanently until he was in his fifties, made Argentina his home but could hardly be said to be an autochthonous "Argentine" scientific hero. Nonetheless, his scientific celebrity and heroification paved the way for Ameghino's and for those who would follow them.

Ameghino's celebrity built on the public scientific cachet developed by Francisco P. Moreno and his museum in La Plata. Moreno diligently worked to include the public in the realm of scientific exploration and knowledge, inaugurating an age of public-oriented museum science in Argentina. The Museo de La Plata appeared in newspaper spreads and magazines and produced its own publications intended for broader dissemination. At the time of Ameghino's death in 1911, Moreno had already forged a highly public reputation for himself as a Patagonian explorer, founded and built the Museo de La Plata, directed it for more than twenty years (1884–1906), served on the Argentine border commission in its boundary dispute with Chile during the 1890s, donated lands in Patagonia (his reward from the national government for his involvement in the border commission) for the creation of Argentina's first national park, and in 1910 embarked upon a second career as an elected representative in the national Congress. Between the 1870s and the 1900s, Moreno's scientific celebrity easily outstripped Ameghino's. His youthful expeditions, funded by the Buenos Aires government and the Sociedad

Científica Argentina, appeared in porteño newspapers; his state-funded museums—both the short-lived Museo Antropológico y Arqueológico in Buenos Aires and the later Museo de La Plata—attracted the attention of high-profile scientific reviewers and floods of public visitors. Meanwhile, Ameghino was forced to support his own private research with the proceeds from his family stationery store. Moreno's interest in public education and access to his museum made him, especially before his departure from La Plata in 1906, a scientist of and for the people, a self-taught naturalist and, in many ways, a slightly more genteel prototype for the model that Ameghino would posthumously epitomize after 1911.

Ameghino's fate was also entwined with Moreno's in a direct personal-professional tangle; after an early period of collegiality, the two descended into rivalry and lasting antipathy. In 1886, Moreno offered the post of vice director of the Museo de La Plata to Ameghino and the position of *naturalista viajero* to his brother and collaborator Carlos, on the condition that the Ameghinos bring their famous paleontological collections with them for display and study in the museum. These collections boasted a virtually unparalleled array of paleontological and paleoanthropological specimens, including visually impressive glyptodont and other megafaunal skeletons that Moreno immediately had mounted and installed in the museum's paleontology halls. Moreno foresaw material and intellectual benefits for both parties in their upcoming collaboration. He wrote to Ameghino, "My intention is to make the Museo de La Plata into the first [museum] of America, and the Government will always assist me. As we are both guided by the same aspirations, we can advance together with complete liberty of action."[26] Ameghino was officially granted the post of vice director by government decree on July 8, 1886, and departed for La Plata, sending his collections ahead of him.

The warmth of the alliance between Moreno and Ameghino did not last, however. By October 1886, Ameghino was already directing stiffly official intramuseum correspondence to Moreno, requesting payment for his collections, which he had agreed to sell to the museum upon his employment in July. "It is clear[ly known] to the Director that my personal financial conditions do not permit me the sacrifice of donating to the province a collection that has cost me so much time, money, and work," Ameghino wrote carefully, "but wishing to facilitate the establishment's acquisition of that collection without being overly burdensome on the funds of the province, the Director can express to the Exmo. Government that I will accept the payment for it [the collection] in installments that it may deem reasonable."[27] These disturbances were minor, but layers of small resentments began to accumulate between the two naturalists, each of them stubborn and accustomed to a high degree of scientific and personal autonomy. Conflict, though certainly not inevitable, was not unprecedented for either man. By January 1888, the friendly collaboration that first bound Ameghino and Moreno together had disintegrated into bitter enmity. Ameghino left the museum in a storm of anger, leaving behind the collections that he had brought with him to La Plata.

Advertently or not, however, Ameghino had his revenge for the loss of his collections to his new enemy; he never provided the Museo de La Plata with the collections' catalogue, which identified each specimen according to provenance, associated stratigraphy, and other information. Without this contextual information, as Moreno lamented in his published review of the museum's collections in 1891, it was impossible to accurately include Ameghino's collections in the catalogue that he hoped to write. He described, with palpable venom, "the unjustifiable refusal on the part of Dr. Florentino Ameghino (ex-Sub-Director of this establishment and who was dismissed from his post by decree of the Exmo. Government, dated February 6, 1888), to deliver, despite being asked for it repeatedly, the catalogue of his collection, which was purchased in the year 1886 for the price of $16,500 *moneda nacional*." Ameghino's defiance caused a serious setback in the creation of a comprehensive collections catalogue, because "those objects do not have labels that indicate their origin nor conventional signs, and . . . many of them are simply plaster molds."[28] Also frustrating, no doubt, was the fact that the Ameghino collections constituted such a sizeable portion of the Museo de La Plata's paleontological collections, which were now significantly less useful for scientific research. This deficiency did not, of course, affect the specimens' exhibit value, and the Ameghinos' fossil skeletons and other finds rapidly became— and some remain to this day—iconic and popular exhibits. The feud between Moreno and Ameghino lasted until Ameghino's death in 1911. Thereafter, Moreno supported the government's bid to purchase Ameghino's collections, library, and personal papers for donation to the Museo Nacional de Ciencias Naturales, perhaps in a gesture of posthumous reconciliation.[29]

Ameghino's legend—as a self-taught Argentine naturalist, a scientific saint and hero standing against the stuffy social and academic conventions of the past, and a representative of what all Argentines might accomplish if they dedicated themselves to learning and to national progress—did not exist in a vacuum, but was rather fashioned in opposition to and in direct dialogue with figures such as Burmeister and Moreno, whose scientific celebrity had been forming for half a century before Ingenieros declared Ameghino to be a "modern saint" at his civil funeral in September 1911. Indeed, Ameghino owed his ability to cultivate a public scientific persona at least in part to these scuffles with fellow museum masters and public scientific figures and to the often dubious publicity he garnered through them.

Pampean Man: Human Evolution and the
Great Ameghinista Debates

Of all the elements that coalesced to lend Ameghino such scientific celebrity and controversy, the most iconic was, without question, his understanding of human evolution. Ameghino developed his ideas on the antiquity and development of humankind in Argentina in a number of prominent scientific publications, most notably *La antigüedad del hombre en el Plata* (1881) and *Filogenía* (1884). He argued, in the face of contrary theories then being proposed in Europe and North America, that *Homo sapiens* had evolved on the South American continent before the beginning of the current Quaternary period (which began approximately 2.6 million years ago), during the late Tertiary period. After assuming the directorship of the Museo Nacional de Ciencias Naturales in Buenos Aires in 1902, Ameghino began to uncover concrete fossil evidence to support his theories. At the Congreso Internacional de Americanistas held in Buenos Aires in July 1910, Ameghino announced that "the year 1909 and what has already transpired of 1910 has been particularly fruitful in finds related to fossil man in Argentine territory," listing the various finds, including human remains and artifacts, all of which, he held, supported the great antiquity of humanity in Argentina. Ameghino argued that humanity had been preceded on Argentine soil by a series of protohuman ancestors, whose remains he identified and classified under new species names, such as *Tetraprothomo argentinus* and *Homo pampaeus*, and who had eventually evolved into the modern human species.

A wave of important paleoanthropological discoveries during the later decades of the nineteenth century set the stage for Ameghino's findings. In 1886, for example, scientists at Spy, Belgium, excavated Neanderthal skeletal remains in association with Pleistocene fauna and Mousterian stone tools, connecting Neanderthals to a specific, and ancient, moment in time. In 1888, Dutch anatomist and paleontologist Eugène Dubois discovered a *Homo erectus* cranium (which he originally identified as an entirely new species,

152 OUR INDIGENOUS ANCESTORS

Pithecanthropus erectus) near Wadjak, Java, followed by a second skullcap near Trinil, Java, in 1891, raising questions about the global locations of ancient human occupation and evolution.[30] By the first decade of the twentieth century, this atmosphere of enthusiasm was sharpening in national directions. In England, fragments of a skull, mandible, and molars discovered in a gravel pit in Sussex between 1908 and 1912—known to science as Piltdown Man—were declared to be the "missing link" between modern humans and ancestral apes and placed Great Britain at the forefront of the international search for humanity's cradle.[31]

Argentines read avidly about these scientific debates in leading newspapers, including *La Nación*, which devoted full pages to photograph-saturated pieces on new discoveries, such as the March 18, 1909, story "Man of the Stone Age—The Fossil Cranium Found in Correze" (fig. 19). It detailed the recent discovery of a fossil skull uncovered in La Chapelle-aux-Saints, France. This story, like many others intended for a popular audience, combined a clear effort at public education—seen here through the museum-like, side-by-side comparison of famous craniums, including the Feldhofer Neanderthal skull, the Mousterian skull, and Dubois's Javanese skullcap, through which the pages of *La Nación* were transformed into a globe-spanning photographic museum case—with more sensational elements, including an artistic re-creation of primitive man entitled "The Origins of Humanity. The Inhabitant of the Cave of La Chapelle-aux-Saints, in the Mousterian Epoch" and a larger-than-life, leering skull on the next page.[32] Another story printed in *La Nación* on September 15, 1913, detailed the discovery of the Piltdown Man and declared that the surprising age attributed to the find—approximately at the boundary between the Tertiary and the Quaternary periods—"again confirms, in a manner as undeniable as the preceding [finds], the perspicacious and profound science of Dr. Florentino Ameghino."[33]

The controversial nature of Ameghino's ideas, however, also attracted a great deal of skepticism and attack. An important early turning point in the debates surrounding his theories came in 1912 with the publication of Smithsonian physical anthropologist Aleš Hrdlička's analysis of Ameghino's finds and theories, following his own expedition to Argentina in 1910. Hrdlička, in collaboration with geologist Bailey Willis, anthropologist W. H. Holmes, and petrologists Fred Eugene Wright and Clarence N. Fenner, concluded that "the evidence is, up to the present time, unfavorable to the hypothesis of man's great antiquity, and especially to the existence of man's predecessors in South America; and it does not sustain the theories of the evolution of man

Europeo   Negro australiano   Chimpancé
CRANEOS MOSTRANDO LAS DIFERENCIAS ENTRE EL HOMBRE DE RACE SUPERIOR, EL HOMBRE INFERIOR
MONO ANTROPOIDEO

Fig. 19a–b   Newspaper pages as a circulating, portable museum display case. The artist's rendering of "ancient man" appeared in the *Illustrated London News* on February 27, 1909, making the Atlantic crossing to Buenos Aires in less than a month. "El hombre de la edad de piedra—El craneo fósil hallado en Correze," *La Nación*, March 18, 1909.

CRANEO FOSIL DEL NEAUDERTHAL   CRANEO FOSIL DE MONSTIER   CRANEO FOSIL DE JAVA

EL CRANEO DEL MAS VIEJO DE LOS ANTEPASADOS CONOCIDOS

Fig. 19b

in general, or even of that of the American man alone, in the southern continent. The facts gathered attest everywhere merely the presence of the already
differentiated and relatively modern American Indian."[34] While historians
have argued quite correctly that Hrdlička's publication did not constitute the
first moment of criticism of Ameghino's theories, either inside or outside of
Argentina, his study was an important watershed in the debate. Published
shortly after Ameghino's death in 1911, it provided focus to already existing
international critiques of his ideas about South American human and protohuman evolution, with the result that by the mid-1910s the international scientific community had largely discounted his ideas as unlikely, poorly supported,
and debunked.

In Argentina, however, Ameghino's theoretical afterlife went very differently. Although his theories of human evolution had been essentially rejected
by the international scientific community, they continued to inspire fervent
interest within Argentina well into the twentieth century, within professional
scientific circles and among a broader network of adherents whose interest
layered science with national, political, social, and other agendas. North
American paleontologist George Gaylord Simpson captured the feeling of
Ameghinismo during a 1931 visit to Buenos Aires: "Twenty years after that
death not only were children singing his praises but also, as I soon learned,
among nonscientists in Argentina any suggestion that Florentino had ever
been mistaken was met with unbelief and resentment."[35] In the decades after
Ameghino's death, debates over the value of his human evolution theories
within Argentina took on an intensely meaning-laden tenor. While Argentine scientists struggled to negotiate a professionally acceptable path between
defending Ameghino as a founding hero of Argentine science and retreating
from his now-unpopular theories, the division between those who adhered to
these theories and those who did not—camps identified as "Ameghinophiles"
and "Ameghinophobes"—became rooted in emotion and patriotism as much
as scientific proof or approach.

A remarkable discovery along the bonaerense coast further sharpened and
ultimately embittered the debate over Ameghino's theories. Late in 1913, on
the heels of Hrdlička's damaging publication and in the glow of Ameghinista
fervor in Argentina, a prehistoric human habitation site was discovered on the
coast of Buenos Aires province, near the seaside resort town of Miramar.
Newspaper readers in Buenos Aires were informed of the "sensational discovery" of human artifacts and the remains of ancient fire pits at Miramar,
which, according to *La Nación*, constituted "the oldest remains of tertiary

man in the world." "It is a shame," the newspaper correspondent went on to
say, "that D. Florentino Ameghino has not been able to witness this definitive
proof of his theories; this triumph of his last battle in the scientific field."[36]
The discoveries at Miramar did not stop in December 1913, but continued
through the decade and into the 1920s, and their increasingly sensational
nature sparked a radicalization of the larger debates surrounding Ameghino's
theories of evolution. Miramar became a controversial proving ground on
which the scientific legitimacy and the patriotic merit of these theories were
tested, again and again, from the 1910s through the 1930s.

Newspapers presented new discoveries along the coast near Miramar in
constellation with previously reported facts and images, recycling and spin-
ning the same elements into different arrangements to appeal to a readership
eager for news.[37] A June 7, 1914, story entitled "Prehistoric Finds," printed in
La Nación, offers an example. This article, which included several photographs and sketches, discussed a parade of artifacts uncovered at Miramar
and elsewhere, supporting Ameghino's theories and defending their scientific
soundness. The article was written as a comprehensive and informative tour
de force for the responsible public reader, the Argentine of conscience, whose
interest in paleoanthropology was construed in the pages of La Nación as
natural and patriotic.[38] Images from this story, as from others, reappeared
later as stock imagery in the illustration of Miramar's sensational landscape
and finds. Every new discovery prompted coverage in the press, and virtually
every story was accompanied by a patriotic message, an homage to Ameghino
and to the industrious, indefatigable Argentine spirit. "The latest, new, and
clear proof of the extremely remote antiquity from which man has existed in
Argentine territory, proving his origin in this soil, has just been discovered,"
an anonymous correspondent for La Nación announced on November 22,
1914. "Any slow-acting or incredulous spirit for whom the previous proof
would not have been enough . . . will have to surrender to the evidence of the
sensational find that today we will make public." This find, a projectile point
discovered embedded in the fossilized femur of an ancient toxodont (a genus
of large herbivorous mammals of the late Pliocene and Pleistocene epochs,
endemic to South America), proved that human beings had occupied the site
contemporaneously with toxodonts, allowing for more concrete dating of the
human artifacts discovered thus far. The find also demonstrated, the article
asserted, that the human inhabitants of the prehistoric bonaerense pampas
had been organized hunters, and therefore intelligent beings, at a very early
date relative to demonstrable signs of similar intelligence in Europe. The

article concluded on a palpably patriotic note. "Today science in Europe has been silenced by the war, only América works," the correspondent reminded readers, effectively throwing down a national scientific gauntlet. The discoveries at Miramar presented Argentine science with, it seemed, a tremendous opportunity for the country to prove the capacity of its national science and for its scientific institutions to take up positions of leadership on the changing global stage.[39]

Crucially, however, while newspaper writers exhorted national museum scientists and scientific institutions to represent Argentina in this debate on the world stage, they distinctly saw themselves as the purveyors of scientific knowledge to nonscientific Argentine readers. Between the 1910s and 1930s, a division of labor between professional science and the popular press effected a sharp bifurcation in which authors wrote for distinctly prescribed audiences. Consider, for example, a piece written for *La Razón* in August 1915, in which the prominent newspaper interviewed Luís María Torres, an anthropologist at the Museo de La Plata (later its director), and presented the public with his thoughts. The unnamed author framed the purpose of the piece in frank and revealing terms:

> As is natural, the public, attracted by admiration for genuinely scientific doctrines that, in honor of truth, it must be said that they do not entirely understand, desire to inform themselves, in an accessible and easy manner, regarding that which in reality is the central point of Ameghino's work: his revolutionary scientific theories. And it is responding to this just desire of the public that we have proposed to make known the conclusions to which we have come, after rigorous scientific analysis, with respect to one of the most [well-]known theories of Ameghino: the American origin of man. To this end, we have interviewed the doctor Luís María Torres.

Invoking Torres as an authority on the basis of his museum and university credentials, the article acted as a scientific intermediary between the museum and the public, outlining Torres's position on Ameghino's theories, the recent finds at Miramar, and the criticism of European and North American scholars on both fronts, all "in an accessible and easy manner." Torres himself expressed some reservations about Ameghino's theories, research into which was certainly still ongoing in 1915. Yet the correspondent for *La Razón* concluded emphatically, "The foundational studies prove Ameghino correct with respect to the archaic character of the indigenous cultures of the South of the province of Buenos Aires, although detailed confirmation is still lacking with relation to the anthropological characteristics of the human remains discovered recently in the region of Miramar. . . . And, as the reader will comprehend, this is no small thing for the solidification of the glory of Ameghino."[40]

The implications of such an article are twofold. First, the opinions of a professional museum anthropologist such as Torres were deemed relevant to a public audience and worthy of considerable time and page space by the editors of *La Razón*. This story represents a common type, frequently printed in the early decades of Argentina's twentieth century, in which museum anthropologists were approached to give their opinions on a topic or even, although less often, commissioned to write such pieces themselves.[41] Torres was a scientific celebrity in Argentine culture, so well known that his face was repeatedly caricatured in newspapers and popular magazines during the 1910s and 1920s (see fig. 20). Second, in printing these stories, *La Razón* clearly saw itself, along with other newspapers of the time, as filling a void unsatisfied by museums themselves. Museums were, it seems, not open enough by public standards, nor their publications accessible enough. The public demanded greater measures of cultural utility from anthropological science, and newspapers stepped forward to fill the void. It is interesting to note, in this context, that museum scientists such as Torres were willing participants in such appropriations, offering their opinions for quotation and publication in daily papers on a fairly regular basis.

The bifurcation between professional scientific and popular press writers, and the kinds of authority they wielded, led to a scientific-popular fusion in newspaper accounts, producing a doubly compelling, if sometimes contradictory, whole. In the May 1916 article "Prehistoric Man," an unnamed writer for *La Nación* stated with unmistakable authority that "science is not obscure, but most simply clear." In this light, he contended, the evidence from Miramar was indisputable: "The finds are undeniable. . . . The only ones who cannot see it are the blind." The article further hailed Ameghino as "the greatest of the Argentine sabios, . . . [who] dedicated two-thirds of his life to the study of geology and wrote volumes in which he studied the formations and established the plan of the layers of our soil." The author then made his case for the strategic importance of science in the daily press: "As it is our custom to speak familiarly with our readers, we offer today some simple and clear points regarding geography and geology, with respect to the situation and character of the hillsides of Miramar, a point which is currently of public

Fig. 20 Caricatures of Luís María Torres. Left: "Importante es el descubrimiento de E. R. Wagner: El Dr. Torres, director del Museo de Historia Natural de La Plata, contesta a la encuesta de *Crítica*," *Crítica*, September 12, 1929. Right: "Doctor Luis M.ª Torres, director del Museo de La Plata," *Caras y Caretas*, October 2, 1920. This caricature is accompanied by a lighthearted poem: "One fossil of the museum, very joyful / said to a skeleton of another race: /— Torres is an active and scholarly man, / and, besides, a guardian so caring / that, when no one is looking, he hugs us." (Un fósil del museo, muy gozoso, / le dijo a un esqueleto de otra raza: /—Torres es hombre activo y estudioso, / y, además, un tutor tan cariñoso / que, cuando no hay ninguno, nos abraza.)

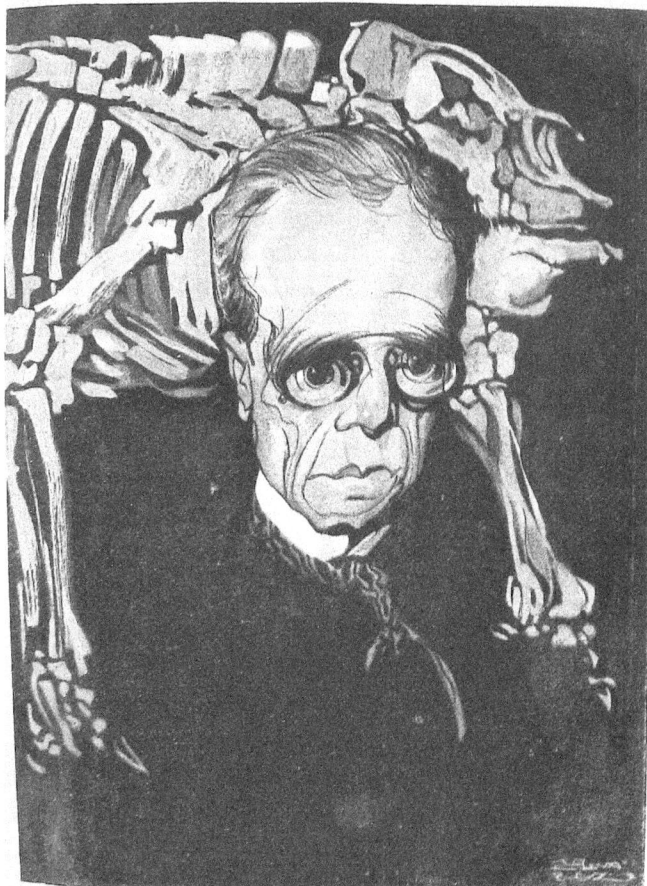

curiosity and of highest scientific interest." This article expertly fused scientific and popular appeals, balancing the emotional tone of praise for Ameghino with maps, stratigraphical cross sections, charts, and images designed to educate the public in the scientific basics of Ameghino's theories, the finds at Miramar, and the principles of geology underlying the debate surrounding them (see fig. 21).[42]

The popular press's appropriation of scientific language and authority in the Ameghinista debate, however, drew strong criticism from certain quarters. Some, irked by what they saw as too free a mixture of emotional and scientific languages in the pro-Ameghino press, accused museum and university scientists of ignoring the issue at their peril and of allowing Argentina's national and innate scientific inclinations to decay into vapid hero worship and unthinking sensationalism. One editorialist wrote, "The extremely small world of the men of science ignores almost absolutely the pseudoscientific pseudo-discussions conducted through the newspapers. . . . Sabios, in general, ignore everyone who is marginal to the science that they cultivate and dominate."[43]

By the beginning of the 1920s, the emotional payload of these debates between pro-Ameghino and anti-Ameghino factions was intensifying palpably. The April 19, 1920, publication in *El Diario* of an editorial entitled "The Tertiary Man of Miramar: It Is Necessary for the Honor of the Country That the Farce of This Find Finish" sparked an explosion of controversy on both sides of the issue. "It is time," the author proclaimed, "that the ridiculous story affirming the existence of tertiary man in Miramar was finished once and for all." The article laid out several objections to the Miramar discoveries, including the question also raised by some professional scientific critics about the Miramar artifacts' morphological similarity to objects of historical and even contemporary indigenous societies from nearby regions. In other words, the artifacts discovered at Miramar looked virtually the same as those associated with nearby indigenous cultures from the recent past and those still living in the present. How was it possible, the article challenged, that humankind's most ancient members had inhabited Argentina over two million years ago and had continued to live there without making any technological progress of any kind over the entire history of the human species? To believe such an argument, the author contended, was contrary to the dictates of evolutionary science and anathema to national pride: "It is necessary to reflect that the country cannot be at the mercy of this scientific misery, because it weakens us. . . . The country cannot meekly witness the destruction of our cultural

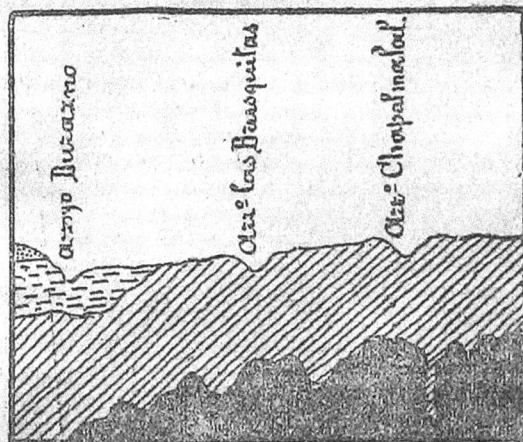

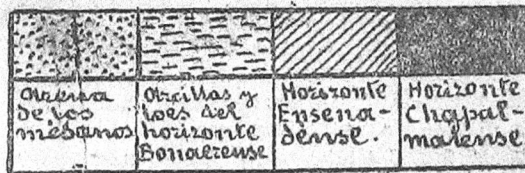

Fig. 21 Stratigraphy cross section and map. "El hombre prehistórico," *La Nación*, May 15, 1916.

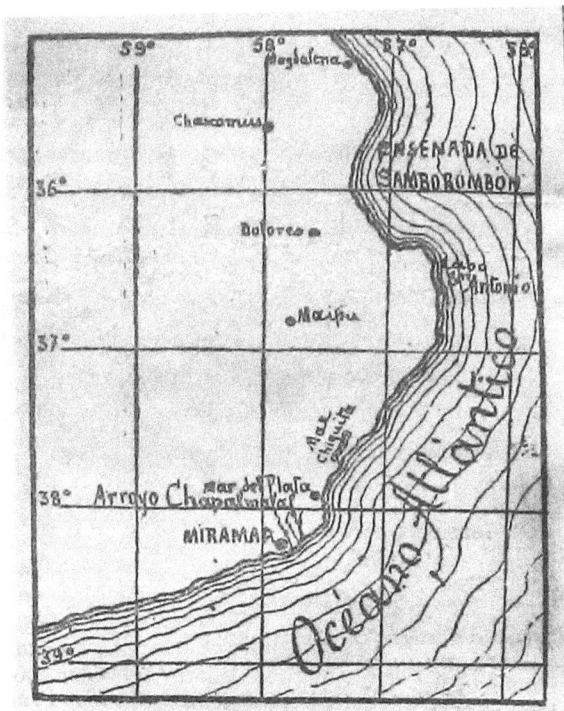

process, without leaving record of their protest; and we say this, because these errors have been spread even in teaching texts." Argentines needed to stand up to this distortion of their own national scientific heritage and show themselves worthy of their national legacy. "Tertiary man does not exist in Miramar, nor [do] traces of his existence," the article insisted. "If there is some problem that requires elucidation with respect to this question, leave it to the specialist men of science, for them to elucidate it, and do not mystify the public, with publications that lack mastery [of the topic] and seriousness."[44] This author's connection of the "ancient man" of Miramar to indigenous cultures of Argentina's past and present represented a rarity in the popular press. Unlike displays of pampean indigenous bodies in the Museo de La Plata or of pre-Columbian indigenous archaeology in the Museo Etnográfico in Buenos Aires and the Instituto de Etnología in Tucumán, discussions about human evolution in Argentina did not commonly invoke indigenous culture, instead envisioning these early humans as ape-like protohumans, without a discernible culture or connection with human groups more specific than "humankind."

An article published ten days later in the newspaper *El Argentino* responded vehemently to *El Diario*'s anonymous editorialist. It was signed by an anonymous author in Dolores, Buenos Aires province, who used the telling nom de plume "Un Ameghinofilo." He wrote of the *El Diario* editorial,

> I am accustomed to learning about the most ardent controversies surrounding this theme and related subjects, such that I would not [normally] greatly bother myself with the scant and already worn-out framework of that string of stupidities. But the excesses of discourtesy of language used anonymously by the arguers, such as "scientific farce" and "blackmail," carry grave charges for that respectable institution that is the Museo Nacional de Historia Natural de Buenos Aires, and even the honesty of that most modest man of science who directs it [Florentino's brother Carlos was then acting as interim director], that must not be allowed to pass without an energetic reply.[45]

The author's invocation of the Ameghino family honor and respectability, as compared to the dishonor and discourtesy of the author of the editorial in *El Diario*, captured an important element of the developing controversy. By 1920, the concrete scientific authority of Ameghino's theories of human evolution was, at best, arguable. The emphasis of the conversation was shifting, at least in part, away from purely scientific debate and toward patriotic and cultural rhetoric; in this context, the rejection or adherence to Ameghinista doctrine made a statement about a person's political, national, and cultural priorities.

By the 1920s, the finds at Miramar—the keystone of scientific and sensational debates surrounding Ameghino's theories of human evolution after his death—were also becoming the subject of intensifying controversy. In January 1922, the newspaper *El Pueblo* reprinted an article from the *Revista Chilena de Historia y Geografía*, in which Chilean naturalist and intellectual Ramón Laval attacked what he saw as the unscientific proceedings at Miramar and especially the problematic figure of Lorenzo Parodi, the Museo Nacional's dedicated naturalista viajero in residence at the site. Laval's article, which formed the first part of a series entitled "El Ameghinismo: Antiscientific Charlatanism and Machiavellian Industrialization. The Word of Men of Science," attacked Parodi as emblematic of the base motivations he saw lurking behind the sensationalism of Miramar, as well as the damage it stood to inflict on Argentina's scientific reputation. It seemed incredible, Laval wrote, that Parodi was finding precisely what he was sent to find: "This naturalista viajero has incredible luck and continues to discover in tertiary deposits of the hillsides of Miramar, fossils and archaeological objects, especially 'bolas' of stone, with or without equatorial groove, that, naturally, must proceed from human industry and, thus, are evident proof that man existed during that epoch and that F. Ameghino was in the right in affirming so." The suspicious regularity of Parodi's success between 1913 and 1922 had, Laval argued, ultimately undermined the trustworthiness of the finds: "But now the result is that in the Argentine Republic, and even more so in the world beyond, the truth of the said sites is being doubted, and a legion of sabios of Europe and América is already forming that sees in all this nothing more than a farce, a sad farce, that discredits the good name and the fame that the cultivators of science had so deservedly attained in the institutions and academies of the neighboring republic [of Argentina]." In other words, Ameghinista enthusiasm over the Miramar finds was not a harmless mistake; it was materially harming the reputation that Argentine anthropologists had worked to build and which brought international respect and stature to the nation. There was a patriotic imperative, then, to ending this "antiscientific charlatanism." Laval also praised the *El Diario* editorial of April 19, 1920 (which had so incensed the "Ameghinofilo" of Dolores), quoting it at length.[46]

Swedish archaeologist and scholar and longtime Argentine resident Eric Boman contributed to the same series in *El Pueblo* the next day, declaring his moral and intellectual compulsion to speak out as a scientist:

> Rarely have scientific theories been the object of a rejection so unanimous and universal as has been the case with the anthropogenetic theories of Ameghino and the osteological pieces on which they are founded. Not even in Buenos Aires, among the few anthropologists who exist here, is there anyone who accepts them. But it is truly curious, as señor Laval observes with good reason, that none of them has published their opinions in this respect, to make known to the public what Ameghino's theories consist of and what specialists argue with respect to them, two things of which the aficionados and uninformed persons [*profanos*] who compose the "ameghinistas" are entirely ignorant, who are guided by the calls of newspapers and the propaganda of certain persons who exploit those theories with political purposes or other purposes alien to science.[47]

Boman called Laval to task for his overly personal attacks on Parodi and yet seemed unable to resist the temptation to add his own fuel to the fire. He reported that "various trustworthy people have informed me, there [in Miramar] as well as here in Buenos Aires," that Parodi was committing the ultimate sin of mixing science and commerce, augmenting his museum-paid wages as a naturalista viajero "by serving as guide to people who pass the season at the seaside resort of Miramar": "The visitors to the baths, curious to see something of the traces of the famous 'tertiary man,' call Parodi, who takes them to the hillsides in a small car that he owns and frequently indicates that they should dig in such or such a place, where it seems they almost always have the great luck to find some object, such as a bola or worked stone, etc. According to what I have heard, [people] customarily pay twenty or thirty pesos for one of these excursions, including tip."[48] Not only, then, did Parodi seek to profit from his scientific work, in itself reprehensible to the sensibilities of contemporary scientific professionalism, but he went so far as to seed the field with false artifacts for tourists to discover. The moral consequences of such an action in the field of scientific excavation were profound; if Parodi felt no compunction about playing such a trick on tourists paying him for his services, what was to stop him from playing the same trick on his scientific employers?

Boman, certainly understanding the implications of the accusations he was not quite making, and perhaps not wanting to shoulder responsibility for them, attempted the following bizarre gloss: "I have no personal reason to doubt the honesty of Parodi, but generally speaking, the intervention in discoveries of this class of a person of his conditions, whom it is impossible should be guided by scientific interests, but only by pecuniary interests and the conservation of employment, cannot but instill suspicions of possible fraudulence." Parodi's class background—compounded, perhaps, by the fact that he was uneducated, an illiterate Italian immigrant with an imperfect command of Spanish—meant to Boman that he could not possibly be interested in the scientific questions that underlay the work he had been employed to oversee. In the end, Boman argued that although Ameghino's theories might have merit and the finds at Miramar might be genuine, the fact that Parodi had been the one to uncover many of them placed them in insurmountable doubt. Boman explained that "the science of our times requires a strict scientific control of the deeds that must serve to found its conclusions, [and must] not allow affirmations and tales of the uninitiated, nor be persuaded by the claims of the newspapers." In a sense, Parodi became emblematic in Boman's mind of the inappropriate overlap of professional science and popular enthusiasm taking place in Argentina.[49]

Argentines beyond the scientific academy, however, often seemed less convinced by scientists' arguments, and the bifurcation between scientist and nonscientist became, at times, openly confrontational. In May 1923, porteño newspapers announced the arrival in Buenos Aires of a fossilized human cranium, uncovered not by professional museum anthropologists but by a nonscientist named Juan Vinría, who had brought his find from southern Santa Cruz province to the director of the Buenos Aires Zoological Garden, Clemente Onelli. *La Razón* ran a photograph of Vinría sitting beside his wife on a park bench, with the skull, wrapped in a cloth, sitting in his lap (fig. 22). Onelli, in his comments to *La Razón*, which ran below this photograph, painted a plainly unflattering picture of the couple, citing their ignorance of law 9080, which required them to freely surrender the skull to a state-affiliated scientific body. Rather than fulfill their legal and patriotic duty, Onelli charged, they "dreamed of millions." They thought not at all of the higher questions to which their find pertained, which he referred to by alluding to (and apparently misquoting) Hamlet, in English: "to be al [*sic*] not to be." Onelli assured *La Razón* that a meeting of "true geologists and paleontologists and petrologists" was to be held immediately to assess the specimen, though he himself suspected it to be a skull-shaped stone rather than an actual cranium.[50]

In its afternoon edition of the same day, *La Razón* ran a cartoon of Onelli holding the cranium—which had been found in Paso Ibáñez and rapidly acquired the moniker "el cráneo Ibáñez"—aloft in Shakespearean contemplation (fig. 23). The cartoon's caption read, "Onelli (parodying Hamlet)—To be or not to be." The purpose of the very brief article that accompanied this rapidly produced cartoon was to update the public on the status of the cra-

Fig. 22   Señor and Señora Juan Vinría. "El craneo que da que decir. Manifestaciones del director del Zoológico," *La Razón*, May 3, 1923.

Fig. 23   Cartoon of Clemente Onelli. "El cráneo fósil," *La Razón*, May 3, 1923.

nium's verification, still in process. It reported, "This afternoon, señor Onelli, the owner of the cranium, and some geologists and paleontologists held a meeting with the purpose of examining the cranium and determining what it truly was. At the moment of printing of the present edition the meeting of the referred-to experts was still in session, supposing, nonetheless, that they are dealing with a stone in the form of a human skull."[51] This was, in fact, the entire text of the article, but this very brief piece suggested that the skull commanded enough public interest to merit running two stories about it on the same day.

The following day, both *La Nación* and *Crítica* ran stories proclaiming that the committee of scientists who had met to examine the cráneo Ibáñez agreed that it was not a skull at all, but a stone shaped like a cranium. *La Nación* announced, "The piece found in Paso Ibáñez is not a cranium, but a stone. It is simply a 'caprice of nature.' Such is the opinion of a group of experts"—who included Robert Lehmann-Nitsche, Félix Outes, Eric Boman, José Imbelloni, and Onelli.[52] Vinría would not be returning to Santa Cruz with a fortune earned by selling his priceless fossil, but with a mildly interesting curiosity that offered no serious interest for the scientists who gathered to examine it.

The story that ran on May 4, 1923, in *Crítica*, written by Argentine poet and self-styled "viscount" Emilio Lascano Tegui, presented the case somewhat differently. The article's flamboyant title, "The Sabios Recognize the Existence of a New Cobblestone. Regarding a Millenarian Cranium. The Fortune of a Naive Man, Evaporated.—The Golden Coins Transformed into Fig Leaves," set the tone for an irreverent account of the committee's proceedings, which Lascano Tegui witnessed, as well as its treatment of Vinría and his wife. Having listened to the scientists chat with one another before the examination began, Lascano Tegui noted, "Sabios are don Juans with theories. They love them like their Dulcineas and live in speaking well of them, like post office employees speak well of the Harrods girls." Once it became clear that the committee did not believe his find to be a cranium at all, Vinría, according to Lascano Tegui, responded with the following outburst: "'Do you not see,' the disconsolate proprietor returned then to join me—in my quality as an ignoramus—'that my cranium lacks for nothing? It has the palate, it has the orbits, it has its parietal well marked and it has that which no other skull has: it has a nose?'" Lascano Tegui quipped in reply that Vinría's skull had "an excess of nose, it is what they disdain. The skull of Cyrano, in life, would not have merited less ridicule." Later, Lascano Tegui attempted to console Vinría's wife, assuring her that because of the press attention their "skull" had attracted in recent days, someone would without doubt offer to buy it, making them rich. "And the sabios?" she asked. Lascano Tegui replied,

> "The sabios are the test weight with which universal ignorance plays. 'The sabios play at [being] the blind rooster in the path of truth.' Have you ever known a rich sabio despite what he knew?"

"No."

"Then, have faith in him [your husband]. They say to possess the truth is not at all interesting. By contrast you are the owner of a lie that is the spur [literally, whip (*látigo*)] of life and the spectacle par excellence until the end of the world. Amen."[53]

It seems that nobody did step forward to buy the craneo Ibáñez, but Lascano Tegui's point was nonetheless a poignant one during the 1920s, when the gulf between professional science and popular enthusiasm yawned wide and the opinion of museum scientists and sabios could be discounted by the importance—expressed here in a decidedly tongue-in-cheek fashion—of popular interest, patriotism, and celebrity.

•

Conclusion

Although professional science sought quietly to forget Ameghino's more controversial theories and the sensationalized associations of discoveries such as those at Miramar and "finds" such as the cráneo Ibáñez, the enormous symbolic weight and power of Ameghino and his ideas in Argentine national culture were not forgotten. Ameghinistas continued to hail him as a scientific hero and to champion his theories well into the 1930s. Professional science also participated in Ameghino's continuing sanctification in ritualized and symbolic ways—celebrating the anniversary of his death or commemorating his memory with a monument or plaque.

Ameghino's celebrity and popular appropriations of his scientific legacy reflected the changing social life of anthropology in the 1930s, as Argentina's dominant political and cultural ideas began to change. By the end of the decade, a crescendo in conservative nationalism would inspire new searches for national heritage and culture that challenged liberal models; indigenous cultures of the ancient past and present and the anthropologists who studied them would fall from imaginings of national identity, to be replaced by more Hispanic imagery and historical figures. In the early decades of the century, however, newspapers, monuments, and public commemorations attested to the powerful cultural utility of anthropology beyond the realm of museums and, in particular, to the appeal of scientific heroes such as Ameghino, who captured the public imagination and expressed something authentically Argentine that professional museum anthropologists were unable to control.

Ameghino's theories of human evolution, the spectacular and scientific ramifications of the finds at Miramar, and Argentines' conflicted quests to embrace and distance themselves from their "greatest sabio" reveal the profound importance of museum anthropology in twentieth-century creole Argentine culture and national identity. The very success of museum anthropologists' grand-scale scientific project, in fact, could often be measured in the ability of scientific ideas to escape from their control and to develop new meanings in broader circles of Argentine society.

.

Epilogue: Reflections and Remaining Questions

Although widely varied in form, all of the expressions of creole Argentine interest in indigenous cultures explored in this study share four crucial commonalities. First, creole Argentines, from museum curators to newspaper editors, provincial statesmen to public schoolteachers, shared a conviction that indigenous cultures of the past and present (or, in the case of early twentieth-century Ameghinistas, protohumans who gave rise to all humankind, including indigenous peoples) were valuable, interesting, and important. Second, for the actors discussed here, the inherent importance of indigenous cultures was directly and consciously connected with preoccupations about national identity. Third, all of the expressions of interest in indigenous cultures examined here offered a privileged position to a creole present, as distinct from a glorified indigenous past (even the northwestern Generación del Centenario, in its strategic embrace of indigenous ethnographies, retained the present-day creole core of its identity project). Finally, all of these actors underlined the indispensability of science as a way of knowing about indigenous cultures in Argentina's past and present, and they stressed the importance of science that served the nation and society. From the Museo de La Plata's physical displays of indigenous bodies collected during the Conquest, to romantic evocations of the ancient northern past in the Museo Etnográfico and Instituto de Etnología, to celebrations of Ameghino's controversial ideas in public monuments and commemorations, late nineteenth- and early twentieth-century museum anthropology offered a scientific lens through which members of Argentina's consciously progressive creole nation-state could embrace a shared indigenous heritage, while still maintaining their national modernity and ethnic Europeanness.

Moreover, as social interest in indigenous cultures escaped the bounds of professional museum science—appearing in newspapers, magazines, popular societies, public celebrations, congressional sessions, and antiquities markets—scientists and nonscientists debated how and by whom Argentines' inherent scientific curiosity could best be explored. Sensational newspaper stories vied against more somber professional studies, and museum scientists countered popular actors' accusations about their own elitism with laments about the uninformed hobbyism of the masses. Entangled in the technicalities of these debates we can see the underlying importance of science to creole understandings of indigenous cultures during the late nineteenth and early twentieth centuries; even as newspaper editors, regionalist elites, private collectors, statesmen, schoolteachers, women's groups, and others attempted to leverage control over the scientific institutions and languages of Argentina's anthropological world, they acknowledged and underscored science's authority. Although histories of Argentine national identity most often focus on the emergence of a "white" or European national community, this book has argued that understanding creole engagement with indigenous cultures reveals an important element of Argentina's national identity formation—that is, creole Argentines actively embraced narratives of their own whiteness and yet strategically constructed their nation's indigenous heritage as part of the identity formation process. This calculated balancing act between romantic indigenous inheritance and modern creole destiny strongly connects Argentina with broader hemispheric trends of national identity formation.

The meanings of indigenous cultures within creole Argentine society—civic, regional, and national—are perhaps uniquely visible in the everyday interactions between museum anthropologists and their various publics. Commonplace actions such as visiting museums or reading newspapers revealed the active meaning making that surrounded indigenous cultures and objects in Argentine anthropology museums, as well as the often heated debates over which interpretations were correct and who decided. The Vinrías, returning to Paso Ibáñez with their stone skull in 1923, could certainly attest to the power of these debates (see chapter 4), as could the tucumano government in its campaign to halt the removal of its menhir in 1936 (see chapter 3) and Debenedetti as he publicly turned his Museo Etnográfico's attention to Egypt's Valley of the Kings (see chapter 2). A cultural historical approach to museum practice, objects, and scientific ideas allows us to explore not only the scientific theories that anthropologists developed in their museums, but also the social life of those ideas among nonscientists. As museums attracted greater and more demanding attention from outside actors during the late nineteenth and early twentieth centuries, the separation between an inner scientific academy and an outer uninformed public threatened to break down, and museums became both scientific and social platforms where the meanings of indigenous cultures could be debated by scientists and nonscientists alike.

The social utility of creole Argentines' strategic embrace of indigenous heritage also begins to explain why, by the end of the 1930s, the importance of indigenous cultures to Argentina's imagined national heritage dimmed in the face of rising conservative political and cultural thought. This conservative nationalism was often anti-foreigner, anti-communist, and anti-liberal, with elements of pro-fascist, anti-immigration, and anti-Semitic sympathies. Conservative nationalists in the 1930s rehabilitated Catholic and Hispanic traditions that had been marginalized by earlier liberal and radical regimes, reframing these elements as distinguished and authentic customs of Argentina's ancestral past. Conservative nationalists also restyled liberal narratives of Argentine history, vilifying previously heroized liberal statesmen such as Bartolomé Mitre and Domingo Faustino Sarmiento as overly Europeanized, and identifying the epitome of authentic Argentine leadership in military leaders such as the mid-nineteenth-century caudillo Juan Manuel de Rosas. In conjunction with rejecting liberalist politics, conservatives took an anti-imperialistic stance against foreign involvement in Argentine affairs and accused the liberal oligarchy of surrendering Argentina's economic interests and natural resources to foreign interests.[1]

In this new climate, institutions created by earlier governments—including many anthropology museums—gradually lost state and popular support, becoming stigmatized as overly steeped in foreign intellectual traditions. As Nicola Miller writes, "From the 1930s onwards in Argentina, even to identify oneself as an intellectual was to invite accusations of supporting the *vendepatria* oligarchy and imperialism against the interests of the people."[2] Visions of Argentina's indigenous heritage, as strategically produced by museum anthropology, were displaced by newly ascendant symbols of national culture such as the Juan Manuel de Rosas Institute for Historical Research, established in 1938. Although anthropologists in museums and in new professional organizations (such as the Sociedad Argentina de Antropología, established in 1936) continued to pursue anthropological and archaeological research into the indigenous cultures of Argentina, this new conservative way of imagining the country's heritage and past remained dominant throughout the decade and beyond, turning scientific attention and funding toward criollo folk culture and Spanish colonial history.[3] Histories of anthropology in twentieth-century Argentina often begin in the 1930s and 1940s and examine an anthropological community that operated within a different intellectual and social world than its predecessors of the later nineteenth and early twentieth centuries.[4]

As do all histories, this study contains significant silences and unanswered questions, the most prominent of which are the voices of indigenous peoples. Indigenous peoples in Argentina underwent traumatic and varied experiences of violence during the later nineteenth and twentieth centuries. They were targets of military conquest and physical violence, were often physically displaced and relocated to territories not of their own choosing, worked under exploitative conditions for low wages, and were denied political rights and even recognition as culturally distinct communities. It is within this context that creole Argentines used museums and science to reincorporate indigenous cultures into national and regional pasts, locating themselves as the true inheritors of indigenous culture. Anthropology in Argentina developed, as elsewhere in the Americas, in response to scientific and political imperatives to understand and control the existence of indigenous peoples within a growing country in search of a unifying identity and path. Scholars of colonialism and settler colonialism have noted that anthropology—in addition to creating a sense of national heritage by connecting indigenous peoples with the natural landscapes claimed by the nation-state—could be used to exoticize and control indigenous peoples, through the rationalizing media of science. Through museum spaces in particular, colonial powers and nation-states possessed and distanced themselves from non-Western cultures by removing bodies and objects from their original context in space and time, hence disempowering or emptying them and recreating them as trophies, art objects, and ciphers in the hands of Western possessors.[5] This process, as María Luz Endere, Plácido Cali, and Pedro Paulo A. Funari have noted, "made archaeological heritage an intellectual property owned exclusively by academic institutions, thus depriving indigenous descendants of all access to their ancestors' cultural heritage."[6] This adoption, then, while it reveals the conflicted importance of indigenous cultures to creole identity building, also denied the participation of indigenous voices in the interpretation of their own cultures.

In conducting the research for this study, it became clear that although museum anthropologists in the late nineteenth and early twentieth centuries spent their careers studying indigenous cultures in Argentina's past and present, they did not see individual indigenous perspectives as an important part of their work. Indigenous voices appear in museum journals and newspapers of this period as tellers of folk stories and singers of ritual songs, but not as voices commenting on their own transformation into scientific objects and data. Where I have found indigenous voices, I have worked conscientiously to include them, but this does not entirely or even largely resolve the absence of these voices elsewhere. Scholars have fruitfully addressed indigenous peoples' relationships with anthropology, museums, and repatriation in late twentieth- and twenty-first-century Argentina, but their studies lay well outside the chronological bounds of this book.[7] In calling attention to the absence of such voices in this history, I hope to inspire further work that may be able to incorporate more indigenous voices into the historical study of this crucial period in Argentine indigenous-state relations, and even to uncover contemporary indigenous perspectives of anthropologists' work.

On a related note, scholarship on memory, as a way of understanding and addressing experiences of social trauma and violence, has shown the power of collective and individual meaning making in times of dislocation and forgetting.[8] This study examines processes of what might be described as external or projected memory making—referring not to the memories of indigenous peoples, but to their transformation *into* memory by creole Argentine scientists and others. To use memory as a central analytical tool here would perhaps be anachronistic, since the ideas supporting memory scholarship only emerged in the later twentieth century. However, the earlier history told here may well offer insights into the origins of memory politics among Argentina's indigenous peoples today.

In recent decades, the important legacies of the nineteenth- and early twentieth-century museum anthropologists examined here have made themselves felt in indigenous communities' often tense relationships with the Argentine state and with state-affiliated museums. The indigenous material culture collections and human remains held by museums in Argentina began to attract sharpening interest in the late twentieth century, in connection with the cultural and patrimonial demands of indigenous revitalization movements. The Museo de La Plata has been a particular focus of repatriation efforts due to its sizeable collections of indigenous human remains dating from the late nineteenth century and, especially, the remains of well-known indigenous individuals (see chapter 1). Indigenous and nonindigenous parties have petitioned the Museo de La Plata to release remains in its collections for return and reburial since the mid-1970s, but no request was successful until the 1990s. In 1994, the remains of the Tehuelche cacique Incayal, who died in captivity at the Museo de La Plata in 1888 and was retained as part of its collections, were transferred to Tecka, in the province of Chubut, after a four-year campaign to establish a legally recognized connection between Incayal and the indigenous community requesting his return. Incayal's remains were interred in a monument built for the purpose.[9] To date, the Museo de La Plata has participated in two other repatriation projects, returning the remains of Rankülche (or Ranquel) cacique Panquitruz Guor (also known as Mariano Rosas) to Leuvucó, in the province of La Pampa, in 2001, and transferring the remains of an Aché girl named Damiana, among other Aché remains, to the Federación Nativa Aché de Paraguay for reburial in 2010.[10]

A 2006 document approved by the Facultad de Ciencias Naturales y Museo of the Universidad Nacional de La Plata captures the museum's changing philosophy and practices toward human remains in its collections at the beginning of the twenty-first century. The document suggests that recent developments in museum practice and ethics, alongside indigenous rights legislation, have prompted museums to "open their doors to a policy of co-management, creating a new space for interaction with both indigenous cultures and the general public." Like their predecessors at the turn of the twentieth century, museum scientists of the early twenty-first century underscore "the important role that museums have today as disseminators and informal educational spaces," now in an effort to promote multiculturalism in marked contrast to practices in Argentine museums a century earlier.[11]

Despite such important steps, however, much work remains. María Luz Endere points out that although the national and various provincial governments have passed legislation supporting indigenous rights, their efforts are not yet coordinated nationwide, and "Congress still needs to pass a whole set of new laws to put into practice these new constitutional rights and guarantees that relate to indigenous cultural heritage."[12] Moreover, the difficulties that have so often marked repatriation debates in museums such as the Museo de La Plata reveal the ongoing legacies of nineteenth-century museum anthropology and an unfortunate continuity in indigenous relations with the Argentine state: while the state is officially prepared to return these remains to their descendants, the onus rests on indigenous communities to prove their genealogical connection with the remains—to the state's satisfaction. In other words, the narratives of indigenous possession and inheritance built by creole Argentines in the late nineteenth and early twentieth centuries still influence state policy today. It is an indigenous community's claim that must be proven; the Argentine state's claim, until proven otherwise, is unquestioned. The connections between nineteenth- and twentieth-century anthropology and present-day repatriation campaigns will repay future scholars' efforts to uncover and understand them.

The history of museum anthropology in Argentina, and through this history a greater understanding of creole Argentines' strategic adoption and possession of indigenous cultures, places these recent events in greater historical context. This book has argued that narratives of national whiteness, which have so influentially shaped Argentina's historiography, were complemented and complicated by creole Argentines' strategic incorporation of indigenous cultures within their own national identity. Museum anthropology, in revealing several conflicting narratives of indigenous heritage produced by creole Argentines during the late nineteenth and early twentieth centuries, uncovers new elements in Argentina's nation-making project that add depth to traditional ideas about total indigenous erasure. If this book exposes some of this complexity and thereby begins to place Argentina in more dynamic relationship with broader Latin American and global historical studies of race, science, and identity, then it will have served its purpose. As Francisco Moreno wrote in 1907, "Without its own science, there is not a strong Nation."[13] Over the course of the seventy years considered in this study, creole Argentines of all walks of life—from museum scientists to newspaper writers, from schoolteachers in Buenos Aires to politicians in San Miguel de Tucumán—transformed anthropology into a nationally useful science that linked indigenous cultures to their own national heritage and landscapes, changing them from racially and politically marginalized others into strategically embraced indigenous ancestors.

Notes

INTRODUCTION

1. "Hace más de 5.000 años que el hombre habitaba en el Chaco Santiagueño"; "¿Una raza desconocida habia dominado en el norte Argentino?"

2. Arenas, "'En la noche de los tiempos'"; Martínez, Taboada, and Auat, "Wagner Brothers"; Ocampo, "La interpretación del descubrimiento."

3. Guy, *Sex and Danger in Buenos Aires*; Plotkin, *Freud in the Pampas*; Rodriguez, *Civilizing Argentina*.

4. Bennett, *Birth of the Museum*; Conn, *Museums and American Intellectual Life*; Sheets-Pyenson, *Cathedrals of Science*; Yanni, *Nature's Museums*.

5. In this book, I use the word "creole" to denote Argentines who self-identified as ethnically European but were born in Argentina. This is a very different category from what historians often describe as "criollo," which denotes the traditional rural culture associated with gauchos and Argentina's colonial cattle frontiers. This distinction avoids describing the liberal and progressive ethos spreading through nineteenth-century Argentina as *porteño*, which suggests that national identity was exclusively defined and practiced in the capital, in contrast to the rural criollo country beyond. I prefer "creole" to "white" because making a distinction between "natives" and immigrants was increasingly important to this emerging national identity in the late nineteenth and twentieth centuries.

6. Earle, "Padres de la Patria."

7. Bueno, "Forjando Patrimonio"; de la Cadena, *Indigenous Mestizos*; Earle, *Return of the Native*; Poole, *Vision, Race, and Modernity*; Appelbaum, Macpherson, and Rosemblatt, *Race and Nation in Modern Latin America*.

8. Castillo Ledón, *El Museo Nacional de Arqueología, Historia, y Etnografía*.

9. Bueno, "Forjando Patrimonio," 220. See also Craib, *Cartographic Mexico*, 19–54.

10. López, *Crafting Mexico*; Poole, "Image of 'Our Indian.'"

11. Shumway, *Invention of Argentina*, x. See also Sommer, *Foundational Fictions*.

12. Jorge M. Mayer, *Las "Bases" de Alberdi*, 239–41, quoted in Shumway, *Invention of Argentina*, 141.

13. Guy, *Sex and Danger in Buenos Aires*; Andrews, *Afro-Argentines of Buenos Aires*; Ariel de la Fuente, *Children of Facundo*; Rodriguez, *Civilizing Argentina*; Moya, *Cousins and Strangers*.

14. Podgorny, *Arqueología de la educación*; Sutton, "Contesting Racism"; Shumway, *Invention of Argentina*; Sommer, *Foundational Fictions*.

15. Quijada, "Ancestros, ciudadanos, piezas de museo."

16. Califano, *Evolución de las ciencias en la República Argentina*; *Obra del centenario del Museo de La Plata*; Arenas, "La antropología en la Argentina"; de Pilar Babot, "La arqueología argentina"; Berberian and Capuano, *El Instituto de Antropología de la Universidad Nacional de Tucumán*; Cáceres Freyre, *Juan B. Ambrosetti*; J. Fernández, *Historia de la arqueología argentina*; Hosne, *Francisco Moreno*; Lascano Gonzalez, *El Museo de Ciencias Naturales de Buenos Aires*; Márquez Miranda, *Ameghino*; Morosi, *Los creadores del edificio del Museo de La Plata y*

su obra; Novoa and Levine, *From Man to Ape*; Podgorny, "De razón a facultad"; Roca, "El Museo Etnográfico 'Juan B. Ambrosetti'"; Teruggi, *Museo de La Plata*; Ygobone, *Francisco P. Moreno*.

17. Recent outstanding examples of cultural history include Bunker, *Creating Mexican Consumer Culture*; Dean, *Culture of Stone*; López, *Crafting Mexico*; Pilcher, *¡Que Vivan Los Tamales!*; and Rubenstein, *Bad Language, Naked Ladies, and Other Threats*.

18. Burke, *What Is Cultural History?*

19. French, "Imagining and the Cultural History."

20. B. Anderson, *Imagined Communities*, 3–7.

21. A. D. Smith, *National Identity*, 11–12, 40; Sabato, *The Many and the Few*.

22. Earle, *Return of the Native*, 3–4.

23. Pratt, *Imperial Eyes*, 6–9; Conn, *Museums and American Intellectual Life*; Earle, *Return of the Native*; López, *Crafting Mexico*; Tenorio-Trillo, *Mexico at the World's Fairs*; Widdifield, *Embodiment of the National*.

24. Foucault, *Order of Things*; Bennett, *Birth of the Museum*; Andermann, *Optic of the State*.

25. Andermann, *Optic of the State*; Coombes, *Reinventing Africa*; Poole, *Vision, Race, and Modernity*; Shaw, *Possessors and Possessed*.

26. Conn, *Museums and American Intellectual Life*, 11–12.

27. Joseph and Nugent, "Popular Culture and State Formation," 17; Beezley and Curcio-Nagy, *Latin American Popular Culture*, xi; Parker, "Toward a Definition of Popular Culture."

28. Joeph and Nugent, "Popular Culture and State Formation," 17.

29. Conn, *Museums and American Intellectual Life*, 4.

30. Appadurai, "Introduction," 13.

31. Bourdieu, "Forms of Capital."

32. Garrigan, *Collecting Mexico*, 2, 4, 13; Tenorio-Trillo, *Mexico at the World's Fairs*; Widdifield, *Embodiment of the National*.

33. George W. Stocking cites Sturtevant's definition of the museum age as spanning from 1840 to 1890, though he takes issue with the earlier end of this period, arguing that it seems "somewhat anachronistic," with which I agree. Steven Conn, studying museums in the United States, has defined the museum age as 1876–1926, and H. Glenn Penny, in the case of German ethnographic museums, identifies 1868–1914 as the period of museums' greatest impact.

34. Hooper-Greenhill, *Museums and the Shaping of Knowledge*; MacGregor, *Curiosity and Enlightenment*; Impey and MacGregor, *The Origins of Museums*; Pearce, *On Collecting*; Yanni, *Nature's Museums*.

35. Iglesias Utset, *Cultural History of Cuba*, 3–4.

36. Ley 947, in *Registro Nacional 1878*, 57–58.

37. Jones, "Conflict and Adaptation in the Argentine Pampas," 167, 191; Lazzari, "Aboriginal Recognition, Freedom, and Phantoms," 63.

38. Quijada, "Ancestros, ciudadanos, piezas de museo"; Quijada, "La *ciudadanización* del 'indio bárbaro.'"

39. Rock, "Intellectual Precursors of Conservative Nationalism"; Miller, *In the Shadow of the State*.

40. Chamosa, *Argentine Folklore Movement*.

CHAPTER 1

1. Quesada, "Memoria of the Ministro Secretario de Gobierno," vii.

2. Governmental decree, November 13, 1877, fols. 75–76, legajo 3096, Fondo Moreno, AGN.

3. Sarmiento, *Discursos Populares*, 2:135.

4. Ibid., 141. Emphasis in the original.

5. Moreno, *Viaje a la Patagonia austral*, 13.

6. Ley 947, in *Registro Nacional 1878*, 57–58.

7. Roca, introductory letter in *La Conquista de Quince Mil Leguas*.

8. For more on the Argentine state's campaigns against indigenous populations in the north, see Bonaudo, Sonzogni, and Klatt, "To Populate and to Discipline."

9. Quijada, "Ancestros, ciudadanos, piezas de museo."

10. Foucault, *History of Sexuality*.

11. Zeballos, *La Conquista de Quince Mil Leguas*, 325.

12. See Lazzari, "Aboriginal Recognition, Freedom, and Phantoms," where Lazzari explores the history and contemporary implications of one such erasure. It should be noted, however, that the legacy of the Conquest's erasure is still felt in the scholarship of indigenous revitalization movements. Argentine indigenous movements and cultures are, for example, infrequently represented in works considering indigenous movements in the Americas.

13. Exceptions to this trend include Lenton, "*Malón de la Paz* of 1946," and Quijada, Bernand, and Schneider, *Homogeneidad y nacio'n*.

14. See Quijada,"Ancestros, ciudadanos, piezas de museo."

15. See Ariel de la Fuente, "Federalism and Opposition to the Paraguayan War" and *Children of Facundo*.

16. See Bethell, *Paraguayan War (1864–1870)*; Kraay and Whigham, *I Die with My Country*; and Leuchars, *To the Bitter End*.

17. Cicerchia, *Journey, Rediscovery, and Narrative*; Jones, "Nineteenth Century British Travel Accounts of Argentina"; Pratt, *Imperial Eyes*; Strobel, *European Women and the Second British Empire*.

18. Bernardo de Yrigoyen to Francisco P. Moreno, June 2, 1877, fol. 1, legajo 3098, Fondo Moreno, AGN.

19. Zeballos, *La Conquista de Quince Mil Leguas*, 296–97.

20. Conn, *History's Shadow*; Coombes, *Reinventing Africa*; Graham, *Idea of Race in Latin America*; Henare, *Museums, Anthropology, and Imperial Exchange*; Hinsley, *Savages and Scientists*; Starn, *Ishi's Brain*; Stocking, *Bones, Bodies, Behavior*; D. H. Thomas, *Skull Wars*.

21. Vallejo, "La Plata y la ideología del progreso," 371.

22. Ward, "Los museos argentinos," 146.

23. Ibid., 146–47.

24. Sheets-Pyenson, *Cathedrals of Science*, 63. See also Lydekker, "La Plata Museum."

25. Sarmiento, "El Museo La Plata," in *Discursos Populares*, 2:300–302.

26. See Andermann, *Optic of the State*, 45–57.

27. Ibid., 47–48.

28. Moreno, "El Museo de La Plata," 40.

29. Ward, "Los museos argentinos," 148. See also Andermann, *Optic of the State*, 49.

30. Moreno, "El Museo de La Plata," 39.

31. Yanni, *Nature's Museums*.

32. Sheets-Pyenson, *Cathedrals of Science*; Yanni, *Nature's Museums*; Andermann, *Optic of the State*, 45–57.

33. Earle, *Return of the Native*.

34. Teruggi, *Museo de La Plata*, 122–23.

35. Moreno, "El Museo de La Plata," 49.

36. Francisco P. Moreno to Oficina de Estadística de la Provincia de Buenos Aires, October 24, 1887, fols. 83–85, legajo 3096, Fondo Moreno, AGN.

37. Lehmann-Nitsche, *Catálogo de la Sección Antropológica*.

38. C. S. Smith, "Philosophy of Museum Display."

39. Rotker, *Captive Women.*

40. Moreno, *Viaje a la Patagonia austral,* 13.

41. Lehmann-Nitsche, *Catálogo de la Sección Antropológica,* 54, 80, 81.

42. Francisco P. Moreno to his father, April 5, 1875, in Moreno, *Reminiscencias de Francisco P. Moreno,* 53–54.

43. Francisco P. Moreno to his brother Josué, April 5, 1875, in ibid., 54–56.

44. Levaggi, *Paz en la frontera,* 448.

45. For a discussion of the notion of "emptying" and recoding objects, see Garrigan, *Collecting Mexico,* 2, 4, 13. For a discussion of recent repatriation efforts connected with Catriel's remains, see Endere, "Reburial Issue in Argentina."

46. See Gavirati, "La vida de un colono gales," 347.

47. Ten Kate, "Matériaux pour servir à l'anthropologie," 35–36; Politis and Podgorny, "Que sucedió en la historia?"

48. Francisco P. Moreno to Antonio Muratorio, October 2, 1886, in Moreno, *Reminiscencias de Francisco P. Moreno,* 208.

49. Francisco P. Moreno to Marcelino Vargas, October 2, 1886, in ibid., 207.

50. Ten Kate, "Matériaux pour servir à l'anthropologie," 36.

51. Ibid., 40, 52. For useful discussions of photography in anthropology, see Penhos, "Frente y perfil"; Poole, *Vision, Race, and Modernity,* esp. 107–41; and Edwards, *Anthropology and Photography.*

52. Ten Kate, "Matériaux pour servir à l'anthropologie," 40–41.

53. Ibid., 39.

54. Ibid., 38–40.

55. Ibid., 37.

56. Moreno, "Reconocimiento de la Región Andina," 108.

57. Quijada, "Ancestros, ciudadanos, piezas de museo," 35–36.

58. Andermann, *Optic of the State,* 55.

59. Podgorny and Politis, "¿Qué sucedió en la historia?"

60. Draft of a speech written by Francisco P. Moreno, October 15, 1907, fols. 11–13, legajo 3099, Fondo Moreno, AGN.

61. See Ariel de la Fuente, *Children of Facundo*; Andrews, *Afro-Argentines of Buenos Aires*; de Liboreiro, *No hay negros argentinos?*; and Mases, *Estado y cuestio'n indi'gena.*

62. For more on Moreno's second career, see Hosne, *Francisco Moreno*; Ygobone, *Francisco P. Moreno*; "Doctor Francisco P. Moreno"; Torres, "Dr. Francisco P. Moreno"; and Ludueña, *Labor parlamentaria del perito doctor Francisco P. Moreno.*

CHAPTER 2

1. An earlier version of some materials in this chapter appeared in the article "'The Ashes of Our Ancestors': Creating Argentina's Indigenous Heritage in the Museo Etnográfico, 1904–1930," *The Americas* 69, no. 4 (2013): 467–92. My thanks to the editors of *The Americas* for their permission to use this material here.

2. Ambrosetti, *Memoria del Museo Etnográfico,* 8.

3. Hudson, *Social History of Museums,* 74.

4. Manuel Antequeda to Salvador Debenedetti, January 15, 1918, Caja 6, MEA.

5. Ibid.

6. Conn, *Museums and American Intellectual Life,* 4.

7. Stocking, "Essays on Museums and Material Culture," in *Objects and Others,* 5.

8. Rabinow, *Foucault Reader*.

9. Bourdieu, "Forms of Capital." See also Garrigan, *Collecting Mexico*.

10. Ambrosetti, "La Facultad de Filosofía y Letras," 984.

11. Ambrosetti, *Trabajos publicados*.

12. De Pilar Babot, "La arqueología argentina," 170.

13. Ambrosetti, "La Facultad de Filosofía y Letras," 984. Emphasis mine.

14. See Graham, *Idea of Race in Latin America*; Stepan, *Hour of Eugenics*; and A. M. Stern, *Eugenic Nation*.

15. Ambrosetti, "La Facultad de Filosofía y Letras," 983.

16. See Arenas, "La antropología en la Argentina"; de Pilar Babot, "La arqueología argentina"; J. Fernández, *Historia de la arqueología argentina*; and Ramundo, "Los aportes de los investigadores pioneros."

17. Endere and Podgorny, "Los gliptodontes son argentinos"; Podgorny, *El argentino despertar de las faunas y de las Gentes Prehistóricas*; Podgorny, "Portable Antiquities."

18. See Solberg, "Immigration and Urban Social Problems," and Rock, *Politics in Argentina*.

19. García and Podgorny, "El sabio tiene una patria."

20. "Inauguración del Museo Etnográfico," Recortes XII, MEA. Debenedetti's comments were also reproduced in *El Diario* and *La Época* on September 28, 1927.

21. De Pilar Babot, "La arqueología argentina."

22. Poole, *Vision, Race, and Modernity*, 107–41.

23. Ambrosetti, *Memoria del Museo Etnográfico*, 4.

24. Ibid., 5.

25. Clark Wissler to Juan B. Ambrosetti, July 6, 1908, legajo "American Museum of Natural History," Caja 1.10, MEA.

26. Clark Wissler to Juan B. Ambrosetti, March 20, 1909, legajo "American Museum of Natural History," Caja 1.10, MEA.

27. Exchange records, 1913, Caja 4.54, MEA.

28. Memoranda, March 28, 1924, Caja Debenedetti Institucional, MEA.

29. Samuel Lafone Quevado (director of the Museo de La Plata [MLP]) to dean of Facultad de Filosofía y Letras (FFyL), Universidad Nacional de Buenos Aires (UBA), April 23, 1906, Caja 1.5, MEA.

30. Dean of FFyL, UBA, to Samuel Lafone Quevado (director of MLP), July 20, 1908, fol. 7, Caja 5, MEA.

31. MLP to Juan B. Ambrosetti, March 18, 1914, Caja Debenedetti 3, MEA.

32. Luis María Torres (director of MLP) to Salvador Debenedetti, December 4, 1922, Caja Debenedetti 3, MEA.

33. Secretary of MLP to Salvador Debendetti, May 16, 1921, Caja Debenedetti Cartas, MEA.

34. Cristian Nelson (director of the Provincial Museum of Salta) to Salvador Debenedetti, April 21 1923, Caja Debenedetti, MEA.

35. Ambrosetti, *Memoria del Museo Etnográfico*, 33.

36. Ibid., 4. See also *El Museo Etnográfico*, 45.

37. Ambrosetti, *Memoria del Museo Etnográfico*, 33.

38. Ibid., 3–4.

39. Alfredo González Garaño to Salvador Debenedetti, September 14, 1927, Caja 7, MEA.

40. Tomás Le Breton to Salvador Debenedetti, September 13, 1927, Caja 7, MEA.

41. "La tumba de Tut-Ankh-Amon"; "La revolución religiosa y su aspecto sexual. Taras de Aj-en-Aton."

42. "Inauguración del Museo Etnográfico."

43. Franz Kühn to Juan B. Ambrosetti, October 12, 1916, Caja Fondo Museo Ambrosetti, MEA; business card, October 17, 1916, Caja Fondo Museo Ambrosetti, MEA.

44. Ambrosetti, *Memoria del Museo Etnográfico*, 8.

45. Calvo and Arenas, "El Museo Etnográfico."

46. "Inauguración del Museo Etnográfico."

47. "Better use" and "public access": "El 28 del corriente será inaugurado el Museo de Etnografía"; "specialization": "El mañana se abrira al publico el Museo Etnográfico de la Facultad de Filosofía y Letras." See also "El Museo Etnográfico de la Facultad de Filosofia. Será inaugurado"; "Museo Etnográfico de la Facultad de Filosofía y Letras"; "Mañana sera inaugurado el Museo Etnográfico."

48. "Fué inaugurado ayer el Museo Etnográfico de la Facultad de Filosofia y Letras"; untitled announcement; "Ashes of Our Ancestors Are Found in the Museo Etnográfico, Inaugurated Today"; "Se inauguraron esta mañana las nuevas instalaciones del Museo de Etnografía"; "Esta mañana quedo inaugurado el nuevo local del Museo Etnográfico de la Facultad de Filosofia y Letras"; "Se inauguro el Museo Etnográfico de la F. Filosofia y Letras"; "Fue inaugurado ayer el Museo Etnográfico de la F. de Filosofía y Letras"; "Hoy será inaugurado en su nuevo local el Museo Etnográfico de la Facultad de Letras"; "Fue inaugurado en su nuevo local del Museo Etnográfico de la Facultad de Letras"; "Il Museo Etnografico della Facoltà di Filosofia e Lettere"; "Se efectuara hoy la inauguración de las instalaciones del Museo de Etnografía"; "Realizose ayer en acto solemne la inauguración del Museo Etnográfico"; "Fue inaugurado hoy el Museo Etnográfico de la Facultad de Filosofia y Letras"; "Las diversas instalaciones del Museo Etnográfico"; "Hoy quedó inaugurado el nuevo local del Museo Etnográfico de la F. de Fliosofía"; "Se abrirá al publico el Museo Etnográfico HOY"; "Visita al Museo Etnográfico."

49. Ambrosetti, "La Facultad de Filosofía y Letras," 985.

50. Clemente Zamora to Juan B. Ambrosetti, August 12, 1914, Caja 4.58, MEA.

51. Arturo R. Frutos to Juan B. Ambrosetti, May 19, 1906, Caja 1, MEA.

52. Carlos Brackibux to Juan B. Ambrosetti, June 25, 1914, Caja 5.69, MEA.

53. Héctor Nuñez to Salvador Debenedetti, June 27, 1928, Caja 8, MEA.

54. Caja Visitas, MEA.

55. Comisión de "Ayuda Social del Consejo Nacional de Mujeres" to the director of the Museo Etnográfico, May 1920, Caja Visitas, MEA.

56. Comisión de "Ayuda Social del Consejo Nacional de Mujeres" to Salvador Debenedetti, May 3, 1920, Caja Visitas, MEA.

57. Ambrosetti, "La Facultad de Filosofía y Letras," 985.

58. Juan Paglia to Juan B. Ambrosetti, September 7, 1909, Caja 2.16, MEA.

59. W. O. Oldman to Juan B. Ambrosetti, September 8, 1910, Caja 3.30, MEA.

60. Ibid.

61. Aguirre, *Informal Empire*; Garrigan, *Collecting Mexico*.

62. Abt, *American Egyptologist*, 310–11; Goode, *Negotiating for the Past*, 70.

63. See Earle, *Return of the Native*, 137–40, and Stiebing, *Uncovering the Past*, 75–78.

64. Cámara de Diputados, Reunion num. 40, September 11, 1912, in *Congreso Nacional*, 673–75, BCN.

65. Cámara de Diputados, Reunion num. 39, September 10, 1912, in *Congreso Nacional*, 637–38, BCN.

66. Cámara de Diputados, Reunion num. 40, September 11, 1912, 673–75.

67. "Yacimientos arqueologicos y paleontologicos"; "Las antiguedades del suelo argentino: Su conservacion."

68. Augusto Scala (director of MLP and director of the Comisión de Yacimientos) to Félix Outes (director of the Museo Etnográfico "Juan B. Ambrosetti" [MEA]), May 12, 1933, Caja Debenedetti Cartas, MEA.

69. Eduardo Casanova to Francisco de Aparicio (director of MEA), August 16, 1944, Caja Debenedetti Cartas, MEA.

70. Transcribed from a photograph taken by the author at the Museo de La Plata, October 25, 2007.

71. Endere and Podgorny, "Los gliptodontes son argentinos."

72. Podgorny, *El argentino despertar de las faunas y de las Gentes Prehistóricas*, 14–15.

73. Cámara de Diputados, Reunion num. 29, July 2, 1913, in *Congreso Nacional*, 384, BCN.

74. For reference, in 1930 the Museo Etngoráfico received a total of 16,400 pesos to fund collections development for the entire fiscal year. "Fondos destinados a investigaciones, publicaciones, fomento y gastos, con exclusion de sueldos," Caja Outes, MEA.

75. *La Libertad*, August 21, 1928, Caja 8, MEA.

76. See receipts and letters recording donations in the archives of MEA: *La Prensa*, September 13, 1928, 500 pesos; Ernesto Tornquist y Cía, October 5, 1927, 1,000 pesos; Francisco Chelia, September 29, 1928, 500 pesos; Caledonio Pereda, August 27, 1928, 5,000 pesos; Sr. Goti (president of the Banco Hipotecario Nacional), September 5, 1928, unknown amount; all located in Caja 8. Banco Hipotecario Nacional, October 4, 1928, 1,000 pesos, fol. 4023, Caja Debenedetti Institucional. Carlos Madariaga's donation of 10,000 pesos is noted in a letter to Debenedetti from the Decano de la Facultad de Filosofia y Letras, March 21, 1928, Caja 8.

77. Piccardo y Cia to Salvador Debenedetti, August 17, 1928, Caja 8, MEA.

78. Dean of FFyL, UBA, to Salvador Debenedetti, October 6, 1928, Caja 8, MEA.

CHAPTER 3

1. "Suspendieron el traslado de un menhir a Buenos Aires."

2. Doello Jurado to Félix Outes, January 15, 1935, Caja Debenedetti Cartas, MEA.

3. The northwest as a region has been defined differently by a host of historians, anthropologists, literary critics, geographers, politicians, and other region-minded authors. I have chosen to identify the region by its most frequently included provinces in order to give the reader a reasonable sense for its geographical extent, but I do not pretend that this is a definitive definition of the northwest. Visions of the region as a space are clearly multiple, and that very multiplicity lies at the core of my argument in this chapter.

4. J. C. Brown, *Socioeconomic History of Argentina*.

5. See Ariel de la Fuente, *Children of Facundo*.

6. Guy, *Argentine Sugar Politics*; Rutledge, *Cambio agrario e integración*; Arenas, "Alfred Métraux"; Chamosa, *Argentine Folklore Movement*.

7. Salvador Debenedetti, field journal entry, January 14, 1918, 14th Expedition, Pucará de Tilcara, Jujuy, December 1917–February 1918, MEA.

8. Terán, *La universidad y la vida*, 35.

9. Ibid.; Coviello, *Geografía intelectual de la República Argentina*, 23–24.

10. Perilli de Colombres Garmendia, "Lo regional, instrumento de equilibrio de la nación," 206.

11. Chamosa, *Argentine Folklore Movement*, 184, 3, 56, 11, 90. See also Chamosa, "Indigenous or Criollo."

12. Tuan, *Space and Place*, 6.

13. Casanova, "Disertación del profesor de arqueología americana," 7.

14. Debenedetti, field journal entry, December 25, 1923, 20th Expedition, December 1923–January 1924, MEA.

15. Debenedetti, field journal entry, December 19, 1927, 23rd Expedition, La Ciénaga, Catamarca, December 1927–January 1928, MEA.

16. Debenedetti, field journal entry, December 27, 1917, 14th Expedition, Pucará de Tilcara, Jujuy, December 1917–February 1918, MEA.

17. Debenedetti, field journal entry, December 21, 1917, 14th Expedition, Pucará de Tilcara, Jujuy, December 1917–February 1918, MEA; Debenedetti, field journal entry, January 20, 1919, 15th Expedition, Jujuy, December 1918–February 1919, MEA; Debenedetti, field journal entry, December 24, 1928, 24th Expedition, Tilcara, Jujuy, December 1928–January 1929, MEA.

18. Debenedetti, field journal entry, October 29, 1914, 11th Expedition, October–November 1914, MEA.

19. Debenedetti, field journal entry, December 22, 1917, 14th Expedition, Pucará de Tilcara, Jujuy, December 1917–February 1918, MEA.

20. Debenedetti, field journal entry, January 20–28, 1918, 14th Expedition, Pucará de Tilcara, Jujuy, December 1917–February 1918, MEA.

21. Debenedetti, field journal entry, December 24, 1923, 20th Expedition, December 1923–January 1924, MEA.

22. Debenedetti, field journal entry, December 20, 1918, 15th Expedition, Jujuy, December 1918–February 1919, MEA.

23. Debenedetti, field journal entry, December 22, 1927, 23rd Expedition, La Ciénaga, Catamarca, December 1927–January 1928, MEA.

24. Debenedetti, field journal entry, December 27, 1917, 14th Expedition, Pucará de Tilcara, Jujuy, December 1917–February 1918, MEA.

25. Debenedetti, field journal entry, February 4, 1918, 14th Expedition, Pucará de Tilcara, Jujuy, December 1917–February 1918, MEA.

26. Debenedetti, field journal entry, January 14, 1919, 14th Expedition, Pucará de Tilcara, Jujuy, December 1918–February 1919, MEA.

27. Debenedetti, field journal entry, January 7, 1928, 23rd Expedition, La Ciénaga, Catamarca, December 1927–January 1928, MEA.

28. Perilli de Colombres Garmendia, "Lo regional, instrumento de equilibrio de la nación," 205.

29. Arenas, "Alfred Métraux"; Formoso, "Padilla, Rougés y la cultura folklórica." See also Wohl, *Generation of 1914*; Lucie-Smith, *Arte latinoamericano del siglo XX*; and Plotkin, *Freud in the Pampas*.

30. Terán, *La universidad y la vida*, 16; Coviello, *Geografía intelectual de la República Argentina*, 23.

31. Terán, *La universidad y la vida*, 35.

32. See Vasconcelos, *The Cosmic Race / La raza cósmica*. See also Joseph and Nugent, *Everyday Forms of State Formation*, and Boyer, *Becoming Campesinos*.

33. This was also the result of a longer and more intense colonial history of Spanish monastic contact with indigenous communities, in missions, schools, and *reducciones*. See Arenas, "Alfred Métraux," and Gordillo, *Landscapes of Devils*.

34. See Guy, *Argentine Sugar Politics*, and Arenas, "Alfred Métraux."

35. Berberian and Capuano, *El Instituto de Antropología de la Universidad Nacional de Tucumán*, 10.

36. Terán, *La universidad y la vida*, 51.

37. Paul Rivet to Juan B. Terán, January 6, 1928, quoted in Berberian and Capuano, *El Instituto de Antropología de la Universidad Nacional de Tucumán*, as well as Auroi and Monnier, *De Suiza a Sudamérica*, 19. Emphasis in the original.

38. Contract of employment between Alfred Metraux and the Universidad Nacional de Tucumán, December 19, 1928, fol. 1, Legajo Metraux, DP-UNT.

39. Metraux's plan for an ethnographic museum, sent to the Rectorate of the Universidad Nacional de Tucumán, June 7, 1928, fol. 7, Legajo Metraux, DP-UNT. Emphasis in the original.

40. Arenas, "Alfred Métraux."

41. Alfred Metraux to Karl Schreiter, December 13, 1932, Archivo M. Lillo, San Miguel de Tucumán, quoted in Perilli de Colombres Garmendia, "Alfred Metraux y la Universidad Nacional de Tucumán," 149–50.

42. Quoted in Krebs, "Un Argentino universal," as well as Perilli de Colombres Garmendia, "Alfred Metraux y la Universidad Nacional de Tucumán," 149.

43. See Arenas, "Alfred Métraux," for further discussion of modern ethnography in relation to salvage ethnography, especially p. 125.

44. *Memoria correspondiente al año 1933*, 178.

45. Alfred Metraux to the Rector of the Universidad Nacional de Tucumán, June 27, 1935, cited in Berberian and Capuano, *El Instituto de Antropología de la Universidad Nacional de Tucumán*, 13–14.

46. Altieri, "La gramatica yunga de F. de la Carrera," 4.

47. Caja 1948, Archivo, IAM.

48. Alfred Metraux to Manuel Doello Jurado (director of the Museo Nacional de Ciencias Naturales), July 28, 1931, Caja 9, MEA; Alfred Metraux to Manuel Doello Jurado, August 24, 1931, Caja 9, MEA.

49. Internal memorandum, Museo Nacional de Ciencias Naturales, September 18, 1934, Caja 8, MEA.

50. Surviving examples of Outes and Metraux's correspondence can be found in the archives of the MEA, especially in Cajas 8 and 9 and Caja Outes.

51. *Memoria correspondiente al año 1939*, 61.

CHAPTER 4

1. "Los triunfos de Ameghino."

2. "Ameghino y la antigüedad del hombre. Resultados de los nuevos estudios."

3. "Los triunfos de Ameghino."

4. Brunk, *Posthumous Career of Emiliano Zapata*; Stephen, *¡Zapata Lives!*; Brunk and Fallaw, *Heroes and Hero Cults in Latin America*.

5. See Farro and Podgorny, "Frente a la tumba del sabio," and Podgorny, "De la santidad laica del científico Florentino Ameghino."

6. "La santidad moderna: Discursa pronunciada anoche en el funeral civil de Florentino Ameghino." Also printed in Ameghino, *Obras completas y correspondencia científica*.

7. Márquez Miranda, *Ameghino*; González Arrili, *Vida de Ameghino*; Lugones, *Elogio de Ameghino*; Ambrosetti, "Doctor Florentino Ameghino"; Farro and Podgorny, "Frente a la tumba del sabio"; Podgorny; "De la santidad laica del científico Florentino Ameghino"; Podgorny and Politis, "It Is Not All Roses Here."

8. See Glick, "Reception of Darwinism in Uruguay"; Montserrat, "Evolutionist Mentality in Argentina"; and Novoa and Levine, *From Man to Ape*.

9. "La santidad moderna."

10. Rock, *Politics in Argentina*, 86–87.

11. Florencia Mallon's notion of local intellectuals offers another approach to this idea; it is one that has influenced my interpretation of the word *sabio* here and my decision to use it in the original Spanish with accompanying explanation, rather than simply translating it into its English approximate. See Mallon, *Peasant and Nation*.

12. "La nacionalidad de Florentino Ameghino."

13. "Las antiguedades del suelo argentino."

14. "Los pequeños monumentos a proposito de Ameghino."

15. "Ameghino—2a aniversario de su fallecimiento."
16. Di Yorio, "A un paso de Ameghino."
17. "Homenaje al Doctor Ameghino—Inauguración de un busto del sabio."
18. Márquez Miranda, *Ameghino*, 222. See also Podgorny, "De la santidad laica del científico Florentino Ameghino," 46, and Barrancos, *La escena iluminada*.
19. Sheets-Pyenson, *Cathedrals of Science*. See also Alexander, *Museum Masters*.
20. Perazzi, "La nación deshuesada," 33.
21. Quoted in Auza, "Germán Burmeister y la Sociedad Paleontológica," 138.
22. "Severe character": Raffino, *Burmeister*, 72; "meticulous man": Biraben, *German Burmeister*, 30.
23. Florentino Ameghino, letter 133, in *Obras completas y correspondencia científica*, 20:107–13.
24. "El hombre fosil de Miramar. Recuerdos y notas de turista."
25. "Monumento Burmeister," Cámara de Diputados, May 22, 1896, 6a Sessión ordinaria, in *Congreso Nacional*, 126, BCN.
26. Francisco P. Moreno to Florentino Ameghino, March 30, 1886, letter 396, in Ameghino, *Obras completas y correspondencia científica*, 20:364–65.
27. Francisco P. Ameghino to Florentino Moreno, October 27, 1886, letter 431, in Ameghino, *Obras completas y correspondencia científica*, 20:390.
28. Moreno, "El Museo de La Plata," 40–41.
29. Proyecto de ley, August 23, 1911, in Ludueña, *Labor parlamentaria del perito doctor Francisco P. Moreno*, 45–47.
30. See Stocking, *Bones, Bodies, Behavior*; Conn, *History's Shadow*; Penny, *Objects of Culture*; and primary treatments in Flower, *Essays on Museums and Other Subjects*, and Stocking, *Shaping of American Anthropology*.
31. See Jones, Martin, and Pilbeam, *Cambridge Encyclopedia of Human Evolution*, 448. The Piltdown Man played an important and contentious role in paleoanthropology until the 1950s, when the remains were declared to be forgeries.
32. See Tattersall and Schwartz, *Extinct Humans*, 26–29, 148–51, and Jones, Martin, and Pilbeam, *Cambridge Encyclopedia of Human Evolution*, 250, 243, 245.
33. "Un hombre terciario."
34. Hrdlicka, preface to *Early Man in South America*, viii.
35. Simpson, *Discoverers of the Lost World*, 76.
36. "Notas científicas, una revelación antropológica: Descubrimiento sensacional."
37. "Una revelación antropológica"; "El hombre terciario"; "Hallazgos prehistóricos"; "Revelaciones prehistóricas"; "Descubrimiento arqueológico en Miramar"; "El origen del hombre—Revelación sensacional"; "El hombre del chapalmalal"; "El hombre prehistórico"; "Nuevos hallazgos"; "Un descubrimiento sensacional"; "Nuevas revelaciones de Miramar: La pesca con redes"; "En las barrancas de Miramar"; "Los yacimientos de Miramar"; "El hombre fósil de Miramar. Recuerdos y notas de turista"; "El hombre de Chapalmalal," April 12, 1920; "El hombre de Chapalmalal," April 14, 1920; "Miramar: Excursión científica"; "El hombre fósil de Miramar: Nuevos hallazgos de reliquias, comisión científica organizada por el Museo Nacional"; "Los artifactos de la industria indígena de los antiguos paraderos de Miramar"; "A proposito de los vestigios de industria humano encontrados en Miramar."
38. "Hallazgos prehistóricos."
39. "El origen del hombre—Revelación sensacional."
40. "Ameghino y la antigüedad del hombre."
41. For example, José Imbelloni—professor of anthropology at the Universidad de Buenos Aires during the early twentieth century—published a series of articles for *La Prensa* on a wide variety of topics related to American and Old World archaeology and ethnography, including

(but certainly not limited to) "El pueblo más misterioso de la tierra" (by which he meant the Etruscans), May 14, 1922; "Historia animistica del retrato. El busto en los dos mundos," August 20, 1922; "La cerámica prosopomorfa en Europa y América," August 27, 1922; "Pinturas rupestres del noroeste de Córdoba," December 17, 1922; "La fauna de las sierras en el verismo y el impresionismo de los pintores indígenas," December 24, 1922; and "Testimonios gráficos de la conquista en los frescos de los naturales," January 1, 1923.

42. "El hombre prehistórico."

43. Gualberto Pelliza, "Ameghinismo and Ameghinofobia."

44. "El hombre terciario de Miramar."

45. "El hombre fosil de Miramar y la afición al macaneo."

46. "El Ameghinismo. Charlatanismo anticientífico e industrialización maquiavelica. La palabra de los hombres de ciencia," *El Pueblo*, January 7, 1922.

47. "El Ameghinismo. Charlatanismo anticientífico e industrialización maquiavelica. La palabra de los hombres de ciencia," *El Pueblo*, January 8, 1922. Boman's claim that there were few anthropologists in Buenos Aires was a somewhat strange comment to make in 1922, in light of the multiple prominent museums and universities in the city housing anthropology sections at that time, including those discussed in this book.

48. "El Ameghinismo. Charlatanismo anticientífico e industrialización maquiavelica. La palabra de los hombres de ciencia," *El Pueblo*, January 10, 1922.

49. Ibid.

50. "El craneo que da que decir. Manifestaciones del director del Zoológico."

51. "El cráneo fósil."

52. "La pieza hallada en Paso Ibáñez no es un craneo, sino un a piedra. Se trata simplemente de un 'capricho de la naturaleza.' Tal es la opinión de un grupo de personas entendidas."

53. Vizconde de Lascano Tegui, "Los sabios reconocen la existencia de un nuevo adoquín. Alrededor de un craneo milenario. La fortuna de un hombre iluso, se evapora.—Las monedas de oro cambiadas en hoias de higuera."

EPILOGUE

1. Endere, Cali, and Funari, "Archaeology and Indigenous Communities," 159; Miller, *In the Shadow of the State*; Rock, "Argentina, 1930–1946."

2. Miller, *In the Shadow of the State*, 224–25.

3. Endere, *Management of Archaeological Sites and the Public*, 32.

4. See, for example, Gonzalez, "A cuarto decadas del comienzo de una etapa," and Perazzi, *Hermenéutica de la barbarie*.

5. W. Anderson, *Cultivation of Whiteness*; Coombes, *Reinventing Africa*; Kirshenblatt-Gimblett, "Objects of Ethnography"; Penny, *Objects of Culture*; Roque, *Headhunting and Colonialism*; Stocking, *Objects and Others*; Wolfe, *Settler Colonialism and the Transformation of Anthropology*.

6. Endere, Cali, and Funari, "Archaeology and Indigenous Communities," 159.

7. Ametrano, "Historia de una restitución"; Curtoni, Lazzari, and Lazzari, "Middle of Nowhere"; Lazzari, "Aboriginal Recognition, Freedom, and Phantoms."

8. For an outstanding discussion of memory scholarship in Latin America, see Steve J. Stern's trilogy *The Memory Box of Pinochet's Chile*, especially "Introduction to the Trilogy: The Memory Box of Pinochet's Chile," in *Remembering Pinochet's Chile*, xix–xxxi.

9. See Endere, "Reburial Issue in Argentina," 266, and Endere, Cali, and Funari, "Archaeology and Indigenous Communities," 161–64.

10. Ametrano, "Historia de una restitución"; Curtoni, Lazzari, and Lazzari, "Middle of Nowhere"; Lazzari, "Aboriginal Recognition, Freedom, and Phantoms."

11. "Los restos humanos en las colecciones del Museo de La Plata," Museo de la Plata, Facultad de Ciencias Naturales y Museo, http://www.museo.fcnym.unlp.edu.ar/restituciones.

12. Endere, "Reburial Issue in Argentina," 268; see also 276–77.

13. Draft of a speech written by Francisco P. Moreno, October 15, 1907, fols. 11–13, legajo 3099, Fondo Moreno, AGN.

Bibliography

PRIMARY SOURCES

Archives Consulted

Buenos Aires
    Academía Nacional de la Historia de la República Argentina (ANH)
    Archivo General de la Nación (AGN)
        Fondo Moreno (legajos 3096–3100)
        Fototeca
    Biblioteca del Congreso de la Nación (BCN)
        Congreso Nacional
        General Collections
        Periodicals
        Special Collections
    Biblioteca Nacional de la República Argentina (BN)
    Museo Etnográfico "Juan B. Ambrosetti," Universidad de Buenos Aires (MEA)
        Archivo Documental
            Cajas 1–11
            Caja Ambrosetti—Investigación
            Caja Archivos MEA
            Caja Debenedetti
            Caja Debenedetti (3)
            Caja Debenedetti Cartas
            Caja Debenedetti Institucional
            Caja Fondo Museo Ambrosetti
            Caja Outes
            Caja Visitas
            Diarios de Campo (Field Journals)
            Recortes 1–12
        Archivo Fotográfico
        Biblioteca "Raúl A. Cortazar"
La Plata
    Museo de Ciencias Naturales de La Plata, Universidad Nacional de La Plata (MLP)
        Archivo Documental
        Biblioteca "Florentino Ameghino"
San Miguel de Tucumán
    Archivo Miguel Lillo (AML)
    Centro Cultural Rougés, Fundación Miguel Lillo (CCR)
        Biblioteca "Dr. Ernesto E. Padilla"

Dirección de Personal de la Universidad Nacional de Tucumán (DP-UNT)
Instituto de Arqueología y Museo, Universidad Nacional de Tucumán (IAM)
 Archivo
 Biblioteca y Hemeroteca "C. Reyes Gajardo"
Universidad Nacional de Tucumán (UNT)
 Archivos
 Biblioteca Arqueológica
 Biblioteca Central

Museum and University Periodical Publications

Actas de la Sociedad Paleontológica de Buenos Aires
Anales de la Sociedad Científica Argentina
Anales del Museo de La Plata
Anales del Museo Público
Archivos de la Universidad de Buenos Aires
Biblioteca de Difusión Científica del Museo de La Plata
Boletín de la Academia Nacional de Ciencias Exactas
Boletín de la Sociedad Argentina de Antropología
Boletín del Instituto Geográfico Argentina
El Naturalista Argentino (1878)
Physis (Revista de la Sociedad Argentina de Ciencias Naturales)
*Publicaciones de la Sección Antropológica, Facultad de Filosofía y Letras, Universidad de
 Buenos Aires*
Publicaciones del Museo Etnográfico (1931)
Revista de la Universidad de Buenos Aires
Revista del Instituto de Antropología de la Universidad Nacional de Tucumán
Revista del Instituto de Etnología de la Universidad Nacional de Tucumán
Revista del Museo de La Plata
Revue d'Anthropologie
Solar (1931)

Newspapers and Magazines

Argentina
El Argentino
Capital (Buenos Aires)
Caras y Caretas (Buenos Aires)
Le Courier
Crítica (Buenos Aires)
El Día (San Salvador de Jujuy)
El Diario (Buenos Aires)
La Época (Buenos Aires)
La Flecha (San Miguel de Tucumán)
Fray Mocho (Buenos Aires)
La Fronda
La Gaceta (San Miguel de Tucumán)
El Hogar (Buenos Aires)
La Libertad (Avellaneda)
La Nación (Buenos Aires)

El Norte Argentino (San Miguel de Tucumán)
El Orden (San Miguel de Tucumán)
Patria degli Italiani
La Prensa (Buenos Aires)
El Pueblo (Buenos Aires)
La Razón (Buenos Aires)
La República (Buenos Aires)
El Telegrafo (Buenos Aires)
El Tiempo (Buenos Aires)
La Vanguardia (Buenos Aires)

Newspaper Articles

"Ameghino—2a aniversario de su fallecimiento." *La Nación*, August 6, 1913.
"Ameghino y la antigüedad del hombre. Resultados de los nuevos estudios. Lo que dice el doctor Torres." *La Razón*, August 5, 1915.
"Las antiguedades del suelo argentino: Su conservacion." *La Nación*, September 14, 1912.
"Los artifactos de la industria indígena de los antiguos paraderos de Miramar. Una excursión interesante." *El Diario*, December 13, 1920.
"The Ashes of Our Ancestors Are Found in the Museo Etnográfico, Inaugurated Today. Millenarian Civilizations Are Represented by Valuable Collections." *Crítica*, September 28, 1927.
"El cráneo fósil." *La Razón*, May 3, 1923.
"El craneo que da que decir. Manifestaciones del director del Zoológico." *La Razón*, May 3, 1923.
"Descubrimiento arqueológico en Miramar." *La Prensa*, October 24, 1914.
"Un descubrimiento sensacional." *La Nación*, August 3, 1916.
"Las diversas instalaciones del Museo Etnográfico. Sintesis historica de la epoca pasada del museo." *La República*, September 28, 1927.
di Yorio, Rafael. "A un paso de Ameghino." *El Hogar*, December 1, 1918.
"En las barrancas de Miramar." *La Razón*, February 25, 1918.
"Esta mañana quedo inaugurado el nuevo local del Museo Etnográfico de la Facultad de Filosofia y Letras." *La Época*, September 28, 1927.
"Fué inaugurado ayer el Museo Etnográfico de la Facultad de Filosofia y Letras." *Argentina*, September 29, 1927.
"Fue inaugurado ayer el Museo Etnográfico de la F. de Filosofía y Letras." *La Libertad*, September 29, 1927.
"Fue inaugurado en su nuevo local del Museo Etnográfico de la Facultad de Letras. Prestigió el acto con su presencia el presidente de la República, e hicieron uso de la palabra los Dres. Rojas, Alberini, Sagarna, Rivet, y Debendedetti. Todos recordaron al sabio fundador del museo." *La Nación*, September 29, 1927.
"Fue inaugurado hoy el Museo Etnográfico de la Facultad de Filosofia y Letras." *La Razón*, September 28, 1927.
Gualberto Pelliza, Juan. "Ameghinismo and Ameghinofobia." *La Razón*, December 11 and 12, 1917.
"Hace más de 5.000 años que el hombre habitaba en el Chaco Santiagueño." *Crítica*, September 5, 1929.
"Hallazgos prehistóricos." *La Nación*, June 7, 1914.
"El hombre de Chapalmalal." *La Nación*, April 12, 1920.
"El hombre de Chapalmalal." *La Nación*, April 14, 1920.

"El hombre de la edad de piedra—El craneo fósil hallado en Correze." *La Nación*, March 18, 1909.

"El hombre del chapalmalal." *La Nación*, May 10, 1916.

"El hombre fósil de Miramar: Nuevos hallazgos de reliquias, comisión científica organizada por el Museo Nacional." *La Prensa*, December 5, 1920.

"El hombre fosil de Miramar. Recuerdos y notas de turista." *La Razón*, April 7, 1920.

"El hombre fosil de Miramar y la afición al macaneo." *El Argentino*, April 29, 1920.

"El hombre prehistórico." *La Nación*, May 15, 1916.

"El hombre terciario." *La Nación*, January 18, 1914.

"Un hombre terciario." *La Nación*, September 15, 1913.

"El hombre terciario de Miramar: Es necesario para honor del país que termine la farsa de su hallazgo." *El Diario*, April 19, 1920.

"Homenaje al Doctor Ameghino—Inauguración de un busto del sabio." *La Nación*, October 27, 1912.

"Hoy quedó inaugurado el nuevo local del Museo Etnográfico de la F. de Fliosofía." *El Telegrafo*, September 28, 1927.

"Hoy será inaugurado en su nuevo local el Museo Etnográfico de la Facultad de Letras." *La Nación*, September 28, 1927.

Imbelloni, José. "La cerámica prosopomorfa en Europa y América." *La Prensa*, August 27, 1922.

———. "La fauna de las sierras en el verismo y el impresionismo de los pintores indígenas." *La Prensa*, December 24, 1922.

———. "Historia animistica del retrato. El busto en los dos mundos." *La Prensa*, August 20, 1922.

———. "Pinturas rupestres del noroeste de Córdoba." *La Prensa*, December 17, 1922.

———. "El pueblo más misterioso de la tierra." *La Prensa*, May 14, 1922.

———. "Testimonios gráficos de la conquista en los frescos de los naturales." *La Prensa*, January 1, 1923.

"El mañana se abrira al publico el Museo Etnográfico de la Facultad de Filosofía y Letras." *La Época*, September 27, 1927.

"Mañana sera inaugurado el Museo Etnográfico." *La Razón*, September 27, 1927.

"Miramar: Excursión científica." *La Nación*, November 25, 1920.

"El Museo Etnográfico de la Facultad de Filosofia. Será inaugurado en su nuevo local el 28 del actual." *La Nación*, September 20, 1927.

"Museo Etnográfico de la Facultad de Filosofía y Letras." *La Libertad*, September 17, 1927.

"Il Museo Etnografico della Facoltà di Filosofia e Lettere." *Patria degli Italiani*, September 29, 1927.

"La nacionalidad de Florentino Ameghino." *La Razón*, September 8, 1916.

"Notas científicas, una revelación antropológica: Descubrimiento sensacional." *La Nación*, December 1, 1913.

"Nueva sala en el Museo de La Plata." *La Nación*, March 27, 2009.

"Nuevas revelaciones de Miramar: La pesca con redes." *La Nación*, July 20, 1917.

"Nuevos hallazgos." *La Nación*, July 26, 1916.

"El origen del hombre—Revelación sensacional." *La Nación*, November 22, 1914.

"Los pequeños monumentos a proposito de Ameghino." *La Nación*, October 28, 1912.

"La pieza hallada en Paso Ibáñez no es un craneo, sino una piedra. Se trata simplemente de un 'capricho de la naturaleza.' Tal es la opinión de un grupo de personas entendidas." *La Nación*, May 4, 1923.

"A proposito de los vestigios de industria humano encontrados en Miramar." *Capital*, April 25, 1922.

"¿Una raza desconocida habia dominado en el norte Argentino?" *La Crítica*, September 6, 1929.

"Realizose ayer en acto solemne la inauguración del Museo Etnográfico. Concurrieron el presidente de la nación, el ministro de instrucción pública, diplomaticos y altas autoridades universitarias—Síntesis de los discursos pronunciados." *La Prensa*, September 29, 1927.

"Una revelación antropológica." *La Nación*, December 1, 1913.

"Revelaciones prehistóricas." *La Nación*, June 21, 1914.

"La revolución religiosa y su aspecto sexual. Taras de Aj-en-Aton." *La Prensa*, February 25, 1923.

"La santidad moderna: Discursa pronunciada anoche en el funeral civil de Florentino Ameghino." *La Nación*, September 19, 1911.

"Se abrirá al publico el Museo Etnográfico HOY." *El Telegrafo*, September 28, 1927.

"Se efectuara hoy la inauguración de las instalaciones del Museo de Etnografía." *La Prensa*, September 28, 1927.

"Se inauguraron esta mañana las nuevas instalaciones del Museo de Etnografía. Asistieron a la ceremonia el presidente de la nacion y el ministro de instruccion publica." *El Diario*, September 28, 1927.

"Se inauguró el Museo Etnográfico de la F. Filosofia y Letras. Al acto de ayer asistió el presidente Alvear y numerosos universitarios." *La Fronda*, September 29, 1927.

"Suspendieron el traslado de un menhir a Buenos Aires." *La Gaceta*, August 28, 1936.

"Los triunfos de Ameghino." *La Nación*, July 13, 1913.

"La tumba de Tut-Ankh-Amon." *La Prensa*, May 13, 1923.

Untitled announcement. *Le Courier*, September 29, 1927.

"El 28 del corriente será inaugurado el Museo de Etnografía." *La Prensa*, September 26, 1927.

"Visita al Museo Etnográfico." *La Vanguardia*, October 17, 1927.

Vizconde de Lascano Tegui. "Los sabios reconocen la existencia de un nuevo adoquín. Alrededor de un craneo milenario. La fortuna de un hombre iluso, se evapora.—Las monedas de oro cambiadas en hoias de higuera." *Crítica*, May 4, 1923.

"Yacimientos arqueologicos y paleontologicos." *La Nación*, September 12, 1912.

"Los yacimientos de Miramar." *La Nación*, April 1, 1919.

Published Primary Sources

Altieri, Radames A. "La gramatica yunga de F. de la Carrera, estudio bibliográfico, con todos los modernos vocabularios." In *Publicación No. 257*. San Miguel de Tucumán: Instituto de Antropología, 1939.

Ambrosetti, Juan B. *El diablo indígena: Supersticiones y leyendas en la Argentina*. Buenos Aires: Editorial Convergencia, 1976.

———. "Doctor Florentino Ameghino, 1854–1911." In *Anales del Museo Nacional de Historia Natural de Buenos Aires*, vol. 22. Buenos Aires: J. A. Alsina, 1912.

———. *Exploraciones arqueológicas en la Pampa Grande (Provincia de Salta)*. Publicaciones del Seccion Antropológica 1. Buenos Aires: Imprenta "Didot," 1906.

———. "La Facultad de Filosofía y Letras de la Universidad Nacional de Buenos Aires y los estudios de arqueología americana." *Anthropos* 3 (1908): 983–87.

———. *Memoria del Museo Etnográfico, 1906 á 1912*. Buenos Aires: Compañía Sud-Americana de Billetes de Banco, 1912.

———. "Resultado de las exploraciones arqueológicas en el Pucará de Tilcara (Provincia de Jujuy)." *Actas del XVII Congreso Internacional de Americanistas*, 1912, 497–98.

———. *Segundo viaje á Misiones (por el Alto Paraná é Iguazú)*. Buenos Aires: Imp. y Enc. "Roma," 1894.

———. *Trabajos publicados*. Buenos Aires: Imprenta de Juan A. Alsina, 1904.

———. "Los vasos del pukará de Tilcara del tipo pelike comparados con los de Machu Pichu." *Proceedings of the Second Pan American Scientific Congress* 1 (1917): 38–39.

Ameghino, Florentino. *La antigüedad geológica del yacimiento antropolítico de Monte Hermoso*. Buenos Aires: Imprenta y Casa Editora "Juan A. Alsina," 1910.

———. *Descubrimiento de un esqueleto humano fossil en el Pampeano Superior del Arroyo Siasgo*. Buenos Aires: Imprenta y Casa Editora "Juan A. Alsina," 1910.

———. *Obras completas y correspondencia científica*. Edited by Alfredo J. Torcelli. La Plata: Taller de Impresiones Oficiales, 1935.

Aramburu, Julio. *Tucumán*. Buenos Aires: M. Gleizer, 1928.

Boas, Franz. "Some Principles of Museum Administration." *Science* 25, no. 650 (1907): 921–33.

Boman, Eric. *Antiquités de la Région Andine de la République Argentine et du Désert d'Atacama*. Vol. 2. Paris: Imprimerie National, 1908.

———. *Los ensayos para establecer una cronología prehispánica en la Región Diaguita*. Buenos Aires: Imprenta Municipal, 1923.

Burmeister, Hermann. *Descripción de Tucumán, por Germán Burmeister: Capítulos traducidos del Alemán por el Señor Cesáreo Wessel, y prólogo del doctor Ángel Gallardo. Publicaciones de la universidad con ocasión del centenario del Congreso de Tucumán de 1916*. Buenos Aires: Coni Hermanos, 1916.

Carrizo, Juan Alfonso. *Cantares tradicionales del Tucumán*. 1939. San Salvador de Jujuy: A. Baiocco y Cía, 1994.

Casanova, Eduardo. "Disertación del profesor de arqueología americana, Doctor Eduardo Casanova." In *Homenaje al Doctor Salvador Debenedetti. Resoluciones de las autoridades de la Facultad de Filosofía y Letras y Disertaciones pronunciadas en el acto académico realizado en el Aula Magna*, 6–24. Buenos Aires: Imprenta y Casa Editora "Coni," 1950.

———. *Restauración del Pucará*. Buenos Aires: Universidad de Buenos Aires, 1950.

Coviello, Alfredo. *Geografía intelectual de la República Argentina*. San Miguel de Tucumán: Grupo Septentrion, 1941.

Debenedetti, Salvador. "La restauración del Pucará." *Archivos del Museo Etnográfico*, vol. 1. Buenos Aires: Museo Etnográfico, 1929.

———. "Las ruinas del Pucará. Tilcara, Quebrada de Humahuaca (Provincia de Jujuy)." *Archivos del Museo Entográfico*, vol. 2. Buenos Aires: Museo Etnográfico, 1930.

"Doctor Francisco P. Moreno (1852–1919), fundador y primer director del museo, homenaje a su memoria." *Revista del Museo de La Plata* 28 (1924): 1–18.

Flower, William Henry. *Essays on Museums and Other Subjects Connected with Natural History*. 1898. Freeport: Books for Libraries Press, 1972.

González, Joaquin V. *Obras completas de Joaquin V. González*. Buenos Aires: Universidad Nacional de La Plata, 1935.

González Arrili, Bernardo. *Vida de Ameghino*. Santa Fe, Argentina: Catellví, 1954.

Goode, George Brown. "On the Classification of Museums." *Science* 3 (1896): 154–61.

Guide to Field Museum of Natural History. Chicago: Field Museum, 1964.

Homenaje al Doctor Salvador Debenedetti. Resoluciones de las autoridades de la Facultad de Filosofía y Letras y Disertaciones pronunciadas en el acto académico realizado en el Aula Magna. Buenos Aires: Imprenta y Casa Editora "Coni," 1950.

Hrdlicka, Ales. Preface to *Early Man in South America*. Smithsonian Institution Bureau of American Ethnology Bulletin 52. Washington: Government Printing Office, 1912.

Inauguración de la Universidad de Tucumán, 25 de Mayo de 1914. San Miguel de Tucumán: Imprenta A. Prebisch, 1914.

"Inauguración del Museo Etnográfico." *Archivos de la Universidad de Buenos Aires* 2, no. 2 (1927): 434–39.

Krebs, Edgardo. "Un Argentino universal." *La Nación*, July 28, 2002.

Lehmann-Nitsche, Robert. *Catálogo de la sección antropológica*. Buenos Aires: Imprenta Coni, 1910.

Lugones, Leopoldo. *Elogio de Ameghino*. Buenos Aires: Otero y Cía, 1915.

Lydekker, Richard. "The La Plata Museum." *Natural Science* 4 (1894): 27–35, 117–28.

Memoria correspondiente al año 1933. Cuadros estadísticas de los años 1930, 1931, y 1932. Proyectors de ley para la organización de la universidad y memoria correspondiente al año 1929. Buenos Aires: Imprenta y Casa Editora Coni, 1931.

Memoria correspondiente al año 1939. San Miguel de Tucumán: Imp. Miguel Violetto, 1940.

Márquez Miranda, Fernando. *Ameghino: Una vida heroica*. Buenos Aires: Editorial Nova, 1951.

———. "Recordando a Felix Outes." *Runa* 10 (1967): 68–82.

Moreno, Francisco P. "El Museo de La Plata. Rápida ojeada sobre su fundación y desarollo." *Revista del Museo de La Plata* 1 (1890–91): 28–54.

———. "Notes on the Anthropogeography of Argentina." *Geographical Journal* 18, no. 6 (December 1901): 574–89.

———. "Reconocimiento de la Región Andina. I. Apuntes preliminaries sobre una excursión á los territorios del Neuquén, Río Negro, Chubut y Santa Cruz." *Revista del Museo de la Plata* 8 (1897): 108.

———. *Reminiscencias de Francisco P. Moreno. Versión propia documentada*. Buenos Aires: Plantié Talleres Gráficos, 1942.

———. *Viaje a la Patagonia austral*. 1st ed. Buenos Aires: El Elefante Blanco, 2004.

Museo de la Provincia de Tucumán, sección etnográfica. Catálogo de arqueología y paleontología. San Miguel de Tucumán: Imprenta Prebisch y Violetto, 1916.

El Museo Etnográfico. Buenos Aires: Universidad de Buenos Aires, 1948.

Outes, Félix. *Palabras pronunciadas en la session inaugural de la Sociedad Argentina de Antropología*. Buenos Aires: Estudio de Artes Gráficas "Futuro," 1936.

Outes, Félix, and Carlos Bruch. *Los Aborígenes de la República Argentina. Manual adaptado á los programas de las escuelas primarias, colegios nacionales y escuelas normales*. Buenos Aires: Ángel Estrada y Cía, 1910.

Parker, William Belmont, ed. *Argentines of To-day*. Vol. 1. New York: Hispanic Society of America, 1920.

Publicaciones del Museo Etnográfico. Buenos Aires: Universidad Nacional de Buenos Aires, 1939.

Quesada, Vicente G. "Memoria of the Ministro Secretario de Gobierno de la Pvia de Buenos Aires, Dr. don Vicente G. Quesada." In *Revista del Museo de La Plata* 1 (1890–91): vii.

Quiroga, Ada'n. *Folk-lore Calchaqui'*. Buenos Aires: Impr. y Papeleri'a "La Buenos Aires," 1897.

Registro Nacional 1878. Buenos Aires: Biblioteca del Congreso Nacional, 1878.

Roca, Julio A. Introductory letter in *La Conquista de Quince Mil Leguas: Estudio sobre la translación de la frontera sud de la Republica al Río Negro dedicado a los jefes y oficiales del ejército expedicionario*, by Estanislao Zeballos, 23. 1878. Buenos Aires: Librería Hachette, 1958.

Sarmiento, Domingo Faustino. *Discursos Populares*. Vol. 22 of *Obras completas de Sarmiento*. 2 vols. Buenos Aires: Editorial Luz del Día, 1951.

Simpson, George Gaylord. *Discoverers of the Lost World: An Account of Some of Those Who Brought Back to Life South American Mammals Long Buried in the Abyss of Time*. New Haven: Yale University Press, 1984.

Ten Kate, Herman. "Matériaux pour servir à l'anthropologie des Indiens de la République Argentine." *Revista del Museo de La Plata* 12 (1905): 33–57.

Terán, Juan B. *La universidad y la vida*. Buenos Aires: Imprenta y Casa Editora Coni, 1921.

Torres, Luis María. "Dr. Francisco P. Moreno, fundador y primer director del museo, noticia bio-bibliográfica." *Revista del Museo de La Plata* 26 (1921): 1–16.

———. *Guía para visitar el Museo de La Plata. Publicado bajo la dirección del Dr. Luis María Torres, director del museo.* La Plata: Museo de La Plata, 1927.

Uhle, Max. "Las relaciones prehispánicas entre Perú y la Argentina." *Actas del Congreso Internacional de Americanistas* 27 (1910): 509–40.

La Universidad de Tucumán, 1914–1979. San Miguel de Tucumán: Imprenta de la Universidad Nacional de Tucumán, 1979.

Universidad Nacional de Tucumán, memoria año 1948. San Miguel de Tucumán: Universidad Nacional de Tucumán, 1948.

Vasconcelos, José. *The Cosmic Race / La raza cósmica.* Translated by Dider T. Jaén. Baltimore: Johns Hopkins University Press, 1997.

Vignati, Milciades Alejo. *Los restos de industria humana de Miramar. A propósito de los despropósitos del Comandante Romero.* Buenos Aires: Est. Gr. "Oceana," 1919.

Ward, Henry A. "Los museos argentinos." *Revista del Museo de La Plata* 1 (1890–91): 145–51.

Zeballos, Estanislao. *La Conquista de Quince Mil Leguas: Estudio sobre la translación de la frontera sud de la Republica al Río Negro dedicado a los jefes y oficiales del ejército expedicionario.* 1878. Buenos Aires: Librería Hachette, 1958.

SECONDARY SOURCES

Abt, Jeffrey. *American Egyptologist: The Life of James Henry Breasted and the Creation of His Oriental Institute.* Chicago: University of Chicago Press, 2011.

Aguirre, Robert D. *Informal Empire: Mexico and Central America in Victorian Culture.* Minneapolis: University of Minnesota Press, 2005.

Alexander, E. P. *Museum Masters: Their Museums and Their Influence.* Nashville: American Association for State and Local History, 1983.

Amati, Mirta Alicia. "Museo y etnografía. La imaginación museístico-etnográfica y su aporte en la construcción de la nación argentina y sus sujetos." M.A. thesis, Universidad Nacional de Buenos Aires, 2003.

Amenta, Sara Graciela. "Carlos Rodolfo Schreiter (1877–1942). Discípulo y colaborador del Dr. Miguel Lillo." In *La Generación del Centenario" y su proyección en el noroeste Argentino, 1900–1950. Actas de las IV Jornadas, realizadas en San Miguel de Tucumán del 3 as 5 de octubre de 2001,* edited by Florencia Aráoz de Isas, Elena Perilli de Colombres Garmendía, and Elba Estela Romero de Espinosa, 34–42. San Miguel de Tucumán: Fundación Miguel Lillo, Centro Cultural Alberto Rouge's, 2002.

———. *Carlos Rodolfo Schreiter (1877–1942): Notas biográficas y epistolario de un naturalista.* San Miguel de Tucumán: Centro Cultural Alberto Rougés, 2008.

Ametrano, Silvia. "Historia de una restitución." *MUSEO (Museo de Ciencias Naturales de La Plata)* 3, no. 24 (2010): 61–67.

Andermann, Jens. *The Optic of the State: Visuality and Power in Argentina and Brazil.* Pittsburgh: University of Pittsburgh Press, 2007.

Anderson, Benedict. *Imagined Communities: Reflections on the Origin and Spread of Nationalism.* London: Verso, 1983.

Anderson, Warwick. *The Cultivation of Whiteness: Science, Health, and Racial Destiny in Australia.* New York: Basic Books, 2003.

Andrews, George Reid. *The Afro-Argentines of Buenos Aires, 1800–1900.* Madison: University of Wisconsin Press, 1980.

Appadurai, Arjun. "Introduction: Commodities and the Politics of Value." In *The Social Life of Things: Commodities in Cultural Perspective*, edited by Arjun Appadurai, 3–61. Cambridge: Cambridge University Press, 1986.

Appelbaum, Nancy A., Anne S. Macpherson, and Karin Alejandra Rosemblatt, eds. *Race and Nation in Modern Latin America*. Chapel Hill: North Carolina University Press, 2003.

Arenas, Patricia. "Alfred Métraux: Momentos de su paso por Argentina." *Mundo de Antes* 1 (1998): 121–36.

———. "La antropología en la Argentina a fines del siglo XIX y principios del XX." *Runa* 19 (1989–90): 147–60.

———. *Antropologia en la Argentina: El aporte de los científicos de habla Aleman*. Buenos Aires: Institución Cultural Argentino-Germana, Museo Etnográfico J. B. Ambrosetti, Facultad de Filosofía y Letras de la Universidad de Buenos Aires, 1991.

———. "Documentos para la historia de la anthropologia." *Runa* 19 (1989–90): 223–27.

———. "'En la noche de los tiempos: Emilio y Duncan Wagner en el campo de profesionalización de la arqueología." *Mundo de Antes Instituto de Arqueología Museo* 4 (2005): 159–87.

Asma, Stephen T. *Stuffed Animals and Pickled Heads: The Culture and Evolution of Natural History Museums*. Oxford: Oxford University Press, 2001.

Auroi, Claude, and Alain Monnier, eds. *De Suiza a Sudamérica: Etnologías de Alfred Metraux*. Translated by Jorge Fondebrider. Geneva: Museo Etnográfico de Ginevra, Suiza, 1998.

Auza, Néstor Tomás. "Germán Burmeister y la Sociedad Paleontológica, 1866–1868." *Investigaciones y Ensayos* 46 (1996): 137–55.

———. "El Museo Nacional de la Confederación." *Investigaciones y Ensayos* 15 (1973): 181–206.

Barba, Enrique Mariano. "La fundación del museo y el ambiente científico de la epoca." In *Obra del centenario del Museo de La Plata*, vol. 1, *Reseña Histórica*, 3–48. La Plata: Universidad Nacional de La Plata, 1977.

Barrancos, Dora. *La escena iluminada: Ciencias para trabajadores 1890–1930*. Buenos Aires: Editoral Plus Ultra, 1996.

Beezley, William H., and Linda A. Curcio-Nagy, eds. *Latin American Popular Culture: An Introduction*. Lanham: SR Books, 2000.

Bennett, Tony. *The Birth of the Museum: History, Theory, Politics*. London: Routledge, 1995.

Berberian, Eduardo E., and Eugenia Capuano. *El Instituto de Antropología de la Universidad Nacional de Tucumán: Sus etapas y aportes a la cultura argentina*. Buenos Aires: Ediciones Cabargon, 1974.

Bethell, Leslie, ed. *Argentina Since Independence*. Cambridge: Cambridge University Press, 1993.

———. *The Paraguayan War (1864–1870)*. London: Institute of Latin American Studies, University of London, 1996.

Biraben, Max. *German Burmeister, su vida, su obra*. Buenos Aires: Ministerio de Cultura y Educación, Ediciones Culturales Argentinas, 1968.

Bonaudo, Marta, Elida Sonzogni, and Andrew Klatt. "To Populate and to Discipline: Labor Market Construction in the Province of Santa Fe, Argentina, 1850–1890." *Latin American Perspectives* 26, no. 1 (1999): 65–91.

Bourdieu, Pierre. "The Forms of Capital." In *Handbook of Theory and Research for the Sociology of Education*, edited by John G. Richardson, 241–58. New York: Greenwood, 1986.

Boyer, Christopher. *Becoming Campesinos: Politics, Identity, and Agrarian Struggle in Postrevolutionary Michoacán, 1920–1935*. Stanford: Stanford University Press, 2003.

Brooke, John Hedley. *Science and Religion: Some Historical Perspectives*. Cambridge: Cambridge University Press, 1991.

Brown, J. Andrew. *Test Tube Envy: Science and Power in Argentine Narrative*. Lewisburg: Bucknell University Press, 2005.

Brown, Jonathan C. *A Socioeconomic History of Argentina, 1776–1860*. New York: Cambridge University Press, 1979.

Brunk, Samuel. *The Posthumous Career of Emiliano Zapata: Myth, Memory, and Mexico's Twentieth Century*. Austin: University of Texas Press, 2008.

Brunk, Samuel, and Ben Fallaw, eds. *Heroes and Hero Cults in Latin America*. Austin: University of Texas Press, 2006.

Bueno, Christina. "Forjando Patrimonio: The Making of Archaeological Patrimony in Porfirian Mexico." *Hispanic American Historical Review* 90, no. 2 (2010): 215–45.

Bunker, Steven B. *Creating Mexican Consumer Culture in the Age of Porfirio Díaz*. Albuquerque: University of New Mexico Press, 2012.

Burckhardt, Frederick, and Sydney Smith, eds. *The Correspondence of Charles Darwin*. 10 vols. Cambridge: Cambridge University Press, 1985–97.

Burke, Peter. *What Is Cultural History?* 2nd ed. Cambridge: Polity Press, 2008.

Cáceres Freyre, Julián. *Juan B. Ambrosetti*. Buenos Aires: Ediciones Culturales Argentinas, 1967.

Califano, Mario, ed. *Evolución de las ciencias en la República Argentina 1872–1972*. Vol. 10, *Antropología*. Buenos Aires: Sociedad Científica Argentina, 1985.

Calvo, Silvia, and Patricia Arenas. "El Museo Etnográfico: Aportes para su historia." Unpublished manuscript, 1987.

Camp, Roderic. *Los intelectuales y el estado en el México del siglo XX*. Mexico: Fondo de Cultura Economica, 1988.

Carrazzoni, José Andrés. "El doctor Francisco J. Muiz y las ciencias naturales." *Todo Es Historia* 28, no. 324 (June 1994): 76–89.

Carrizo, Sergio. "Carlos Rodolfo Schreiter: Generador de la tarea arqueológica en la Provincia de Tucumán." In *La generacio'n del centenario y su proyeccio'n en el noroeste Argentino, 1900–1950. Actas de las VI Jornadas*, edited by Elena Perilli de Colombres Garmendía, Elba Estela Romero, 200–208. San Miguel de Tucumán: Fundación Miguel Lillo, Centro Cultural Alberto Rougés, 2005.

Castillo Ledón, Luis. *El Museo Nacional de Arqueología, Historia, y Etnografía, 1825–1925*. Mexico: Imprenta del Museo Nacional, 1924.

Chamosa, Oscar. *The Argentine Folklore Movement: Sugar Elites, Criollo Workers, and the Politics of Cultural Nationalism, 1900–1955*. Tucson: University of Arizona Press, 2010.

———. "Indigenous or Criollo: The Myth of White Argentina in Tucumán's Calchaquí Valley." *Hispanic American Historical Review* 88, no. 1 (February 2008): 71–106.

Cicerchia, Ricardo. *Journey, Rediscovery, and Narrative: British Travel Accounts of Argentina*. London: Institute of Latin American Studies, University of London, 1998.

Coleman, Laurence Vail. *Directory of Museums in South America*. Washington, D.C.: American Museum Association, 1929.

Conn, Steven. *History's Shadow: Native Americans and Historical Consciousness in the Nineteenth Century*. Chicago: University of Chicago Press, 2004.

———. *Museums and American Intellectual Life, 1876–1920*. Chicago: University of Chicago Press, 1998.

Coombes, Annie E. "Museums and the Formation of National and Cultural Identities." *Oxford Art Journal* 11, no. 2 (1988): 57–68.

———. *Reinventing Africa: Museums, Material Culture, and Popular Imagination in Late Victorian and Edwardian England*. New Haven: Yale University Press, 1994.

Cope, R. Douglas. *The Limits of Racial Domination: Plebeian Society in Colonial Mexico City, 1660–1720*. Madison: University of Wisconsin Press, 1994.

Craib, Raymond B. *Cartographic Mexico: A History of State Fixations and Fugitive Landscapes.* Durham: Duke University Press, 2004.

Crane, Susan A. "Memory, Distortion, and History in the Museum." *History and Theory* 36 (1997): 44–63.

Cummins, Tom, and Joanne Rappaport. "The Reconfiguration of Civic and Sacred Space: Architecture, Image, and Writing in the Colonial Northern Andes." In "Colonial Latin America: A Multidisciplinary Approach," special issue, *Latin American Literary Review* 26, no. 52 (1998): 174–200.

Curtoni, Rafael, Axel Lazzari, and Marisa Lazzari. "Middle of Nowhere: A Place of War Memories, Commemoration, and Aboriginal Re-emergence (La Pampa, Argentina)." *World Archaeology* 35, no. 1 (2003): 61–78.

Dean, Carolyn. *A Culture of Stone: Inka Perspectives on Rock.* Durham: Duke University Press, 2010.

de la Cadena, Marisol. *Indigenous Mestizos: The Politics of Race and Culture in Cuzco, Peru, 1919–1991.* Durham: Duke University Press, 2000.

de la Fuente, Alejandro. *A Nation for All: Race, Inequality, and Politics in Twentieth-Century Cuba.* Chapel Hill: University of North Carolina Press, 2001.

de la Fuente, Ariel. *Children of Facundo: Caudillo and Gaucho Insurgency During the Argentine State-Formation Process (La Rioja, 1853–1870).* Durham: Duke University Press, 2000.

———. "Federalism and Opposition to the Paraguayan War in the Argentine Interior, La Rioja, 1865–67." In *I Die with My Country: Perspectives on the Paraguayan War, 1864–1870,* edited by Hendrick Kraay and Thomas L. Whigham, 140–53. Lincoln: University of Nebraska Press, 2004.

de Liboreiro, M. Cristina. *No hay negros argentinos?* Buenos Aires: Editorial Dunken, 1999.

Delrio, Walter. "De 'salvajes' a 'indios nacionales.' Interpelaciones hegemónicas y campañas militares en Norpatagonia y la Araucanía (1879–1885)." *Mundo de Antes* 3 (2002): 189–207.

de Pilar Babot, María. "La arqueología argentina de fines del siglo XIX y principios del XX a través de J. B. Ambrosetti." *Mundo de Antes* 1 (1998): 165–92.

Díaz Polanco, Héctor. *Indigenous Peoples in Latin America: The Quest for Self-Determination.* Translated by Lucía Rayas. Boulder, Colo.: Westview Press, 1997.

Dodds, Klaus-John. "Geography, Identity, and the Creation of the Argentine State." *Bulletin of Latin American Research* 12, no. 3 (1993): 311–31.

Dorsey, George A. "The Anthropological Exhibits at the American Museum of Natural History." *Science* 25 (1907): 584–89.

Ducey, Michael T. *A Nation of Villages: Riot and Rebellion in the Mexican Huasteca, 1750–1850.* Tucson: University of Arizona Press, 2004.

Earle, Rebecca. "'Padres de la Patria' and the Ancestral Past: Commemorations of Independence in Nineteenth-Century Spanish America." *Journal of Latin American Studies* 34 (2002): 775–805.

———. *The Return of the Native: Indians and Myth-Making in Spanish America, 1810–1930.* Durham: Duke University Press, 2007.

Edwards, Elizabeth. *Anthropology and Photography: 1860–1920.* New Haven: Yale University Press, 1992.

Endere, María Luz. *Management of Archaeological Sites and the Public in Argentina.* Ann Arbor: University of Michigan Press, 2007.

———. "The Reburial Issue in Argentina: A Growing Conflict." In *The Dead and Their Possessions: Repatriation in Principle, Policy, and Practice,* edited by Cressida Fforde, Jane Hubert, and Paul Turnbull, 266–83. London: Routledge, 2002.

Endere, María Luz, Plácido Cali, and Pedro Paulo A. Funari. "Archaeology and Indigenous Communities: A Comparative Study of Argentinean and Brazilian Legislation." In

Indigenous Peoples and Archaeology in Latin America, edited by Cristóbal Gnecco and Patricia Ayala, 159–77. Walnut Creek, Calif.: Left Coast Press, 2011.

Endere, María Luz, and Irina Podgorny. "Los gliptodontes son argentinos: La Ley 9080 y la creación del patrimonio nacional." *Ciencia Hoy* 7, no. 42 (1997): 54–59.

Farro, Máximo, and Irina Podgorny. "Frente a la tumba del sabio: Florentino Ameghino y la 'santidad' del científico en el Plata." *Ciencia Hoy* 8, no. 47 (1998): 28–37.

Fernández, Jorge. *Historia de la arqueología argentina*. Mendoza: Talleres Gráficos del Centro de Economía, Legislación y Administración del Agua, 1982.

Fernández, Laura. "La utopia oligarquica: Argentina en la Exposición Universal de 1889." *Todo Es Historia* 421 (August 2002): 58–64.

Ferrari, Roberto A. "Cartas inéditas de Francisco P. Moreno a Germán Avé-Lallemant. 1891–1892." *Investigaciones y Ensayos* 48 (1998): 439–62.

Ferrer, Ada. *Insurgent Cuba: Race, Nation, and Revolution, 1868–1898*. Chapel Hill: University of North Carolina Press, 1999.

Findlen, Paula. *Possessing Nature: Museums, Collecting, and Scientific Culture in Early Modern Italy*. Berkeley: University of California Press, 1994.

Forgan, Sophie. "The Architecture of Display: Museums, Universities, and Objects in Nineteenth-Century Britain." *History of Science* 32 (1994): 139–62.

Formoso, Silvia Eugenia. "Padilla, Rougés y la cultura folklórica." In *La generación del centenario y su proyección en el noroeste Argentino (1900–1950). Actas de las IV Jornadas realizadas en San Miguel de Tucumán del 3 al 5 de octubre de 2001*, edited by Florencia Aráoz de Isas, Elena Perilli de Colombres Garmendía, and Elba Estela Romero de Espinosa, 171–81. San Miguel de Tucumán: Fundación Miguel Lillo, Centro Cultural Alberto Rougés, 2002.

Foucault, Michel. *Discipline and Punish: The Birth of the Prison*. Translated by Alan Sheridan. 1977. New York: Vintage Books, 1995.

———. *The History of Sexuality*. Translated by Robert Hurley. Vol. 1. New York: Vintage Books, 1990.

———. *The Order of Things: An Archaeology of the Human Sciences*. New York: Pantheon Books, 1971.

———. *Power/Knowledge: Selected Interviews and Other Writings, 1972–1977*. Edited by Colin Gordon. New York: Pantheon Books, 1980.

French, William E. "Imagining and the Cultural History of Nineteenth-Century Mexico." In "Mexico's New Cultural History: Una Lucha Libre," special issue, *Hispanic American Historical Review* 79, no. 2 (1990): 250.

Gallardo, José M. *El Museo de Ciencias Naturales en la Manzana de las Luces*. Buenos Aires: Imprenta Coni SACIFI, 1976.

García, Susana V., and Irina Podgorny. "El sabio tiene una patria: La Gran Guerra y la comunidad científica argentina." *Ciencia Hoy* 10, no. 55 (2000): 24–34.

Garrigan, Shelley E. *Collecting Mexico: Museums, Monuments, and the Creation of National Identity*. Minneapolis: University of Minnesota Press, 2012.

Gavirati, Marcelo. "La vida de un colono gales en la última frontera. John Daniel Evans." In *Vivir entre dos mundos: Las fronteras del sur de la Argentina. Siglos XVIII y XIX*, edited by Raúl Mandrini, 319–54. Buenos Aires: Taurus, 2006.

Glick, Thomas F. "The Reception of Darwinism in Uruguay." In *The Reception of Darwinism in the Iberian World: Spain, Spanish America, and Brazil*, edited by Thomas F. Glick, Miguel Angel Puig-Samper, and Rosaura Ruiz, 29–52. Dordrecht: Kluwer Academic, 1999.

Glick, Thomas F., Miguel Angel Puig-Samper, and Rosaura Ruiz, eds. *The Reception of Darwinism in the Iberian World: Spain, Spanish America, and Brazil*. Dordrecht: Kluwer Academic, 1999.

Gonzalez, Alberto Rex. "A cuarto decadas del comienzo de una etapa. Apuntes marginales para la historia de la antropología argentina." *Runa* 20 (1991–92): 91–110.

Goode, James F. *Negotiating for the Past: Archeology, Nationalism, and Diplomacy in the Middle East, 1919–1941*. Austin: University of Texas Press, 2007.

Goodwin, Mark. "Objects, Belief, and Power in Mid-Victorian England: The Origins of the Victoria and Albert Museum." In *Objects of Knowledge*, edited by Susan Pierce, 9–49. New Research in Museum Studies Series 1. London: Athlone Press, 1990.

Gordillo, Gastón. *Landscapes of Devils: Tensions of Place and Memory in the Argentinean Chaco*. Durham: Duke University Press, 2004.

Graham, Richard, ed. *The Idea of Race in Latin America, 1870–1940*. Austin: University of Texas Press, 1990.

Grandin, Greg. *The Blood of Guatemala: A History of Race and Nation*. Durham: Duke University Press, 2000.

Guy, Donna. *Argentine Sugar Politics: Tucumán and the Generation of Eighty*. Tempe: Center for Latin American Studies, Arizona State University, 1980.

———. *Sex and Danger in Buenos Aires: Prostitution, Family, and Nation in Argentina*. Lincoln: University of Nebraska Press, 1991.

Habermas, Jürgen. *The Structural Transformation of the Public Sphere: An Inquiry into a Category of Bourgeois Society*. Translated by Thomas Burger. Cambridge: MIT Press, 1989.

Hellman, Geoffrey T. *Bankers, Bones, and Beetles: The First Century of the American Museum of Natural History*. Garden City: Natural History Press, 1969.

Henare, Amira J. M. *Museums, Anthropology, and Imperial Exchange*. Cambridge: Cambridge University Press, 2005.

Hinsley, Curtis M., Jr. *Savages and Scientists: The Smithsonian Institution and the Development of American Anthropology, 1846–1910*. Washington, D.C.: Smithsonian Institution Press, 1981.

Hoberman, Louisa Schell, and Susan Migden Socolow, eds. *Cities and Society in Colonial Latin America*. Albuquerque: University of New Mexico Press, 1986.

Home, R. W., and S. G. Kohlstedt, eds. *International Science and National Scientific Identity*. Boston: Kluwer Academic, 1991.

"Homenaje a Adán Quiroga." *Cuadernos del Instituto Nacional de Antropología* 4 (1963): 11–34.

Hooper-Greenhill, Eilean. *Museums and the Interpretation of Visual Culture*. London: Routledge, 2000.

———. *Museums and the Shaping of Knowledge*. London: Routledge, 1992.

Hosne, Roberto. *Francisco Moreno: Una herencia patagónica desperdiciada*. Buenos Aires: Emecé, 2005.

Hudson, Kenneth. *Museums of Influence*. Cambridge: Cambridge University Press, 1987.

———. *A Social History of Museums: What the Visitors Thought*. Atlantic Highlands: Humanities Press, 1975.

Iglesias Utset, Marial. *A Cultural History of Cuba During the U.S. Occupation, 1898–1902*. Translated by Russ Davidson. Chapel Hill: University of North Carolina Press, 2011.

Impey, Oliver, and Arthur MacGregor, eds. *The Origins of Museums: The Cabinet of Curiosities in Sixteenth- and Seventeenth-Century Europe*. Oxford: Clarendon Press, 1985.

James, Daniel. *Doña María's Story: Life History, Memory, and Political Identity*. Durham: Duke University Press, 2000.

Jenkins, David. "Object Lessons and Ethnographic Displays: Museum Exhibitions and the Making of American Anthropology." *Comparative Studies in Society and History* 36, no. 2 (1994): 242–70.

Jones, Kristine L. "Conflict and Adaptation in the Argentine Pampas, 1750–1880." Ph.D. diss., University of Chicago, 1984.

———. "Nineteenth Century British Travel Accounts of Argentina." *Ethnohistory* 33, no. 2 (1986): 195–211.

Jones, Steve, Robert Martin, and David Pilbeam, eds. *The Cambridge Encyclopedia of Human Evolution.* 1992. Cambridge: Cambridge University Press, 2000.

Joseph, Gilbert M., and Daniel Nugent, eds. *Everyday Forms of State Formation: Revolution and the Negotiation of Rule in Modern Mexico.* Durham: Duke University Press, 1994.

———. "Popular Culture and State Formation in Revolutionary Mexico." In *Everyday Forms of State Formation: Revolution and the Negotiation of Rule in Modern Mexico,* edited by Gilbert M. Joseph and Daniel Nugent, 3–23. Durham: Duke University Press, 1994.

Joseph, Gilbert M., and Mark D. Szuchman, eds. *I Saw a City Invincible: Urban Portraits of Latin America.* Jaguar Books on Latin America 9. Wilmington, Del.: Scholarly Resources, 1996.

Kaplan, Flora E. S., ed. *Museums and the Making of "Ourselves": The Role of Objects in National Identity.* London: Leicester University Press, 1994.

Karush, Matthew B., and Oscar Chamosa, eds. *The New Cultural History of Peronism: Power and Identity in Mid-Twentieth-Century Argentina.* Durham: Duke University Press, 2010.

Kinsbruner, Jay. *The Colonial Spanish-American City: Urban Life in the Age of Atlantic Capitalism.* Austin: University of Texas Press, 2005.

Kirshenblatt-Gimblett, Barbara. *Destination Culture: Tourism, Museums, and Heritage.* Berkeley: University of California Press, 1998.

———. "Objects of Ethnography." In *Exhibiting Cultures: The Poetics and Politics of Museum Display,* edited by Ivan Karp and Steven D. Lavine, 384–443. Washington, D.C.: Smithsonian Institution Press, 1991.

Kohlstedt, Sally Gregory. "Henry A. Ward: The Merchant Naturalist and American Museum Development." *Journal of the Society for the Bibliography of Natural History* 9 (1980): 647–61.

———. "Museums: Revisiting Sites in the History of the Natural Sciences." *Journal of the History of Biology* 28 (1995): 151–66.

Kraay, Hendrik, and Thomas L. Whigham, eds. *I Die with My Country: Perspectives on the Paraguayan War, 1864–1870.* Lincoln: University of Nebraska Press, 2004.

Larson, Brooke. *Trials of Nation Making: Liberalism, Race, and Ethnicity in the Andes, 1810–1910.* Cambridge: Cambridge University Press, 2004.

Larson, Carolyne R. "Natural Athletes: Constructing Southern Indigenous Physicality in Late Nineteenth-Century Argentina." In *Sports in Latin American History,* edited by David Sheinin. Pittsburgh: University of Pittsburgh Press, forthcoming.

Lascano Gonzalez, Antonio. *El Museo de Ciencias Naturales de Buenos Aires.* Buenos Aires: Ediciones Culturales Argentinas, 1980.

Latour, Bruno. *Science in Action: How to Follow Scientists and Engineers Through Society.* Cambridge: Harvard University Press, 1987.

Lazzari, Axel. "Aboriginal Recognition, Freedom, and Phantoms: The Vanishing of the Ranquel and the Return of the Rankülche in La Pampa." *Journal of Latin American Anthropology* 8, no. 3 (2003): 59–83.

Lekan, Thomas M. *Imagining the Nation in Nature: Landscape Preservation and German Identity, 1885–1945.* Cambridge: Harvard University Press, 2004.

Lenton, Diana. "The *Malón de la Paz* of 1946: Indigenous *Descamisados* at the Dawn of Peronism." In *The New Cultural History of Peronism: Power and Identity in Mid-*

Twentieth-Century Argentina, edited by Matthew B. Karush and Oscar Chamosa, 85–112. Durham: Duke University Press, 2010.

Leuchars, Chris. *To the Bitter End: Paraguay and the War of the Triple Alliance*. Westport, Conn.: Greenwood Press, 2002.

Levaggi, Abelardo. *Paz en la frontera: Historia de las relaciones diplomáticas con las comunidades en la Argentina (siglos XVI–XIX)*. Buenos Aires: Editorial Dunken, 2000.

Lockhart, James. *The Nahuas After the Conquest: A Social and Cultural History of the Indians of Central Mexico, Sixteenth Through Eighteenth Centuries*. Stanford: Stanford University Press, 1992.

Lomnitz, Claudio. "Elusive Property: The Personification of Mexican National Sovereignty." In *The Empire of Things: Regimes of Value and Material Culture*, edited by Fred R. Myers, 119–38. Santa Fe: School of American Research Press, 2001.

Lopes, Maria Margaret, and Irina Podgorny. "The Shaping of Latin American Museums of Natural History, 1850–1990." In "Nature and Empire: Science and the Colonial Enterprise," special issue, *Osiris* 15 (2000): 108–18.

López, Rick A. *Crafting Mexico: Intellectuals, Artisans, and the State After the Revolution*. Durham: Duke University Press, 2010.

Lucie-Smith, Edward. *Arte latinoamericano del siglo XX*. Barcelona: Ediciones Destino, 1993.

Ludueña, Felipe. *Labor parlamentaria del perito doctor Francisco P. Moreno*. Buenos Aires: Horable Senado de la Nación, Secretaría Parlamentaria, Dirección Publicaciones, 1995.

Lynch, John. *The Spanish American Revolutions, 1808–1826*. 2nd ed. New York: W. W. Norton, 1986.

MacGregor, Arthur. *Curiosity and Enlightenment: Collectors and Collections from the Sixteenth to the Nineteenth Century*. New Haven: Yale University Press, 2007.

Mah, Harold. "Phantasies of the Public Sphere: Rethinking the Habermas of Historians." In "New Work on the Old Regime and the French Revolution," special issue, *Journal of Modern History* 72, no. 1 (2000): 153–82.

Mallon, Florencia. "La 'doble columna' y la 'doble consciencia' en la obra de Manuel Manquilef." *Revista Chilena de Antropología* 21 (2010): 59–79.

———. *Peasant and Nation: The Making of Postcolonial Mexico and Peru*. Berkeley: University of California Press, 1995.

Mandrini, Raúl J. *Vivir entre dos mundos. Las fronteras del sur de la Argentina. Siglos XVIII y XIX*. Buenos Aires: Taurus, 2006.

Martínez, Ana Teresa, Constanza Taboada, and Luis Alejandro Auat. "The Wagner Brothers: French Archaeologists and Origin Myths in Early Twentieth-Century Argentina." In *Archives, Ancestors, Practices: Archaeology in the Light of Its History*, edited by Nathan Schlanger and Jarl Nordlbladh, 261–71. New York: Berghahn Books, 2008.

Mases, Enrique Hugo. *Estado y cuestión indígena: El destino final de los indios sometidos en el sur del territorio (1878–1910)*. Buenos Aires: Entrepasados/Prometeo Libros, 2002.

Masotta, Carlos. "Almas Robadas. Exotismo y ambigüedad en las postales etnográficas argentinas." *Cuadernos del Instituto Nacional de Antropología y Pensamiento Latinoamericano* 19 (2000–2002): 421–40.

Miller, Nicola. *In the Shadow of the State: Intellectuals and the Quest for National Identity in Twentieth-Century Spanish America*. London: Verso, 1999.

Montserrat, Marcelo, ed. *La ciencia en la Argentina entre siglos: Textos, contextos, e instituciones*. Buenos Aires: Manantial, 2000.

———. "The Evolutionist Mentality in Argentina: An Ideology of Progress." In *The Reception of Darwinism in the Iberian World: Spain, Spanish America, and Brazil*, edited by Thomas F. Glick, Miguel Angel Puig-Sampler, and Rosaura Ruiz, 1–28. Dordrecht: Kluwer Academic, 1999.

Morales-Moreno, Luis Gerardo. "History and Patriotism in the National Museum of Mexico." In *Museums and the Making of "Ourselves": The Role of Objects in National Identity*, edited by Flora E. S. Kaplan, 171–91. London: Leicester University Press, 1994.
———. *Museopatria mexicana*. Mexico: Instituto Nacional de Antropologia e Historia, 1991.
Morosi, Julio A. *Los creadores del edificio del Museo de La Plata y su obra*. La Plata: Fundación Museo de La Plata Francisco Pascasio Moreno, 2004.
Moya, José C. *Cousins and Strangers: Spanish Immigrants in Buenos Aires, 1850–1930*. Berkeley: University of California Press, 1998.
Nacuzzi, Lidia R., ed. *Funcionarios, diplomáticos, guerreros: Miradas hacia el otro en las fronteras de Pampa y Patagonia (siglos XVIII y XIX)*. Buenos Aires: Gráfica Integral, 2002.
Novoa, Adriana, and Alex Levine. *From Man to Ape: Darwinism in Argentina, 1870–1920*. Chicago: University of Chicago Press, 2010.
Obra del centenario del Museo de La Plata. La Plata: Universidad Nacional de La Plata, 1977.
Ocampo, Beatriz. "La interpretación del descubrimiento de la Civilización Chaco-Santiagueña de los Hnos Wagner: La temporalidad en la teoría y en la existencia de los sujetos (arqueólogos)." *Trabajo y Sociedad* 9, no. 9 (2007): 1–13.
Omil, Marta, José Bobovnikov, and Josefina Durango de Cabrera. "Primera Reunión Nacional de Ciencias Naturales." In *La generación del centenario y su projección en el noroeste Argentino, 1900–1950. Actas de las III Jornadas*, 1:43–47. San Miguel de Tucumán: Fundación Miguel Lillo, Centro Cultural Alberto Rougés, 2000.
Orosz, Joel J. *Curators and Culture*. Tuscaloosa: University of Alabama Press, 1990.
Paoletti, Elisa. "Translations as Shapers of Image: Don Carlos Darwin and His Voyage into Spanish on H.M.S. *Beagle*." *Traduction, Terminologie, Redaction* 18, no. 1 (2005): 55–77.
Parker, Holt N. "Toward a Definition of Popular Culture." *History and Theory* 50 (2011): 147–70.
Pearce, Susan M. *Museums, Objects, and Collections*. Washington, D.C.: Smithsonian Institution Press, 1993.
———. *On Collecting: An Investigation into Collecting in the European Tradition*. New York: Routledge, 1995.
Pegoraro, Andrea. "'Instrucciones' y colecciones en viaje. Redes de recolección entre el Museo Etnográfico y los Territorios Nacionales." *Anuario de Estudios en Antropología Social* (2005): 49–64.
Penhos, Marta, Carlos Masotta, Mariano Oropeza, Sandra Bendayán, María Inés Rodríguez Aguilar, Miguel Ruffo, and María Spinelli. *Arte y antropología en la Argentina*. Buenos Aires: Ronor, 2005.
Penhos, Marta Noemí. "Frente y perfil. Una indagación acerca de la fotografía en las prácticas antropológicas y criminológicas en Argentina a fines del siglo XIX y principios del XX." In *Arte y antropología en la Argentina*, 39, 45–50. Buenos Aires: Ronor, 2005.
Penny, H. Glenn. *Objects of Culture: Ethnology and Ethnographic Museums in Imperial Germany*. Chapel Hill: University of North Carolina Press, 2002.
Perazzi, Pablo. *Hermenéutica de la barbarie: Una historia de la antropología en Buenos Aires, 1935–1966*. Buenos Aires: Gráfica Integral, 2003.
———. "La nación deshuesada: Condiciones espaciales y sociales en el orígen de las disciplinas antropológicas en Buenos Aires." In *Historia, poder, y discursos: Antropología sociocultural*, edited by Guillermo Wilde and Pablo Javier Schamber, 27–48. Buenos Aires: Paradigma Indicial, 2005.
Pérez Gollán, José Antonio. "Mr. Ward en Buenos Aires: Los museos y el proyecto de nación a fines del siglo XIX." *Ciencia Hoy* 5, no. 28 (1995): 52–58.

Pérez Gollán, José Antonio, and Gutavo Politis. "Latin American Archaeology: From Colonialism to Globalization." In *A Companion to Social Archaeology*, edited by Lynn Meskell and Robert Preucel, 353–73. Oxford: Blackwell, 2004.

Perilli de Colombres Garmendia, Elena. "Alfred Metraux y la Universidad Nacional de Tucumán." In *Actas del Primer Congreso sobre la historia de la Universidad Nacional de Tucumán*, edited by Florencio Gilberto Aceñolaza, 145–53. San Miguel de Tucumán: Universidad Nacional de Tucumán, 2006.

———. "Lo regional, instrumento de equilibrio de la nación." In *La generación del centenario y su projección en el noroeste Argentino, 1900–1950. Actas de las III Jornadas*, 1:203–15. San Miguel de Tucumán: Fundación Miguel Lillo, Centro Cultural Alberto Rougés, 2000.

Pilcher, Jeffrey M. *¡Que Vivan Los Tamales! Food and the Making of Mexican Identity*. Albuquerque: University of New Mexico Press, 1998.

Plotkin, Mariano Ben. *Freud in the Pampas: The Emergence and Development of a Psychoanalytic Culture in Argentina*. Stanford: Stanford University Press, 2001.

———. *Mañana es San Perón: A Cultural History of Perón's Argentina*. Wilmington: Scholarly Resources, 2003.

Podgorny, Irina. "El acervo histórico de la Facultad y Museo de La Plata: Huesos y flechas para la nación." *Entrepasados* 3 (1992): 157–65.

———. "Antiguedades incontroladas. La arqueología en la Argentina, 1910–1940." In *Intelectuales y expertos. La constitución del conocimiento social en la Argentina*, edited by Federico Neiburg and Mariano Plotkin, 147–74. Buenos Aires: Editorial Paidós, 2004.

———. *El argentino despertar de las faunas y de las Gentes Prehistóricas: Coleccionistas, estudios, museos y universidad en la creación del patrimonio paleontológico y arqueológico nacional (1875–1913)*. Buenos Aires: Gráfica L'Aiglón, 2000.

———. *Arqueología de la educación: Textos, indicios, monumentos: La imagen de los indios en el mundo escolar*. Buenos Aires: Sociedad Argentina de Antropología, 1999.

———. "De la antigüedad del hombre en el Plata a la distribución de las antigüedades en el mapa: Los criterios de organización de las colecciones antropológicas del Museo de La Plata entre 1897 y 1930." *História, Ciências, Saúde—Manguinhos* 6, no. 1 (1999): 81–101.

———. "De la santidad laica del científico Florentino Ameghino y el espectáculo de la ciencia en la Argentina moderna." *Entrepasados* 13 (1997): 37–61.

———. "De razón a facultad: Ideas acerca de las funciones del Museo de La Plata en el período 1890–1913." *Runa* 22 (1995): 89–104.

———. "La mirada que pasa: Museos, educación pública y visualización de la evidencia científica." Supplement, *História, Ciências, Saúde—Manguinhos* 12 (2005): 231–64.

———. "El museo soy yo: Alfred Marbais du Graty en la Confederación Argentina." *Ciencia Hoy* 7, no. 38 (1997): 48–53.

———. "Portable Antiquities: Transportation, Ruins, and Communications in Nineteenth-Century Archeology." *História, Ciências, Saúde—Manguinhos* 15, no. 3 (2008): 577–95.

Podgorny, Irina, and Gustavo Politis. "It Is Not All Roses Here: Ales Hrdlicka's Travelogue and His Trip to Buenos Aires in 1910." *Revista de Historia de Arte e Arqueología* 3 (2000): 95–108.

———. "¿Que sucedió en la historia? Los esqueletos araucanos del Museo de La Plata y la Conquista del Desierto." *Arqueología Contemporánea* 3 (1990–92): 73–79.

Poole, Deborah. "An Image of 'Our Indian': Type Photographs and Racial Sentiments in Oaxaca, 1920–1940." *Hispanic American Historical Review* 84, no. 1 (2004): 37–82.

———. *Vision, Race, and Modernity: A Visual Economy of the Andean Image World*. Princeton: Princeton University Press, 1997.

Postero, Nancy Grey, and Leon Zamosc, eds. *The Struggle for Indigenous Rights in Latin America*. Eastbourne: Sussex Academic Press, 2006.

Pratt, Mary Louise. *Imperial Eyes: Travel Writing and Transculturation*. London: Routledge Press, 1992.

Quijada, Mónica. "Ancestros, ciudadanos, piezas de museo. Francisco P. Moreno y la articulación del indígena en la construcción nacional argentina." *Estudios Interdisciplinarios de América Latina y el Caribe* 9, no. 2 (1998): 21–46.

———. "La *ciudadanización* del 'indio bárbaro.' Políticas oficiales y oficiosas hacia la población indígena de La Pampa y la Patagonia, 1870–1920." *Revista de Indias* 19, no. 217 (1999): 675–704.

Quijada, Mónica, Carmen Bernand, and Arnd Schneider. *Homogeneidad y nación: Con un estudio de caso: Argentina, siglos XIX y XX*. Madrid: Consejo Superior de Investigaciones Científicas, Centro de Humanidades, Instituto de Historia, 2000.

Quiroga, Laura, and Verónica Puente. "Imagen y percepción: Iconografía de las urnas Belén. Colección Schreiter." In *Procesos sociales prehispánicos en el sur andino. La vivienda, la comunidad y el territorio*, edited by Axel E. Nielsen, M. Clara Rivolta, Verónica Seldes, María Vázquez, and Pablo H. Mercolli, 323–45. Córdoba: Editorial Brujas, 2007.

Rabinow, Paul, ed. *The Foucault Reader*. New York: Pantheon Books, 1984.

Racine, Karen. " 'This England and This Now': British Cultural and Intellectual Influence in the Spanish American Independence Era." *Hispanic American Historical Review* 90, no. 3 (2010): 423–54.

Raffino, Rodolfo Adelio. *Burmeister: El dorado y dos Argentinas*. Buenos Aires: Editorial Dunken, 2006.

Rama, Angel. *The Lettered City*. Translated by John Charles Chasteen. Durham: Duke University Press, 1996.

Ramundo, Paola Silvia. "Los aportes de los investigadores pioneros a la arqueología del noroeste Argentino." *Temas de Historia Argentina y Americana* 11 (2007): 179–217.

"Roberto Lehmann-Nitsche (1872–1972)." *Cuadernos del Instituto de Antropología* (1972–78): 7–19.

Roca, Andrea. "El Museo Etnográfico 'Juan B. Ambrosetti': Los usos del tiempo en una colección de pasados." *Anuario de Estudios en Antropología Social* (2005): 65–85.

Rock, David. *Argentina, 1516–1987: From Spanish Colonization to Alfonsín*. Berkeley: University of California Press, 1985.

———. "Argentina, 1930–1946." In *Argentina Since Independence*, edited by Leslie Bethell, 173–242. Cambridge: Cambridge University Press, 1993.

———. "Intellectual Precursors of Conservative Nationalism in Argentina, 1900–1927." *Hispanic Historical Review* 67, no. 2 (1987): 271–300.

———. *Politics in Argentina, 1890–1930: The Rise and Fall of Radicalism*. Cambridge: Cambridge University Press, 1975.

Rodriguez, Julia. *Civilizing Argentina: Science, Medicine, and the Modern State*. Chapel Hill: University of North Carolina Press, 2006.

Roque, Ricardo. *Headhunting and Colonialism: Anthropology and the Circulation of Human Skulls in the Portuguese Empire, 1870–1930*. Basingstoke: Palgrave Macmillan, 2010.

Rotker, Susana. *Captive Women: Oblivion and Memory in Argentina*. Translated by Jennifer French. Minneapolis: University of Minnesota Press, 2002.

Rubenstein, Anne. *Bad Language, Naked Ladies, and Other Threats to the Nation: A Political History of Comic Books in Mexico*. Durham: Duke University Press, 1998.

Rutledge, Ian. *Cambio agrario e integración: El desarrollo del capitalismo en Jujuy, 1550–1960*. San Miguel de Tucumán: COOTGRATUC, 1987.

Rydell, Robert W. *All the World's a Fair: Visions of Empire at American International Exposi-tions, 1876–1916*. Chicago: University of Chicago Press, 1984.

Sabato, Hilda. *The Many and the Few: Political Participation in Republican Buenos Aires*. Stanford: Stanford University Press, 2001.

Said, Edward. *Culture and Imperialism*. New York: Aldine, 1993.

Sánchez Gómez, Gonzalo. *Museo, memoria y nación: Misión de los museos nacionales para los ciudadanos del futuro*. Bogotá: Ministerio de Cultura, 2000.

Secord, J. A., N. Jardine, and E. C. Spray, eds. *Cultures of Natural History*. Cambridge: Cambridge University Press, 1996.

Shaw, Wendy M. K. *Possessors and Possessed: Museums, Archaeology, and the Visualization of History in the Late Ottoman Empire*. Berkeley: University of California Press, 2003.

Sheets-Pyenson, Susan. *Cathedrals of Science: The Development of Colonial Natural History Museums During the Late Nineteenth Century*. Kingston: McGill–Queen's University Press, 1988.

Sherman, Daniel J., and Irit Rogoff, eds. *Museum Culture: Histories, Discourses, Spectacles*. Minneapolis: University of Minnesota Press, 1994.

Shumway, Nicolas. *The Invention of Argentina*. Berkeley: University of California Press, 1991.

Smith, Anthony D. *National Identity*. Reno: University of Nevada Press, 1991.

Smith, Charles Saumarez. "Museums, Artifacts, and Meanings." In *The New Museology*, edited by Peter Vergo, 6–21. London: Reaction Books, 1989.

———. "The Philosophy of Museum Display—The Continuing Debate." *V & A Album* 5 (1986): 3–18.

Solberg, Carl. "Immigration and Urban Social Problems in Argentina and Chile, 1890–1914." *Hispanic American Historical Review* 49, no. 2 (1969): 215–32.

Sommer, Doris. *Foundational Fictions: The National Romances of Latin America*. Berkeley: University of California Press, 1991.

Spencer, Frank, ed. *History of Physical Anthropology*. New York: Garland, 1997.

Starn, Orin. *Ishi's Brain: In Search of America's Last "Wild" Indian*. New York: W. W. Nor-ton, 2004.

Steedman, Carolyn. "Inside, Outside, Other: Accounts of National Identity in the Late Nineteenth Century." *History of the Human Sciences* 8, no. 4 (1995): 59–76.

Steinmetz, George. *The Devil's Handwriting: Precoloniality and the German Colonial State in Qindao, Samoa, and Southwest Africa*. Chicago: University of Chicago Press, 2007.

Stepan, Nancy Leys. *The Hour of Eugenics: Race, Gender, and Nation in Latin America*. Ithaca: Cornell University Press, 1991.

Stephen, Lynn. *¡Zapata Lives! Histories and Cultural Politics in Southern Mexico*. Berkeley: University of California Press, 2002.

Stern, Alexandra Minna. *Eugenic Nation: Faults and Frontiers of Better Breeding in Modern America*. Berkeley: University of California Press, 2005.

Stern, Steve J. *Peru's Indian Peoples and the Challenge of Spanish Conquest: Huamanga to 1640*. 2nd ed. Madison: University of Wisconsin Press, 1993.

———. *Remembering Pinochet's Chile: On the Eve of London, 1998*. Vol. 1 of *The Memory Box of Pinochet's Chile*. Durham: Duke University Press, 2004.

Stewart, Susan. *On Longing: Narratives of the Miniature, the Gigantic, the Souvenir, the Col-lection*. Baltimore: Johns Hopkins University Press, 1984.

Stiebing, William H. *Uncovering the Past: A History of Archaeology*. Amherst: Prometheus Books, 1993.

Stocking, George W., Jr., ed. *Bones, Bodies, Behavior: Essays on Biological Anthropology*. His-tory of Anthropology 5. Madison: University of Wisconsin Press, 1988.

————, ed. *Objects and Others: Essays on Museums and Material Culture.* History of Anthropology 3. Madison: University of Wisconsin Press, 1985.

————. *The Shaping of American Anthropology, 1883–1911: A Franz Boas Reader.* New York: Basic Books, 1974.

————. *Victorian Anthropology.* New York: Free Press, 1987.

Stoler, Laura Ann. *Carnal Knowledge and Imperial Power: Race and the Intimate in Colonial Rule.* Berkeley: University of California Press, 2002.

Strobel, Margaret. *European Women and the Second British Empire.* Bloomington: Indiana University Press, 1991.

Sutton, Barbara. "Contesting Racism: Democratic Citizenship, Human Rights, and Antiracist Politics in Argentina." *Latin American Perspectives* 35, no. 6 (2008): 106–21.

Tattersall, Ian, and Jeffrey H. Schwartz. *Extinct Humans.* Boulder, Colo.: Westview Press, 2001.

Tenorio-Trillo, Mauricio. *Mexico at the World's Fairs: Crafting a Modern Nation.* Berkeley: University of California Press, 1996.

Teruggi, Mario. *Museo de La Plata, 1888–1988. Una centuria de honra.* La Plata: Fundación Museo de La Plata Francisco P. Moreno, 1988.

Thomas, David Hurst. *Skull Wars: Kennewick Man, Archaeology, and the Battle for Native American Identity.* New York: Basic Books, 2000.

Thomas, Nicolas. *Colonialism's Culture: Anthropology, Travel, and Government.* Cambridge: Polity Press, 1994.

Tognetti, Luis, and Sergio Barbieri. *La Academia Nacional de Ciencias en el siglo XIX: Los naturalistas, publicaciones y exploraciones.* Córdoba: Academia Nacional de Ciencias 2004.

Tuan, Yi-Fu. *Space and Place: The Perspective of Experience.* Minneapolis: University of Minnesota Press, 1977.

Valentié, María Eugenia, ed. *La cultura en Tucumán y en el noroeste Argentino en la primera mitad del siglo XX (1900–1950).* San Miguel de Tucumán: Fundación Miguel Lillo, Centro Cultural Alberto Rougés, 1997.

Vallejo, Gustavo. "La Plata y la ideología del progreso: Redes y espacios culturales en la reproducción en un *habitus laicista*, 1882–1916." *Anuario del Instituto de Historia Argentina* 2 (2001): 367–405.

Vasconcelos, José. *The Cosmic Race / La raza cósmica.* Translated by Dider T. Jaén. Baltimore: Johns Hopkins University Press, 1997.

Vaughn, Mary Kay, and Stephen E. Lewis, eds. *The Eagle and the Virgin: Nation and Cultural Revolution in Mexico, 1920–1940.* Durham: Duke University Press, 2006.

Vezub, Julio. *Indios y soldados: Las fotografías de Carlos Encina y Edgardo Moreno durante la "Conquista del Desierto."* Buenos Aires: Elefante Blanco, 2002.

Viñas, David. *Indios, ejército y frontera.* Buenos Aires: Santiago Arcos Editor, 2003.

Visacovsky, Sergio Eduardo, and Rosana Guber, eds. *Historias y estilos de trabajo de campo en Argentina.* Buenos Aires: Editorial Antropofagía, 2002.

Walther, Juan Carlos. *La Conquista del Desierto: Síntesis historica de los principales sucesos ocurridos y operaciones militares realizadas en La Pampa y Patagonia, contra los Indios (años 1527–1885).* 3rd ed. Buenos Aires: Editorial Universitaria de Buenos Aires, 1970.

Widdifield, Stacie. *The Embodiment of the National in Late Nineteenth-Century Mexican Painting.* Tucson: University of Arizona Press, 1996.

Wohl, Robert. *The Generation of 1914.* Cambridge: Harvard University Press, 1979.

Wolfe, Patrick. *Settler Colonialism and the Transformation of Anthropology: The Politics and Poetics of an Ethnographic Event.* London: Continuum, 1998.

Yanni, Carla. *Nature's Museums: Victorian Science and the Architecture of Display.* Baltimore: John Hopkins University Press, 1999.

Ygobone, Aquiles D. *Francisco P. Moreno: Arquetipo de Argentinidad.* Buenos Aires: Editorial Plus Ultra, 1979.

Index

Europe
  export of artifacts to, 84, 87
  immigrants from (*see* immigrants)
  paleoarchaeological discoveries in, 151–52,
    153–54
European-descended Argentines. *See* creole
  Argentines
evolution. *See* human evolution
exchanges, among museums, 67–70, 127–28
exclusion, mythology of, 5–6
expeditions and excavations
  evolution of modern methodologies in, 103,
    105–6
  government regulation of, 88–90
  local workers employed in, 104–5
  by Museo Etnográfico, 63–64, 65–67, 104–5,
    112
  by Museo Nacional de Ciencias Naturales,
    105–6, *109*
  in northwestern Argentina, by coastal
    archaeologists, 97–98, 101–16
  photos of daily life during, 106–11, *110, 111*
  "Exploraciones arqueológicas en la Pampa
    Grande" (Ambrosetti), 63–65, *65, 66*
exportation, of artifacts, regulation of, 84–87

Farro, Máximo, 134
Federación Obrera Regional Argentina,
  60–61
Fenner, Charles N., 152
Filogenía (Ameghino), 151
Flower, William Henry, 26–27
folklore, northwestern, 100
Foyel (cacique), 41, 42, 47–48
frontiers
  expansion of, 21–23
  northwestern Argentina as, 98
  public interest in, 21–22
Frutos, Arturo, 78
Funari, Pedro Paulo A., 174
fundraising, by Museo Etnográfico, to buy
  Nasca Collection, 90–92

Gaceta, La (newspaper), 93–94
Garrigan, Shelley, 11
Garro, Juan M., 70
Gaudry, Albert, 28
Generación del Centenario, 99–100, 116, 119
general strike of 1910, 139
Germany Scientific Society, 79
Gómez, Indalecio, 70
Gonnet, Manuel, 85–88
González Garaño, Alfredo, 71

Gouchón, Emilio, 147–48
Guevara, Che, 134
Gülich, Freiherr von, 146
Gutierrez, Juan María, 146

heresy, cultural, 136
heroes, scientific, 133–51
  Ameghino as, 16, 132, 133–45, 169
  Burmeister as, 145–48
  Moreno as, 148–51
Heynemann, Karl, 26
hierarchies
  among museums, 69
  racial, in skull science, 23
Hogar, El (periodical), 142, *143*
Holmes, W. H., 152
Hrdlička, Aleš, 152–55
Hudson, Kenneth, 53
human evolution, 16, 151–70
  Ameghino's theories on, 151–70; press cov-
    erage of, 131–32, 134, 157–69; publication
    of, 151; scientists on merits of, 131–32, 134,
    152–55, 163–65; summary of, 131, 151
  indigenous cultures missing in discussions
    of, 162
  press coverage of, 151–69; on Ameghino's
    theories, 131–32, 134, 157–69; audience
    for, 157–58; on discoveries in Europe,
    151–52, *153–54*; on discoveries in Mira-
    mar, 155–65, *161*; on discoveries in
    Santiago del Estero, 1–2; on discovery of
    cráneo Ibáñez, 165–69, *166, 167*; as inter-
    mediary between scientists and public,
    157–60; vs. scientific writing, 2–3, 157–
    60; shift from scientific debate to
    patriotic rhetoric in, 160–63
  public interest in, rise of, 34, 132
  religion in debates over, 137
human remains. *See also* skeletons; skulls
  as commodities, 10–11, 40
  difficulty of obtaining, 81, 82
  and human evolution theories, 133
  in Museo de La Plata, 29–41, *32, 33,* 59
  in Museo Etnográfico, 82
  as national patrimony, legislation on,
    84–90, 140
  repatriation of, 175–77
  sources of, 36, 38–39, 82

iconography, indigenous, in Museo de La
  Plata, 27
identity. *See* national identity; regional identity
Illustrated London News, 153

Typeset by
COGHILL COMPOSITION COMPANY

Printed and bound by
SHERIDAN BOOKS

Composed in
ADOBE GARAMOND PRO

Printed on
NATURES NATURAL

Bound in
ARRESTOX

www.ingramcontent.com/pod-product-compliance
Lightning Source LLC
Chambersburg PA
CBHW032133020426
42334CB00016B/1148